RICHELIEU
AND THE COUNCILLORS
OF LOUIS XIII

LE ON BOVTHILIER COMTE DE CHAVIGNY et de Ponts Baron de la Greue,
et d'Antibes Seig.^r des Caues.Gou.^r du bois de Vincennes.Comand.^t et grand Trésorier des Ordres de
sa Ma.^{té} Ministre d'Estat, Nasquit 1607, du Mariage de Claude Bouthillier Con.^{er} du Roy en ses Conseils, Secret.
de ses Comandem.^{ts} Surintendant de ses finances, et Trésorier de ses ordres; et de Magdelaine de Bragelonne fut
receu Con.^{er} au Parlem.^t de Paris 1627. Le Card. de Richelieu connoissant la rareté de son esprit le présenta au
feu Roy, qui l'honora de la charge de Secret.^{re} d'Estat et des autres qu'il a depuis possedées. Il fut aussi nom
mé par sa Ma.^{té} son Plenipotentiaire pour la Paix generale, et l'establit par son Testament 1643, du Conseil
de la Reine Regente son espouse, marquant par là l'estime qu'il en faisoit. ce qui ne fut pas pourtant
entretenu: les affaires ayant changé de face. Mais l'an 1652 s'estant meslé dans les affaires des
Princes et leurs Conseils, mourut le 11 Octobre a Paris. Il avoit espousé Anne Phelippeaux Fille
du Sr de Villesauin Trésorier de l'Espargne.

RICHELIEU
AND THE COUNCILLORS
OF LOUIS XIII

A Study of the Secretaries of State
and Superintendents of Finance
in the Ministry of Richelieu
1635–1642

BY

OREST A. RANUM

GREENWOOD PRESS, PUBLISHERS
WESTPORT, CONNECTICUT

3018

Library of Congress Cataloging in Publication Data

Ranum, Orest A
   Richelieu and the councillors of Louis XIII.

   Reprint of the ed. published by Clarendon Press,
Oxford.
   Bibliography: p. *199-205*
   Includes index.
   1. Richelieu, Armand Jean du Plessis, Cardinal,
duc de, 1585-1642. 2. France--Politics and
government--1610-1643. I. Title.
DC123.3.R3   1976   354'.44'03   76-3762
ISBN 0-8371-8803-2

© *Oxford University Press 1963*

Originally published in 1963 by the Clarendon Press, Oxford

This reprint has been authorized by the Clarendon Press
Oxford.

Reprinted in 1976 by Greenwood Press,
a division of Williamhouse-Regency Inc.

Library of Congress Catalog Card Number 76-3762

ISBN 0-8371-8803-2

Printed in the United States of America

PREFACE

WHEN I was preparing this work from manuscript sources of the early modern period, several questions arose from the documents and the changes of time. Also, grammatical and vocabulary changes appeared as traps when I was translating into either modern French or English. The spelling was very irregular, varying from person to person, and even the same document or letter sometimes contained variants.

Dating presented less difficulty, but for Claude de Bullion, for example, there were many problems because he rarely noted the year when writing the month and day in his letters. The use of abbreviations also made it difficult to determine exactly what word or tense was intended. The room for errors was therefore very great, and even after numerous verifications, it was impossible to remove them all.

An attempt was made to translate the texts into good English and yet retain some of the vigour of seventeenth-century expressions. Except for already well-known historical figures, names were left in their old spelling, but modern terms were used for the secretaries of state in preference to the much longer forms of the seventeenth century, e.g. secrétaire d'estat ayant le département des affaires étrangères. Where French texts were included, the grammar and punctuation were not changed except to clarify the meaning. The same was true in the use of accent marks, which were very irregular in the period under study.

In citing manuscripts, certain abbreviations were used: AAE, Archives du Ministère des Affaires Étrangères; AG, Archives du Ministère de la Guerre; BN, Bibliothèque Nationale (fonds français); and PRO, Public Record Office. Mr. David L. Evans, Keeper of the Public Records in London, very kindly granted permission to quote manuscripts under the Crown Copyright.

I should like to acknowledge my indebtedness to the United States Educational Commission for two Fulbright grants, permitting me to spend two years in research among the original sources in France. I owe much to professors of history on both sides of the Atlantic: to Professors Herbert Heaton, Robert S. Hoyt, David Harris Willson, and particularly my adviser, Professor John B. Wolf, at the University of Minnesota, for their helpful suggestions and useful criticism. In France, the encouragement of Professors Roland Mousnier, René Rémond, and Georges Livet was much appreciated, as was also the help of innumerable friends and archivists, notably the Comte d'Adhémar de Panat, Georges Dethan, and William Newman.

I should also like to express my gratitude to Miss Louise P. Olsen for her help in preparing the manuscript for publication, and for typing it. Last of all, it is my pleasure to acknowledge the assistance of my wife, Patricia M. Ranum, whose help as copyist, typist, and listener was very great.

OREST A. RANUM

Schiltigheim, Bas-Rhin
14 June 1960

CONTENTS

LIST OF PLATES

Introduction

WHAT is the proper term for the governmental relationships that existed between the king, the lesser officials, and the institutions of the royal government in the *ancien régime*? The chancellor, keeper of the seals, superintendent of finance, secretaries of state, ministers of state, and the lesser councillors all had interrelated duties which made them the link between the real source of power, the king, and the lower administration. For the seventeenth century, ministerial government would be a useful term if used in the general sense to describe the above, but the danger of confusing it with modern concepts and existing institutions must be pointed out.

Current ideas of ministerial government do not capture the essence of the government of Louis XIII. It was indeed a team of administrators, royal ministers, working together; but the flexibility within what we think of as administrative departments remained by modern standards very great. This lack of functional divisions—finance, foreign affairs, justice, and so forth—puts the emphasis on the role which each minister played in the government; and it is at this point that the great legal historians of the nineteenth century faltered as they attempted to systematize an administration based on the custom and legislation of centuries. Cutting the government of Louis XIII into chapters on finance, justice, foreign affairs, and war must be done, but the whole must be preserved at the same time by analysing the functions of the major personalities which cut across these lines.

Certain privileged councillors were given the title 'minister of state' by Louis XIII, but this was important only for precedence in council sessions or court ceremonies. The same was true when Cardinal Richelieu became principal minister by letters patent in 1629.[1] It confirmed his superior rank in the councils, but no political power was given him

[1] See the letters patent, pub. by Aubery, *Mémoires pour l'histoire du Cardinal Duc de Richelieu* (Cologne, 1667), i, p. 619; and also L. Batiffol, *Richelieu et le Roi Louis XIII* (Paris, 1935), p. 19.

for the purpose of raising him above the other ministers of state. In the last years of the reign, as older councillors either died or were disgraced, Richelieu dominated the *conseil* in a way resembling political practices in later times. The cardinal virtually appointed the other councillors, directed their labours, and even controlled their relations with the king to such an extent that the central administration of the period 1635 to 1642 may rightly be called a ministerial government. This was reflected in the delineation of administrative functions, particularly on war and financial affairs, to such a point that new ministerial relationships and responsibilities became apparent.

At the same time, the councillors appointed through the cardinal's influence were not made ministers of state. They functioned as officers and councillors in just the same way as the ministers had a decade before, and the king even referred to them occasionally as his ministers, but they did not have the necessary letters patent.[1] The concept of a government of ministers headed by a principal minister did not yet exist, although in fact it accurately describes the political relationships between Richelieu and the other councillors.

Historians have, with few exceptions, mistakenly centred their interpretations of Louis's ministerial government solely on his relationship with Cardinal Richelieu. For many, Richelieu became the real ruler of France in fact if not in name. It was not until the pioneering work of Fagniez had proved the existence of many important men with considerable influence on Richelieu that historians began to examine the whole court of Louis XIII.[2] Fagniez broke new ground by looking beyond the documents strictly pertinent to the king and the cardinal.

Succeeding chapters will point out the futility of trying to determine who was responsible for a given act or decision

[1] A striking example is the famous 'plein pouvoirs' letter written by Louis to Richelieu, 30 June 1642, Aubery, ed. cit. v, p. 366; and Richelieu, *Lettres, instructions diplomatiques et papiers d'État*, ed. by M. Avenel (Paris, 1853–77), vi, p. 957, and Richelieu to Chavigny, 10 Aug. 1637, ibid. v, p. 1049, where the salutation bears the title 'ministre d'estat'.

[2] G. Fagniez, *Le Père Joseph et Richelieu* (Paris, 1894), vols. i and ii, as well as his studies on Fancan, *Revue Historique*, cvii and cviii, 1911.

in the government of Louis XIII. This concept of political responsibility will continue to be intriguing, but its validity and usefulness in studying seventeenth-century government is severely limited. The central principle of monarchy, that the king was the source of political power in the state, did not permit ministers to acknowledge, to their credit or detriment, political decisions. But this does not hinder the attempt to measure the importance of a minister to the affairs of state by analysing his position in the government, his influence on the Crown and on the other ministers. Indeed, the necessity of maintaining the fiction that all administrative action stemmed directly from the king accounts for the almost total absence of acknowledgement for a political decision by ministers even in their private correspondence. The whole range of formulas used to communicate the will of the Crown in writing were legal manifestations of the necessity to attribute all political decisions to the king. Numerous problems involving signature usage on royal letters are a good example of this aspect of royal government; the problem of determining when and under what conditions the king gave the secretaries the right to sign his name has not been solved. From the hundreds of letters which were not sent, because of modifications, and which already have the LOUIS, the signature of the king, upon them, it is obvious that the secretaries of state and even their clerks were signing royal documents and sending them without the king ever having seen them.[1] But at the same time there is ample evidence to indicate that the king alone signed royal letters, and that when he was incapacitated the secretaries were obliged to wait for his signature.[2] Ministerial government

[1] This had been true for several decades with letters signed with the phrase 'par le Roy' (see the *Mémoire de l'establissement des secrétaires d'Estat*, BN, Collection Cinq Cents Colbert, MS. 136, fol. 371). But there are rejected charters and letters patent corrected by a secretary of state, which are already signed, in the AG, A¹, *passim*. See also where the secretaries were practising the royal signature, AG, A¹, 27, fol. 316ᵛ.

[2] Sublet de Noyers, Secretary of State, wrote to his colleague, Chavigny: 'Vous aurés suject de vous plaindre de moy, vous renvoyant si tard une response pressée, mais les aimorroides tourmentant le Roy, il n'a pas esté possible de le faire signer les deux expeditions devant cinq heures du soir, enfin je vous les renvoie signées de sa proprio signo(?). . . .' 17 May 1642, AAE, France, 842, fol. 244.

in the modern sense was a long way off when ministers functioned merely in the shadow of the Crown; their only privilege, and it was carefully watched by Louis, was to speak or write at his pleasure.

Thanks to the admirable works by Mousnier on the royal councils for the reign of Louis XIII, the administrative framework of the ministerial government is now known in detail.[1] 'The council of the king is *par excellence* the sovereign's instrument for government. It is in the council that he legislates, that he judges as final arbiter, that he administers.'[2] Historians who interpreted Richelieu as the real ruler in France, because of his domination of the king, did not analyse the government in the context traditional to the French monarchy. In the *Testament politique* attributed to Richelieu, the steady confirmation of government by council, that is, by a group of councillors who represented different points of view and had the right freely to express them before their sovereign, was in fact merely an expression of what political philosophers had held as an ideal for a long time.[3] Indeed, the king's council did not play a secondary role in the government when Richelieu was principal minister; instead, it provided the means whereby he came to dominate the central administration.

Again in the council of the king, with its complex divisions and jurisdictions, the futility of trying to determine political responsibility and even administrative systems is the lesson to be learned from the articles of Georges Pagès.[4] This supreme instrument of royal power will always remain somewhat of an enigma, especially when historians try to find aspects of it which only characterize the institution in

[1] Roland Mousnier, 'Le Conseil du roi de la mort de Henri IV au gouvernement personnel de Louis XIV', *Études d'Histoire Moderne et Contemporaine*, 1947, where his other works pertinent to the *conseil* are cited.

[2] Roland Mousnier, 'Les Règlements du conseil du roi sous Louis XIII', *Annuaire-Bulletin de la Société de l'Histoire de France*, 1946–7, p. 93.

[3] Richelieu, *Testament politique*, ed. by L. André (Paris, 1947), *passim*. For the problems of authorship, see R. Pithon, 'A Propos du Testament Politique de Richelieu', *Revue Suisse d'Histoire*, vi, 1956.

[4] 'Le Conseil du roi sous Louis XIII', *Revue d'Histoire Moderne*, xii, 1937, and 'Études sur l'histoire administrative et sociale de l'ancien régime', published under the direction of Pagès by the *Société d'Histoire Moderne* (Paris, 1938), pp. 7–38.

later times. A fine example involves the Council of Dispatches. Professor Mousnier's excellent summary of the early mistakes[1] needs only one addition.[2] Councillors worked with great freedom on all problems in the various sections of the council, even though there had been attempts to systematize the labour. In later chapters it will be seen that all of the chief councillors of state held brevets to sit on every branch of the council except for the *Conseil d'en haut*. With nearly the same personnel on every council, the question of whether one councillor or another treated only foreign affairs or internal affairs, and so forth, in a particular council becomes unimportant.[3] It would be of interest to solve the mystery of which *arrêts* came from what branch of the council, but this presupposes that a fixed system for their expedition existed.

Neither Louis XIII nor Richelieu attended the royal councils which took up the legislation of day-to-day government. Were these councils left free to deliberate and administer without royal pressure or influence? This would hardly be the case. It is at this point that ministers possessing brevets as 'councillor of the king in all his councils' provided the vital link which transmitted the royal will to the governmental machinery established to execute it. The chancellor, the keeper of the seals, and the superintendents of finance were in a very real sense responsible to the Crown for the control of the councils, with the exception, of course, of the *Conseil d'en haut*. The chancellor was presiding officer in the king's absence and supervised the mechanical organization and functions of the councils.[4] Cardinal Richelieu relied on him, along with the superintendents, to make

[1] 'Les Règlements du Conseil du Roi sous Louis XIII', loc. cit., pp. 114-19.

[2] See below, p. 60.

[3] A glance at the excellent lists of councillors which have survived shows that in spite of the large turn-over of councillors due to the quarter and semester brevets, there was always an important hard core of non-changing councillors. See the lists in the *Mémoires d'André Lefevre d'Ormesson*, MS. Léber, 5767, Bibliothèque de Rouen. See also the 'conseillers d'estat employés sur l'estat que fut expédié pour l'année 1638', AAE, France 832, fol. 139.

[2] Keeper of the Seals Marillac, by the *règlement* of 1630, ended the long list of council reforms by legislation in the reign of Louis XIII. Chancellor Séguier's supervision of council membership and action can be seen in the manuscript written in his hand in the British Museum, MS. Harleian 4472, fol. 269.

the councils effective instruments in the royal administration.[1]

The duties of various ministers in the councils will be discussed in succeeding chapters, where the importance of interministerial co-operation is explained in detail. It would be inaccurate to imagine all council meetings as solemn dress-up occasions. These most certainly took place; but generally speaking, and that is all that the documentation permits one to do, a group of minister-councillors, and they are one and the same, working together on affairs of state, considered themselves *en conseil*. This deliberate confusion was a source of concern to the English ambassador, who wrote to his superior:

> Besides, I insisted that the place of hearing this affair of importance is not properly *Le Conseil de la Marine* but *Le Conseil du Roy*, which by excellence is meant his Council of State. Monsieur de Chavigny replied that at the hearing of this business there were present Monseigneur le Cardinal [Richelieu], Monsieur de Bullion, and himself, and therefore this was heard in the *Conseil du Roy*. But I told him *Le Conseil de la Marine* is but a species of the *Conseil du Roy*, and is not the Counsell meant by the treaties. In time I gave him to understand that this course of proceeding seemed strange to me. . . .[2]

Sometimes councils were held merely to announce decisions already made and to execute them.[3] The protocol and rules of order provided by custom to fit the various councils on different occasions permitted the councillors to arrange their administrative schedules freely. There was no regular council room; the place and time of sitting were determined by custom and at the convenience of the higher councillors.[4]

---

[1] A fine example of how these officers were in a middle position between Richelieu and the lesser councillors is Richelieu to *Messieurs le chancelier et le surintendant*, 22 Aug. 1641, Avenel, ed. cit. VI. ccccxxx.

[2] De Vic to the Secretary of State, 3/13 Feb. 1635/6, PRO State Papers, Series 78, vol. c, part i, fol. 108.

[3] Bullion, Superintendent of Finance, wrote to Richelieu: 'Nous faisons estat soubz le bon plaisir de Vostre Emminence de tenir un conseil chez Monsieur le Chancelier où Messieurs le duc de Montbazin, Bouthillier, et moy seront pour donner ordre que Messieurs le lieutenant civil, criminel, procureur du Roy . . .', 25 Aug. 1639, AAE, France, 834, fol. 28.

[4] There is considerable evidence to indicate that the elaborate schedules for holding different councils on different days established by the *règlements*

Thus it is not surprising to find references to councils held in sick rooms or in the king's *Cabinet de travail*.[1] Sometimes the ministers themselves drafted legislation immediately after a council decision; Bullion, Superintendent of Finance, wrote to Richelieu: 'This morning the Maréchal de Houssay affair has been resolved following your order. I wrote the instructions with my own hand in the council where it was approved, and [I] am sure that it will be according to the intentions and commands of Your Eminence.'[2]

To the student of politically important men in the *ancien régime*, the multiplicity of offices held by one official is always striking.[3] A criss-cross of duties and personnel characterizes government in the seventeenth century and again makes it difficult to trace traditional administrative patterns. Studying ministerial government by offices would be artificial if it were not combined with an analysis of the other duties carried out by the same officers in other capacities.

Then, too, there is a double nature for every man in office; he possesses certain duties and rights by reason of his office, no matter what it is; and also, he enjoys other powers because of family and economic position. His personality and its consequent influence upon the political machinery around him is a factor to be considered and, if possible, measured. Administrative historians in the nineteenth century stopped with an analysis of the first aspect, simply the office; as a result it is not surprising that they never

was either frequently modified or loosely followed. The schedule made in 1630 (Mousnier, 'Les Règlements du Conseil du Roi sous Louis XIII', loc. cit., pp. 183 f.) planned the *Conseil des finances* for Wednesday (p. 185), whereas it was to take place on a Saturday according to a letter of Claude Bouthillier to Richelieu, 18 Jan. 1635, AAE, France, 813, fol. 35. See further evidence in Bouthillier to Richelieu, Tuesday, 19 Nov. 1641, AAE, France, 839, fol. 356. But at the same time, see Bullion's promise to maintain a council schedule in the *règlement* of 1638, Appendix B, pp. 197 f.

1 Paris remained the centre of government activity even if the king or Richelieu were not there. See Richelieu to Sublet de Noyers, 28 June 1637, Avenel, ed. cit. v. cdli, and Bullion to Richelieu: 'Je suis obligé de dire à Vostre Eminence que nous avons plus que jamais besoin de sa presence proche de Paris estant impossible de faire les affaires ailleurs qu'à Paris, qui est le seul lieu du Royaume où l'on peult faire le service du Roy pour le recouvrement des deniers.' 26 Apr. 1636, AAE, France, 820, fol. 228.

2 24 July 1636, AAE, France, 821, fol. 104.

3 This is partly explained by the granting of minor offices with pensions as a compensation for services rendered.

really grappled with the problem of how offices rose and fell in political importance as time passed.

The assembling of the group which helped Louis XIII and Cardinal Richelieu to rule France is a long and fascinating story. The background needed for beginning in 1635 has been sketched in from relatively few sources and secondary works. When Richelieu entered the king's council in 1624, his friends in the royal government were few indeed, but by the Day of the Dupes in 1630 this was no longer true. Marillac's dramatic disgrace brought several important changes in the government around the king; the flight of the Queen Mother, Marie de Médicis, a few months later, and the disgrace of the new keeper of the seals, Châteauneuf, in 1633, left Richelieu and those loyal to him a free hand to dominate the central administration. Richelieu could thus propose whomever he wished to the king when an officer was to be appointed. It will be obvious in succeeding chapters how carefully and skilfully the cardinal used his influence on appointments.

The detailed analysis of the background and rise to power of Richelieu's friends, his creatures, in Chapter III places the emphasis upon the personalities in the government of Louis XIII.

These favourites merit the epithet which they used themselves when writing to the cardinal. They were creatures of Richelieu, responsible to him for their political power, prestige, and wealth. Though they had considerable influence and ability in politics, it was not for these qualities that Richelieu favoured them. Their obsequious fidelity in thought and deed, even to the point of risking their lives, explains Richelieu's decision to share political power with them.

At this time, new developments changed the position of the secretaries of state just as older officers, such as the constable, disappeared or were brought under more strict surveillance by the Crown. For the councils, the problem of royal control was solved, not by legislation, but by Richelieu's supporters, who dominated their deliberations after 1633. How does one know this? Unfortunately, minutes for the councils do not exist, so one must look for other evidence. Very few of the thousands of minutes for the council *arrêts* from 1633 to 1642 were not signed by Keeper of the Seals Séguier and by one or both of the Superintendents of Finance, Bullion and Bouthillier. Council legislation was only legal with their signatures, and Séguier, in another domain, once wrote to Richelieu that he would 'let things against his sentiment go through so long as justice was not harmed'.[1] Richelieu felt free to use the councils as an instrument whereby his decisions became legally those of the king. This, combined with control of the secretaries of state and influence over Louis to sign the letters they prepared, gave Richelieu the power to act in many ways, but still within the traditional forms and structure of the *ancien régime*.

Through the favour of the king, Richelieu and his creatures were able to dominate the government of France without opposition from factions for almost a decade. His death in 1642 brought into the open partisans whom he had either closely controlled or defeated. Not the least of Richelieu's many qualities was his ability to direct and control a group of ambitious and power-hungry men.

[1] Minute, 1640?, BN, MS. 18158, fol. 145.

I

The King and His Ministers

A STUDY of the last years of the reign of Louis XIII reveals a decided paradox: at a time when French political philosophers and jurists were proclaiming absolutism, there was an absence of absolutist ideology or doctrine in the correspondence and working papers of the king and his ministers.[1] But the paradox is more apparent than real. The idea that the king was the source of all political power and justice was clearly implicit on all occasions when decisions were communicated, whether between ministers or to the lower branches of the administration. All political action was in the king's name, either through institutions such as the Parlement, whose powers had been delegated to them by the Crown long before, or, more directly by the king and his ministers *vis-à-vis* the rest of the administration.

Within the framework of the *Conseil du roi* the principal minister and other councillors made decisions which were transmitted to the realm in the king's name. The traditional phrase, *par le roi en son conseil*, was not just a legal fiction. The centuries of political centralization in the person of the king, a phenomenon much older than absolutism as expressed in the seventeenth century, made commands in the king's name the only effective political power in the realm.[2]

The same was true of relations between the ministers. Commands and political decisions were made for the *service du roi*, a phrase which Richelieu and the creatures used constantly.[3] Often references to the king were simply automatic,

[1] See Roland Mousnier and Fritz Hartung, 'Quelques problèmes concernant la monarchie absolue', *Comitato Internazionale di Scienze Storiche* (Florence, 1958).

[2] The *arrêts du conseil*, which have survived by the thousands in the form of minutes in the Archives Nationales, enable one to measure the great importance of the *Conseil du roi*. No governmental action was too great or too small to come under its jurisdiction.

[3] See Richelieu, *Lettres, instructions diplomatiques, et papiers d'état*, ed. M. Avenel (Paris, 1853–77), v, p. 637. At the height of his power, Richelieu

but even so they reflected the nature of monarchy and maintained even the most powerful ministers in a juridical framework which gave the king unlimited powers over his ministers if he desired to use them. Richelieu made daily requests to ministers in the name of the king; and when they were to come to a political decision themselves, either Louis or the cardinal gave them permission to do so. Richelieu wrote to Chancellor Séguier: 'You will send to us, if you please, with diligence the necessary powers and orders to execute the decisions which you judge that the king must make on such a subject . . . .'[1] A reference to the king was not a mere formality; it properly expressed the nature of the government and was a political necessity.

Often mere references to the king by ministers, or even traditional formulas, were ineffective against rebellious subjects or institutions. The presence of the king, or direct orders from him with his signature boldly visible and his seal affixed, were the only effective instruments of the government. The ministers therefore did not have political identity in themselves; on both the personal and institutional levels their orders were frequently brushed aside. Dupuy, in his letter to Chancellor Séguier, accepted the decision of the ministers, but waited for a royal letter before taking action.[2]

On the institutional level, the position of the minister was also dependent upon the king. When Louis was away from Paris he was obliged to send letters to enforce obedience of the sovereign courts and to make them execute the orders of his ministers, even though they had acted in his name *en conseil*. At a time when new troops were badly needed, Louis

never transgressed the royal prerogative to command; he made commands in his name only where delegated authority was given him to do so, e.g. as grand admiral or governor of Brittany.

[1] 17 Oct. 1635, ibid. v. cxlvi.

[2] 'Mon frere prieur de la Chartreuse de Rouen m'a escrit le dernier ord^e [ordinaire?] que Monseigneur le Cardinal de Lion [the brother of Richelieu] luy avoit fait voir une lettre de Monsieur Bouthillier comme j'estois nommé avec Monsieur Godefroy pour nous trouver à Cologne pres dudit Seigneur Cardinal pour servir le Roi à la conference de la paix. Monsieur de Bullion nous a confirmé cet advis mais je ne l'ai pas directement [*illegible*] de la part du Roy, avant de m'y engager plus avant. . . .' Dupuy continued to wait for orders directly from Louis in spite of the information directly or indirectly transmitted to him by three important officials. 18 Oct. 1636, BN, MS. 17370, fol. 3.

wrote to First President Nicolay of the *Chambre des comptes:*

And I wish to have raised as soon as possible up to eight or ten thousand foot soldiers [in Paris] as well as in the *élection* of that city, and in the neighbouring ones; and because I expect much from the affection of my principal servants in this affair and especially from you, I am writing you this letter to invite you and exhort you as much as I am able, to contribute everything which depends on you for the progress of this levy, addressing orders especially to Monsieur the Chancellor and to the Sieur Bouthillier, Superintendent of my finances, who will make my intentions known to you. . . .[1]

The ministers of Louis XIII did not possess delegated powers in the broad sense, merely rights and traditions which permitted them to act only in limited spheres. As the source of all power, Louis was often compelled to write letters requesting royal officials to execute the orders of his ministers.

In times of severe crisis or revolt, or when the realm was threatened with invasion, not even royal letters, much less the actions of the ministers in the *conseil*, would bring the king's subjects to obey. Only the presence of the king with military force could do so.[2] Louis XIII, many times in his long life as king, was compelled to go to provinces or towns to quell revolts or to force a parlement to register the edicts of his ministers. Even ecclesiastical assemblies were subject to strict surveillance by the Crown. In 1635 Bullion advised Richelieu that the forthcoming Assembly of the Clergy should be held close to the king. He knew all too well the stormy sessions which inevitably occurred between ecclesiastics and royal officials as they determined the size of the 'contribution' of the clergy.[3] As a result, the power of the king alone was legally observable not only in the realm— the exterior administration outside of the king and his

[1] Written from Nesle, countersigned by Sublet de Noyers, 10 July 1641, AN, 3ap, 165, chapter 125, from the Nicolay family archives.

[2] No one realized this better than Richelieu. At critical moments he asked for the king's presence. See his letters to Louis in the summer of 1636, particularly Avenel, ed. cit. v. cclxi and cccviii.

[3] 17 May 1635, AAE, France, 814, fol. 54. Bullion began by carefully reminding Richelieu that the cardinal had decided to do the same thing during the crisis of La Rochelle, when the Assemblée Générale was held in Poitiers, in 1628.

council—but within the council as well. The legal fiction that only the king made political decisions was guaranteed and made effective by old customs which bound the ministers as well as the lower branches of the administration.

Beyond the framework of councils and offices there was a mixture of purely administrative and personal factors which gave the government of Louis XIII its character and determined how it functioned. Traditionally, the king's ministers had formed parties which tended to counterbalance each other in importance and power; but after the Day of the Dupes, the death of Effiat, and the disgrace of Châteauneuf in 1633, Richelieu dominated all of the ministers. From the exterior they seemed to function independently of each other and in direct relationship with the king. With Richelieu as principal minister this was not so. A hierarchy within the ministry, based upon personalities and consequent favouritism, determined the importance of the minister.

This hierarchy, with Richelieu at the top, changed the traditional importance of the officers. As chancellor, Séguier probably enjoyed greater prestige but less real influence in the government than two of the secretaries of state, who held offices which, as will be noted later, had very humble beginnings.[1] Under these circumstances the favour of the king still remained very important, but it was not so decisive as favour with the cardinal. Chavigny openly wrote to a friend that he was out of favour with Louis XIII, but since he was in favour with Richelieu he was sure that his position in the government was safe.[2]

Louis was confronted with a unified ministry as a result of his affection for and confidence in Richelieu and of the consequent acceptance of the latter's creatures. He continued to support the cardinal and to grant him ever greater powers. The king rarely commented on the powers of his ministers, but in the Vendôme affair, where the brother of the king

[1] Only a thorough study of Séguier could determine his influence on Louis XIII and Richelieu; but the lack of references to his views, and the penury of letters from Richelieu to him, indicate that although his tasks were important and great, they nevertheless were generally carried out in a framework of judicial tradition calling for less participation by the king and the principal minister.

[2] See below, p. 83.

was accused of plotting against Richelieu, Louis lucidly explained his support for the principal minister. In the council which had been united to judge Vendôme, Louis said:

> Messieurs, it is Monsieur the Cardinal who requests me to pardon Monsieur de Vendôme; that is not my opinion. I owe protection to those who serve me with affection and fidelity, as does Monsieur the Cardinal; and if I am not careful to have the plots made against his person punished, it will be difficult to find ministers to watch over my affairs with the courage and fidelity that he does.[1]

The personality of the king was in itself the principal reason for the hierarchical relationships between the ministers. Louis was a conscientious worker at affairs of state; he was intelligent and had a marked ability for knowing and respecting the rights of his subjects.[2] Although the government of France was significantly modified during his reign, which meant that a multiplicity of ancient rights, both corporal and personal, were trampled on by the Crown, the king was in no way a political reformer. Louis consented to these changes only when necessity required it. During the crucial years of the war from 1635 to 1640, when the old sovereign courts and minor venal officers protested so violently against the massive creations of new offices, Louis probably remained reticent and accepted such changes only when his ministers offered no other means of increasing the royal revenues.[3] Louis XIII merited his sobriquet 'the Just',

---

[1] 'Procès-Verbal du Prince Vendôme', 17 May 1641, Avenel, ed. cit. vi, p. 793.

[2] He worked daily with at least one or two secretaries of state and his own personal secretaries, primarily Lucas, and he held councils whenever the political situation necessitated them. Louis worked at affairs whenever they demanded his time. His letters addressed to Richelieu and other ministers often include the hour written, and enough of them have survived to indicate that he worked at all times of the day and late at night.

[3] In summarizing a speech made by Séguier before the Parlement, Omer Talon has given the official explanation of the war and its consequences: 'que ceux qui se laissent surprendre à la mollesse ne reçoivent aucune grâce ni bénédiction dans leur État; que le Roi étoit bien informé des grandes charges dont le peuple de son royaume étoit pressé; que c'étoit avec regret de sa part qu'elles avoient été imposées, et qu'elles continuoient; mais que le salut de l'État et la conservation de son royaume l'avoient obligé d'en user de la sorte, et qu'entre les remèdes les plus doux il avoit été conseillé de faire de nouvelles créations d'officiers dans lesquelles ses finances se trouveroient peu chargées, et le peuple ne recevroit peu ou point d'incommodité.' *Mémoires d'Omer Talon*, ed. by Michaud et Poujoulat, séries 3, vi, p. 41.

partly because of the long list of executions which took place during his reign, and also because of his carefulness and respect for the rights of his subjects.[1]

The king's views were made known to his ministers. Louis seems to have had an excellent mind for the details of government. He took special interest in the armies; no detail of provision, troop-raising and payments, or officer appointments was too small for him to consider.[2] The king became angry and sullen whenever he discovered that his ministers, including Richelieu, had planned or executed something without consulting him. This caused an instantaneous reaction among the ministers, who never forgot that in earlier times Louis had brutally disgraced ministers. Claude le Bouthillier wrote to Richelieu:

> His Majesty was surprised when the marshal informed him that the infantry had been reduced to eighty in accordance with an order that [the marshal] says he saw signed by Monsieur de Bullion. As a result, I bore the brunt of a little [of the king's] anger; but after having explained that, in spite of that resolution, Monsieur de Bullion had left funds . . . His Majesty calmed down and only commanded me to send in any case an ordonnance stating that the troops be paid according to the number present. . . .[3]

The *mauvaises humeurs* of the king were the cause of much anxiety on the part of the ministers, including Richelieu; and his desire to review every detail obliged the ministers to prepare dispatches carefully.[4] Louis's real interest in

[1] Louis complained when one of Richelieu's creatures wrote a letter as secretary of state when it was not in his department. Sublet to Chavigny, 3 Feb. 1639, AAE, France, 833, fol. 32. With a sense of justice even about deserting officers, Louis wrote: 'Je vous envoye l'ordonnance contre les officiers absans laquelle j'ay signé, elle est un peu rude, mais aux extremes maux il faut d'extremes remedes', n.d., AAE, France, 244, fol. 126. See also Avenel, ed. cit. v, p. 318, note 2. Once after the Comte de Cramail gave a speech, Louis wrote to Richelieu: 'Je l'avertis ier que il estoit trop rude à la noblesse qui s'en plaint un peu. . . .' 23 Sept. 1635, AAE, France, 244, fol. 148.

[2] He even personally worked out army projects which became plans for the formation of royal armies.

[3] 30 Oct. 1633, AAE, France, 808, fol. 124. This was not the only time when Louis felt obliged to change the orders of the superintendent of finance. He wrote to Richelieu: 'Monsieur de Bullion a reduit la garnison de Bar à 6 monstres qui est trop peu, il la faudrait faire mettre 8.' 10 Aug. 1635, AAE, France, 244, fol. 124ᵛ.

[4] Ordonnances and other forms of royal correspondence were constantly reviewed by Louis. Sublet de Noyers wrote to Chavigny, who was with the

government, even down to the little details, was overlooked by Avenel when he observed that Richelieu requested the king to fix the price of army bread at a moment when the cardinal was enjoying the 'fullness of absolute power'.[1] While the presentation of such details might seem absurd to present-day administrators, nothing could be more misleading. Louis took the *métier du roi* very seriously, and insisted on being informed of everything.

In the complex problems of government, where goals and political policies were defined, Louis's role is more difficult to determine. Little is known about this aspect for either Louis or Richelieu, because their thoughts and actions, as indicated in their correspondence, do not clearly delineate their political personalities. The great affairs of state were usually discussed, and decisions were reached in the *Conseil d'en haut* in the presence of the king, Richelieu, Bullion, Séguier, Chavigny, and Sublet de Noyers. No minutes were taken, and to our knowledge not even a detailed description of one of these sessions is extant.

In correspondence with his ministers, Louis appears as the reviewer of policies. He did this very carefully. Claude le Bouthillier wrote to Richelieu:

I saw by a letter of Monsieur de Noyers to Monsieur the Chancellor that the King was displeased that we created [the office] of provosts generals for the provinces *en son conseil* without talking about it to His Majesty. His Eminence will remember, if it please him, that I gave myself the honour of talking to him about it. . . .[2]

When Louis was displeased, the creatures quickly sought cover under the protection of Richelieu, but as this incident clearly indicates, speaking to the cardinal alone about a political decision was insufficient unless Richelieu in turn presented it to the king.

The letters from Richelieu to Louis—where problems and solutions are briefly explained in forms of alternatives so

king: 'J'adjouste ce mot à ma premiere despesche pour vous prier de faire voir [to the king] deux expeditions cy jointes. L'un est un project d'ordonance que Son Eminence [Richelieu] m'a fait dresser pour obliger la cavallerie à avoir des armes et les porter. Sa Majesté y augmentera et retranchera selon son bon plaisir. . . .' 24 Aug. 1638, AAE, France, 831, fol. 82.
[1] Avenel, ed. cit. vi, p. 723.
[2] 24 Feb. 1642, AAE, 842, fol. 55.

that the king could simply scribble *bon* or *il le fault* in the margin—do not help to determine Louis's initiative in government, for they generally concern only the decisions of daily government routine.[1]

The king was always sensitive when he felt improperly informed by his ministers. He and his ministers were anxious to read dispatches newly arrived from foreign capitals or battlefields. When Richelieu or the particular secretary of state to whom a dispatch was addressed was not present when it arrived, Louis complained.[2] Occasionally he opened such dispatches himself, to the dismay and terror of the secretaries, for they often carried on private correspondence and exchanged court gossip with other royal servants.[3] The importance of letters in the ministry of Louis XIII cannot be over-estimated.

In an age without modern communications, and when customs and exigencies of government often separated the king from his ministers, the letter, its presentation, form, and content all had great significance. The formalities were long and complicated, and tremendously important.[4]

[1] A good example is Richelieu's letter to Louis, 16 Aug. 1636, Avenel, ed. cit. v. ccxc. On one such occasion Louis wrote to Richelieu: 'Mon Cousin, j'ay escrit le billet pour les surintendants lequel je vous envoye, j'ay apostillé votre memoire lequel je vous envoye dans ce pacquet . . . j'ay escrit le tout dans mon lit que est cause que mon escriture est un peu plus difficile à lire, à Monceaux, 12e septembre, 1634.' AAE, France, 244, fol. 64.

[2] Richelieu to Saint-Simon, 5 June 1636, Avenel, ed. cit. v. ccxliv.

[3] Sublet to Chavigny: 'Le Roy m'aiant escript qu'il avoit ouvert les lettres . . . je n'aurai point de repos que vous m'aiés faict l'honneur de me mander s'il n'y avoit rien dedans. . . .' April 1642, AAE, France, 842, fol. 171. Once Louis wrote to Richelieu, 6 July 1636: 'Je commanderay à cette heure que les couriers qui viendront d'Italie et de Dolle passent par icy; j'ouvriray les lettres des secretaires d'estat, mais non pas les vostres. . . .' Archives de Condé, Chantilly, séries I, tome iii, fol. 177. But sometimes Louis respected the letters and did not open them. He wrote to Richelieu: 'Je ne vous feray responce sur ce que avés escrit à Monsieur Boutilier parceque, estant parti ce matin, je n'ay osé ouvrir son paquet.' 18 June 1634, Avenel, ed. cit. iv, p. 573.

[4] Richelieu wrote to Chavigny: 'Je vous envoye un billet d'une nouvelle forme pour le plus obligeant maistre du monde [Louis]. Vous me manderez comme il l'aura receu; et croirez qu'en obmettant les civilités accoustumées, qui ne parlent que de service, rien ne vous est plus asseuré que l'amitié d'une personne qui, par la volx publique, ne peut estre dict le plus impertinent du monde.' 18 Mar. 1634, Avenel, ed. cit. iv. cclxxix. Avenel correctly noted that Richelieu took precautions to ascertain the king's reaction to receiving letters without long formulas of politeness.

The relative informality of Richelieu's letters to Louis, and vice versa, remains the most convincing proof of the affection and mutual respect which existed between the two men. Louis was often subject to fits of ill temper, moments of severe psychological depression; and frequently his attitude or even his decision on a policy was determined or greatly modified by his mood of the moment.[1] Louis's correspondence was controlled by Chavigny, and to a lesser extent by Sublet de Noyers. It was their task to present Richelieu's letters to the king at the times when they were most likely to be well received.[2] Chavigny wrote to Richelieu: 'I showed [the letter] to the King in my accustomed fashion . . .',[3] indicating that he had perhaps developed a system to assure Richelieu that his letters would be favourably received by the king. In a period of difficulty, when the cardinal was not even sure of Louis's favour, Chavigny, after reporting that the king was in a bad mood, wrote: 'I did not believe that I should show the letter of His Eminence [Richelieu] to the King until I am able to determine better in what disposition his thoughts are . . . .'[4]

After 1630 the whole ministry of Louis XIII depended upon Richelieu's personal favour with the king. The cardinal might never have so cleverly dominated the entire government of France if he had not ensured his good relations with Louis through his creatures. The ministers of Louis XIII were in a direct relationship with the king, but they were not free to advise and act as they wished. The personality of Cardinal Richelieu, with his great personal favour, stood between them and the king. Through Richelieu's influence Louis XIII had appointed the other ministers; through Richelieu's favour they remained in office. When Louis was offended at something that Richelieu or the

[1] Louis's moods made him physically ill as well. Chavigny wrote to Richelieu, 21 Sept. 1635: 'La melancolie du Roy n'est que trop veritable; si vous l'aviez veu lorsque Vrilliere arriva à Vitry, vous en eussiez beaucoup de peine, et pour moy, j'avois plus de peur qu'il ne se fist malade. . . .' AAE, France, 815, fol. 232.

[2] Even letters from outside the ministry were occasionally kept from Louis.

[3] 18 Sept. 1635, AAE, France, 815, fol. 214; and below, pp. 79 f.

[4] 7 Nov. 1642, AAE, France, 844, fol. 109 bis. See also Sublet to Chavigny, 12 Sept. 1642, fol. 33 of the same volume.

creatures had done, the cardinal appealed to him as an old and faithful servant and begged forgiveness, yet at the same time he would give the king a verbal spanking.[1] The personality of the king, his health and moods, enabled Richelieu to establish this intermediary position between the ministry as a whole and the king.

If Louis was primarily the reviewer of policy, Richelieu was both the formulator and co-ordinator of it. When differences of views arose between the other ministers, it was Richelieu, not the king, who took the initiative in making the final decision. Louis was then informed, was asked to give his opinion, and the policy was approved or modified according to the king's pleasure; but in most cases the divergence of views between the councillor-ministers was settled before the measure was presented to him.

The hierarchical relationship and subservient position of the other ministers is clearly observable in other ways, and Louis's own actions and statements in regard to his ministers are most indicative. The king made a practice of holding Richelieu responsible for the actions of the other ministers; when one of them displeased him, he wrote to Richelieu, instead of to the offending minister, about it.

I gave all the orders for the levying of the six regiments and also for the two new ones and for the whole cavalry. I am writing to you in anger after a commissioner named Renart cut down all the old regiments by 400 men . . . all done under the orders of Monsieur de Bullion without [his] having spoken to me about it. It is indeed strange that they give such orders without my knowing it. . . . Excuse me if I am speaking to you angrily; it is simply that these things happen often.[2]

Likewise, when the creatures did something that pleased Louis, he informed Richelieu of his approval. Louis fully

[1] 'Apres cela Vostre Majesté a trop de bonté pour n'aprouver pas, qu'un Serviteur ancien, fidelle et confident luy die, avec le respect qui est deu à un Maitre, que si elle s'acoustume à penser, que les intentions de ses plus asseurées Creatures soient autres, qu'ils ne les luy témoignerent, elles apre-henderent tellement ses soupçons à l'avenir, qu'il leur seroit difficile de la servir aussi utilement qu'ils le desirent. Je puis respondre à Vostre Majesté que la liberté que vous leur donnez, fait qu'ils vous disent franchement ce qu'ils estiment estre du bien de vostre service. . . .' n.d., Aubery, *Mémoires pour l'histoire du Cardinal de Richelieu* (Cologne, 1667), v, p. 274.

[2] 29 Oct. 1633, ed. by the Vicomtesse de Galard, *Mélanges publiés par la Société des Bibliophiles François* (Paris, 1903).

understood the relationship between Richelieu and the other ministers, and he acted accordingly. On one occasion he criticized the treasurers and army munitioners, and the cardinal refused to accept the censure for what had been done by someone else.[1]

The relationship between the king and the cardinal, as well as their health, was of the utmost importance to the creatures. The constant references to their health were not simply phrases of courtesy or friendly concern, but political realities.[2]

Only in the king's relationship with Bullion, Superintendent of Finance, was Richelieu's middle position modified. This crafty old minister, who enjoyed much prestige and affection with Louis, did not hesitate to appeal directly to the king when a policy proposed by Richelieu seemed not to be in the best interests of the Crown. His power to control the purse strings was particularly great, and he enjoyed more independence than the other ministers, especially when the financial pinch of war brought France to the brink of bankruptcy.

Even so, both Louis and Richelieu evaded onerous and, if we are to believe Bullion, impossible tasks involving the search for money to pay for the war. Louis probably did not understand the complex financial problems of his government; in his correspondence with the superintendents, there were demands for money without any suggestion about where it was to be found.[3]

[1] Richelieu to Louis: 'Sa Majesté est trop bonne et trop juste pour me rendre responsable des deffauts d'autruy, et a trop d'expérience pour ne considérer pas que jamais aux grandes affaires les effects ne respondent à point nommé à tous les ordres qui ont esté donnez. . . .' 16 Sept. 1635, Avenel, ed. cit. v. cx. This quotation also typifies Richelieu's approach to royal criticism by appealing to Louis's conception of himself as king.

[2] The creatures arranged the meetings between Louis and Richelieu when one of them was ill, especially when the cardinal was unable to perform the customary functions for receiving the king. Chavigny wrote to Richelieu: 'Sa Majesté donnera le temps qu'il fault à Monseigneur pour se preparer à le recevoir et si elle demeure plus d'une heure avec luy elle trouvera bon qu'il se mette au lit. Elle sera tres aise de sejourner ici mardi ou mercredi pour resoudre toutes les affaires avec Son Eminence. . . .' 12 Oct. 1642, AAE, France, 844, fol. 85.

[3] Louis to Bouthillier and Bullion, AAE, France, 244, *passim*. But one must be careful not to draw hasty conclusions, for in writing letters the king might well have considered such problems below his dignity.

Instead of addressing his money requests to the superintendents, Louis often wrote to Richelieu, giving him the task of extracting money from them. Indeed, he sometimes made decisions involving considerable sums of money without taking cognizance of the financial condition of the realm.[1] At the same time, he knew full well that even Richelieu, no matter how devoted the superintendents were to him, also had difficulty in enforcing his decisions. The cardinal was sometimes obliged to solicit the king's aid in compelling the superintendents to carry out policies made by Louis and himself. When the superintendents were particularly difficult, Louis talked with them personally. Yet Louis, who probably did not understand the problems fully, requested Richelieu to instruct him on what to say to Bullion about his own finances.[2] The old superintendent did not fear the jealousy of the cardinal when they failed to agree. He wrote to Louis in a frank, fatherly way to give his views on financial policies, but at the same time he included a good word for the cardinal.[3] When Richelieu feared that Bullion would oppose or hinder a policy, he presented it directly to the king. Chavigny once wrote to the cardinal, after remarking that Louis had accepted Richelieu's suggestions: 'It is true, Monseigneur, that it was much more convenient to have the affair accepted that way than if Monsieur de Bullion had proposed it with some preambles.'[4] The hierarchical relationship was thus maintained, although to a lesser degree than with the other ministers. Richelieu stood supreme above the others, instructing them and limiting their direct initiative with the king.

Louis's freedom to act as he pleased, while theoretically very great, was broadly limited in two ways: the first was institutional and traditional, the second personal. Louis's actions were limited by the traditional rights of his subjects, both individual and institutional; personally, his own

[1] Louis to Richelieu: 'L'ambassadeur de Holande m'est venu voir ce matin pour me representer la grande necessité où sont mes trouppes qui sont par delà, je luy ay promis d'y faire pourvoir promptement, c'est pourquoy vous en parlerés à Messieurs de Bulion et Boutilier comme il faut. . . .' 2 Apr. 1636, ibid., fol. 25.

[2] Richelieu to Louis, 2 Dec. 1635, Avenel, ed. cit. v. clxxv.

[3] Bullion to Louis XIII, 25 Mar. 1637, AAE, France, 826, fol. 227.

[4] 15 June 1634, AAE, France, 810, fol. 218.

initiative was somewhat circumscribed by Richelieu and his creatures. They controlled his correspondence, surrounded him, and sheltered him from other would-be favourites and courtiers opposed to Richelieu and his policies.[1] They exiled the king's favourites who did not remain faithful to the cardinal, and in part even controlled the king's excursions.[2] Letters which might upset the king were kept from him by Sublet de Noyers and Chavigny, and ambassadors complained about the tight circle of ministers around the king, which made it difficult to gain audiences with him.[3]

Chavigny sometimes had real difficulty in managing Louis, especially when he tried to persuade the king to accept a policy which he did not favour.[4] At the same time, the *mauvaises humeurs* of the king were enough to make all the ministers tremble; even Richelieu, when Louis was angry, tip-toed softly under cover of total obeisance.

Louis depended on the creatures to explain to the cardinal not only governmental actions but also the king's views on problems, men, and suggestions made by Richelieu. The king's decisions were often transmitted verbally by the creatures, leaving Richelieu to see to their execution, a practice which, if not observed closely, leads to the old and incorrect interpretation that political decisions were freely made and executed solely by Richelieu.[5] Co-operation

---

[1] Such was the fate of Mesdemoiselles de Lafayette and Hautefort, as well as Cinq-Mars; see J. H. Mariéjol, *Histoire de France*, ed. by E. Lavisse (Paris, 1911), VI, part 2, pp. 442 ff.

[2] Richelieu, appealing to a conscientious king, bade him stay in places where he did not wish to because his counsel was needed, which might well have been true. Avenel, ed. cit. VI. ccclxv, 25 Sept. 1640. The clash between Richelieu and Louis XIII over the former's opposition to the king's intended excursion into Lorraine in 1635 put their affections to a real test. See Richelieu to Louis XIII, 1635, Aubery, ed. cit. v, p. 273.

[3] See Sublet de Noyers to Chavigny, 12 Sept. 1642, AAE, France, 844, fol. 33; and the letters of the Count of Leicester, English ambassador, to Coke, PRO, State Papers, series 78, particularly vol. 100.

[4] Chavigny to Richelieu, 9 Oct. 1635: '. . . ayant fait la proposition d'aller à Nancy avant mesme avoir receu le dernier memoire de Son Eminence, il [Louis] la rejetta fort loin. Il m'a esté impossible de luy faire agreer cette fois, et je ne scay s'il n'est point meilleur qu'il n'y ayt pas esté, parce que sur la moindre melancolie qu'il eust eu là, il s'en fut revenu si brusquement que cela eust esté capable de tout perdre. . . .' AAE, France, 815, fol. 324.

[5] Louis to Richelieu, 20 July 1635: 'Je crois que Monsieur Boutilier vous aura dit ce que se passoit ier entre nous. . . .' AAE, France, 244, fol. 118.

between the secretaries, the chancellor, the superintendents, and finally the principal minister, was a necessity in the period of severe administrative crisis which began with open war in 1635. In this period Richelieu forged a ministry relatively free from intrigue and competition between the ministers; it was their dependence on him for favour which rendered them docile. At his death, jealousy and suspicion soon destroyed the cohesion that he had created among the ministers, resulting in disgrace for all of them in the early years of the minority of Louis XIV.

Under Richelieu a secretary could freely explain to his colleagues how he had fared with Louis, and together they harmonized their efforts to eliminate royal bad humour, and communicated the king's orders to each other for the benefit of the group.[1] They also informed each other when the king was to be given some specific information from their departments.[2] When Louis wanted to communicate with Richelieu on various affairs of state, he requested a secretary of state to come and see him in order to transmit what he had to say to the cardinal.[3] The king had confidence in the men who managed his government. Richelieu and the other ministers were aware of all political policies directed by the king,[4] including the secret details.[5]

[1] De Noyers explained to Chavigny the king's decision to move some troops, but he feared that Louis might change his mind; Noyers to Chavigny, n.d., AAE, France, 828, fol. 236. Chavigny was encouraged by Richelieu to do all in his power to eliminate the king's bad humour, 1 Oct. 1635, Avenel, ed. cit. v. cxxvi. Sublet de Noyers to Chavigny: he explains that he has completed all of the tasks that Chavigny had ordered him to do 'de la part du Roy', 25 Aug. 1636, AAE, France, 821, vol. 228.

[2] Claude le Bouthillier to Chavigny?, 18 Oct. 1636, AAE, France, 822, fol. 49.

[3] Louis to Richelieu, 30 Oct. 1637: 'J'ay plusieurs choses à vous mander, si Monsieur de Noyers n'a que faire, vous me feriés plesir de me l'envoyer ce soir sur les 4 à 5 heures.' AAE, France, 244, fol. 276.

[4] Louis was careful to inform Richelieu directly when he feared that a secretary would change his views or orders. He wrote to Richelieu: 'Monsieur Servien me vient de parler d'une depesche à Monsieur le Conte [Soissons] pour entrer dans le conté de Bourgogne et par ce moyen jetter des vivres dans Colmar et Sélestat. Je luy ay dit de vous dire que je desirois vous voir avant que cette depesche partit, je vous ay voulu escrire cecy de peur que il ne vous dit autrement, que ce que je luy ay dit ou qu'il n'adjoutat quelque chose à la verité.' 19 Dec. 1635, AAE, France, 244, fol. 232.

[5] When secrecy was requested by Louis, it usually concerned his brother Gaston; he specified who was to be informed. Louis to Richelieu, 12 Sept. 1634, ibid., fol. 65.

As to Richelieu's general political relationships with his creatures, he possessed broader powers than they, though no new title was given to institutionalize them;[1] in fact, they needed no institutionalization, for they were based upon the great favour and support of the king, as reflected in the confusion of the roles of king and principal minister in the last years of the reign. These broad powers enabled Richelieu to dominate and direct the whole government.

Richelieu did not hesitate to reprimand his underlings or to insult them with his sarcasm.[2] Yet at the same time he showered them with gifts, political favours, and personal affection. The loss of the cardinal's favour meant disgrace; the threat hung like a pall over all the ministers, obliging them to be obedient and obsequious.[3] At the same time, all knew that the political existence of the entire ministry depended upon the favour of Louis for Richelieu; the king guarded his supreme powers jealously, and Richelieu acted independently only when expressly authorized by Louis to do so.[4]

Richelieu relied heavily on these officers for information and administrative details.[5] He had confidence in them;

[1] The title of Principal Minister, given to him in 1629, does not seem to have changed his ministerial stature, but it gave him precedence over other councillors.

[2] Richelieu wrote to Louis: 'Monsieur de Bullion paiera volontiers ceste despense sur les quinze cens chevaux d'Allemagne, à cause de la dévotion qu'il a eue autrefois à Martin Luther.' 14 Oct. 1634, Avenel, ed. cit. IV. cccxxvi. Was Richelieu joking, or had Bullion once been sympathetic toward the Protestants? Such a comment would appear to be innocent, but considering the emotionalism and political consequences of religious beliefs in the seventeenth century, this type of humour was heavier than it would seem.

[3] There was no exception among the councillors. See Séguier's letter to Chavigny, where he nervously lists the signs of affection shown for him by Richelieu. Some minor offence had made him fear that his position was in danger, but he concluded peacefully that there was no reason to 'prendre créance si légèrement', 28 Apr. 1635, AAE, France, 813, fol. 317.

[4] When considerable distance separated Louis and Richelieu, the latter sometimes felt obliged to act quickly without informing the king. To do so, he asked Louis for special powers which seem to have been only temporary. A good example of this action occurred in 1642, when the king and the cardinal were both campaigning in southern France. See Richelieu to Sublet, 25 June 1642, Avenel, ed. cit. VI. cccclxxxiii; Richelieu to Sublet and Chavigny, 27 June 1642, letter cccclxxxvi of the same volume; and Louis's letter granting the powers cited above, p. 2.

[5] This is most clear in foreign affairs and the army administration; see below, Chapters IV and V.

when he was preparing for war he nervously sent the secretary of state for war a request for a statement of the condition and strength of the army.[1] Their advice was sought, and after humbly apologizing, they gave it quite freely to Richelieu. Even Bullion, the minister second only to Richelieu in prestige and power in the government of Louis XIII, made it a practice to begin with a long apology, which nevertheless did not hide his differences of opinion from the cardinal.[2] In this way the cardinal was able to keep abreast of governmental problems, to make decisions quickly, and with the support of the other ministers to present a unified policy to Louis XIII in the *conseil*. Although his knowledge of detail was vast, he was not an administrative superman.

Haste and efficiency were essential to seventeenth-century government; some of Richelieu's most bitter comments to his creatures concerned their failure to act quickly and forcefully. The ministers worked all hours of the day and night, and travelled almost constantly about the realm.[3] Louis himself insisted on action, and sometimes while on a campaign he took very bad lodgings in his haste to get on with the war.[4] As with the king, the ministers often carried verbal orders from Richelieu to each other to save time and to ensure secrecy.[5] Intrigue against Richelieu by courtiers and would-be parties was constant, but the cardinal's confidence in the other ministers was absolute. Through his influence with the king, the cardinal had made them ministers, not because of their administrative efficiency, nor for that matter because of their knowledge of foreign affairs, finance, or the army, but because affection and fidelity were

[1] Richelieu to Servien, 23 Mar. 1635, Avenel, ed. cit. IV. ccclxi.
[2] Bullion to Richelieu, 1 Sept. 1639?: 'Je suplie Vostre Eminence m'excuser si un serviteur prend la hardiesse d'escripre à Son Maistre avec la liberté dont vous voulez que vos creatures usent vers vous. . . .' AAE, France, 834, fol. 43.
[3] Servien to Richelieu, 9 July 1635, '. . . hyer aussy tost que je receuz vos ordres par la despesche du sieur de Vignolles, je montay en carosse pour aller voir le Révérend Père Joseph où je fus jusques à deux heures apres midy sans avoir disné; au retour je travaillay à la despesche jusques à la nuit. . . .' Avenel, ed. cit. v, p. 101; AAE, France, 814, fol. 255.
[4] De Noyers to Chavigny, 18? Sept. 1636, AAE, France, 821, fol. 341.
[5] Chavigny reported to Richelieu that he had communicated his orders to Bullion and Séguier, 6 May 1635, AAE, France, 814, fol. 20.

the chief personal and political pre-requisites which determined the very nature of government in the last years of
Louis XIII.

How did Richelieu personally envisage his position within
the ministry? In his own correspondence with the ministers
he made very few comments on his role as he saw it. Once
he wrote to Chavigny: 'However, I will leave all the necessary orders at Amiens in fulfilment of my *charge* which, as
you know, is none other than solicitor of diligence . . . .'[1] It
was much more than this. Without creating new offices or
institutions, Richelieu acquired certain powers reserved only
for the king. The force of his personality, first on the king
and next on the ministers whom he selected, was responsible
for the nature of the central government in the last years of
Louis XIII.

[1] 29 Oct. 1636, Avenel, ed. cit. v. ccclii.

II

The Creatures of Cardinal Richelieu

CARDINAL RICHELIEU, like all men in high office, was compelled to choose administrators and secretaries to help him with the affairs of state. The story of how he came to choose the other ministers has never been told, and while historians have always been interested in the influence of men who live in the shadow of great figures, for Richelieu only Père Joseph and Cardinal Mazarin have thus far attracted their attention. Several ministers who played roles of great importance in the last decade of the reign of Louis XIII have only been described in a few pages scattered in various works.

In the seventeenth and eighteenth centuries historians recognized the importance of favouritism, but they looked at it only from the viewpoint of the king. As a result, many histories rarely got beyond anecdotes of Louis XIII's relations with Concini, Luynes, Richelieu, Cinq-Mars, and so forth. Though they were aware of the ministerial circle, its formation and character did not attract them.[1] As a result, in the nineteenth century—with the development of the old interpretation that Richelieu virtually governed France alone—the other ministers, the king himself, and the favouritism which determined their relationship were not given their proper place in the history of the reign of Louis XIII.[2]

[1] Certain historians were very aware of Richelieu's domination of the other ministers. Some notable examples are Aubery, *Histoire du Cardinal de Richelieu* . . . (Paris, 1660); Père Griffet, *Histoire du règne de Louis XIII* . . . (Paris, 1758); and Le Vassor, *Histoire de Louis XIII* . . . (Amsterdam, 1757).

[2] Representative of a whole group of historians who emphasized only the work of Richelieu are A. Bazin, *Histoire de France sous Louis XIII et sous le ministère du Cardinal Mazarin* (Paris, 1846); J. Caillet, *L'Administration en France sous le ministère du Cardinal de Richelieu* (Paris, 1863); and Vicomte d'Avenel, *Richelieu et la monarchie absolue* (Paris, 1895). In the twentieth century historians have dropped the problem after the studies of the Duc de la Force, *Histoire du Cardinal de Richelieu* (Paris, 1933).

To put the ministry of Richelieu into proper perspective, knowledge of royal-patronage practices and detailed family histories of the ministers is necessary. In tracing the history of office appointments, one is confronted with silence in the documents; the intrigues of the various parties in the government itself are frequently impossible to untangle, and yet it was in precisely this domain that councillors and courtiers measured their stature. Even the sketches of the early lives of the ministers of Louis XIII are difficult. Old genealogies and historical dictionaries abound, but they render the problem not so much one of lack of information as of verification of facts.

It is particularly convenient that in the seventeenth century the word *créature* was common usage in the French upper classes. As a term of politeness, it is frequently found in thank-you letters and in the long and formal closing sentences of day-to-day correspondence. In addressing expressions of affection to the king, Richelieu often referred to himself as a creature of Louis XIII.[1] In this way the source of the high position and favour which the cardinal enjoyed in the State was acknowledged.[2] The other ministers also used the term quite naturally when writing to a member of the royal family or to anyone having a rank in society superior to theirs.[3]

The chancellor, superintendents of finance, and secretaries of state—in short, the whole ministry of Louis XIII— frequently wrote letters to Richelieu referring to themselves as his 'creatures'. In addition to honour, the term 'creature'

[1] Richelieu spoke for his party as a whole when he wrote to Louis: 'Je la [sa Majesté] supplie de ne craindre jamais de les [his sentiments] communiquer à ses créatures. . . .' He finished his letter: 'Pour moy, je n'en [contentement] auray jamais qu'en faisant connoistre de plus en plus à Vostre Majesté, que je suis la plus fidèle créature, le plus passionné sujet, et le plus zélé serviteur que jamais roy et maistre ait eu au monde. Je vivray et finiray en cet estat comme estant cent fois plus à Vostre Majesté qu'à moy-mesme. . . .' 12 Nov. 1630, Richelieu, *Lettres, instructions diplomatiques et papiers d'État*, ed. M. Avenel (Paris, 1853–77), IV. iv.

[2] Richelieu used the term when writing to his own creatures about his relationship with the king. He wrote to Claude le Bouthillier: 'J'ay esté très aise de recevoir par vous asseurance de la santé du roy, qui est ce que je désire avec la passion d'une vraie et passionnée créature.' 10 Jan. 1639, ibid. VI. clvii.

[3] See below, p. 82.

also reflected real obligation and affection. The relationships between Richelieu and the other ministers were unlike those usually found in modern times.

The entire ministry, including all the political power exercised by Richelieu, rested upon his personal relationship with Louis XIII. The monarchy, through the centuries, had not only increased the central powers in the State, but had also erected a series of relationships within the government based on the personal will and favour of the king. Louis XIII always had the power to disgrace, even to put to death, any minister, but this theoretically unlimited power vested in the monarchy was in reality limited by the ability of the ministers in power to command factions within the State. The power of the king over his ministers was in a very real sense dependent upon the existence of opposition parties and upon the presence of other influential councillors eager to have a greater voice in the affairs of State. Richelieu, in almost twenty years as the principal favourite of Louis XIII, was able to build his own party in the government and to crush the men plotting his disgrace.

After his entry into the *Conseil du roi* in 1624, Richelieu gradually began to dominate the political will, not only of the king, but of the chief councillors as well. There were certainly numerous trials, setbacks, and even near disgrace, such as the affair of the Day of the Dupes in 1630; but this did not stop Richelieu from extending his powers. The reign to 1624, with its constant upheavals in the central administration, was excellent testing ground for the minister, who well knew and understood how to direct political favouritism in its broadest sense and who did not hesitate to form a circle of favourites himself. In the period from 1635 to 1642 a hierarchy of relationships developed among the men around the king that became politically more significant in determining their powers than the traditional divisions of royal authority by office.

What were Richelieu's relations with Louis's other ministers? Not long after the cardinal's death an anonymous historian of the secretaries of state wrote, in discussing the disfavour of one secretary: 'The disgrace of the Sieur de la Ville-aux-Clercs proceeded from the fact that Cardinal

Richelieu, having made himself master of the King's mind, wanted all those who approached his person to be his creatures and to promise to obey him without reservation.'[1] Richelieu's domination of Louis's other ministers did not slip by unnoticed by his contemporaries.

Although Richelieu had many favourites during his tempestuous career, in this study only the secretaries of state, Chavigny and Sublet de Noyers, and the superintendents of finance, Bullion and Bouthillier, will be considered for the period from 1635 to 1642. In the group closest to the king, Pierre Séguier, Chancellor and Keeper of the Seals, also played a very important role as one of Richelieu's devoted creatures, but any analysis of his position in the government must wait until the Séguier papers now in Leningrad become generally available.[2] Père Joseph and Mazarin have already been extensively studied.[3]

Characteristically, when Richelieu gained the power to influence royal appointments, he turned to his family. As he himself amassed offices and wealth, all the members of his family—both the du Plessis and the La Portes—climbed to positions of political or ecclesiastical power and of social prestige. His brother became a cardinal, one niece a duchess, and a cousin was made a marshal in the French armies, while countless offices were held by his more distant relatives.

[1] *Mémoires de l'establissement des secrétaires d'Estat*, BN, MS. 18236, fol. 115ᵛ. This most important source for the history of the secretaries of state in the sixteenth century and to 1647 was probably the work of one author. To our knowledge, there are six copies of the manuscript in France. At the BN, MSS. 18236 and 18237 from the library of Chancellor Séguier both contain copies. These, along with MS. 136 in the special collection Cinq Cents Colbert in the same library, seem to be the oldest copies. BN MS. 18242 from the library of Louvois is late seventeenth century, while MS. 4191 is an eighteenth-century copy made for Cangé, Secretary of State under Louis XV. Finally, the catalogue of manuscripts for the Bibliothèque de Bordeaux indicates another copy. Interestingly, MS. 18236 and MS. 136 in the Cinq Cents Colbert are in the same hand, although they came from two different private libraries. There are slight differences in the text, which appear to be due to errors of the copyist and which indicate that the two manuscripts were probably copied from another copy or the original text.

[2] For a discussion of the Séguier papers, see R. Mousnier, 'Recherches sur les soulèvements populaires en France avant la Fronde', *Revue d'Histoire Moderne et Contemporaine*, 1958, pp. 82 ff.

[3] See E. Préclin et V. Tapié, *Le XVIIᵉ Siècle* (Paris, 1955), for a bibliography concerning Mazarin and Père Joseph.

Richelieu had difficulty in controlling certain members of his family, notably Maréchal de La Meilleraye; and in other cases the incapacity of his relatives and the resulting confusion caused him some embarrassment and even anger, but never to the point of disgracing a member of his family.[1]

The importance of family in the political career of any statesman is hard to measure, but at least two reasons for Richelieu's appointment of his relatives are obvious. The old framework remaining from what had been feudalism continued to give dynastic ambitions direction and importance. It provided a scale of social values and goals. The importance of an individual in society was determined not only by his position and wealth, but also by the prestige of his family. Inheritance and family relationships as a whole were measured not in family units of father, mother, and children, but in ties much deeper and almost dynastic. A desire for titles with higher prestige became more obvious, not only in the Richelieu family, but in French society as a whole as the seventeenth century wore on. Aided by royal policy, greater numbers of what became *titres de fantaisie*, such as count, marquis, baron, and even duke, caused the nobility and the Richelieus to be content no longer as plain *seigneurs* of their lands. This, however, was only the lighter side of the story. Wealth, political and ecclesiastical powers, great houses, lands, prosperous marriages for their children, and prestige-laden as well as lucrative offices that could be passed on from father to son or nephew, were the goals of the du Plessis and the La Porte families.

The second aspect was the element of control, and ultimately of fidelity, which Richelieu commanded over his family. With his relatives in influential positions, he was fairly safe from opposition in those quarters; and like the king above them all, Richelieu held the supreme threat, that of disgrace, over all their heads.

In many ways the ambitions and positions of Richelieu's friends, the future ministers, were similar to those of his family, for they were second to benefit from his rise to

---

[1] See Richelieu's caustic letter to his nephew, Du Pont de Courlay, *général des galères*, where he upbraids him for his excessive expenditures on servants, &c., 6 June 1636, Avenel, ed. cit. v. ccxlv.

power. The entire Bouthillier family, for example, had played a great role in the cardinal's life from childhood. If one can believe Saint-Simon, Denis le Bouthillier, Seigneur de Fouilletourte, had been a clerk of François de La Porte, Richelieu's grandfather.[1] Upon his death, La Porte left Bouthillier his law practice, 'and recommended to him his grandchildren who no longer had any parents. [Saint-Simon is mistaken; Richelieu's mother lived until 1616.] Bouthillier cared for them like his own children. This is the origin of the Bouthillier fortune.'[2] Thus it was perhaps in gratitude and in confidence that Richelieu recommended the Bouthilliers— particularly Claude, who had become a councillor in the Parlement of Paris in 1613—to Marie de Médicis, to be a secretary of the Queen Mother's commands. Richelieu's influence on the good fortune of his friend was acknowledged in a letter to the king written some ten years later, when Louis had just named Bouthillier Secretary of State.[3]

Denis le Bouthillier, the brother of Claude, was also a secretary to the Queen Mother and a councillor.[4] Beginning together as favourites of the old queen, Richelieu and the Bouthilliers formed a party and placed the interest of the group above those of its particular members. The cardinal, first to break into the royal court, relied on these old friends as they worked together for greater power and prestige. Richelieu's confidential letters to Denis, Seigneur de Rancé, indicate how he relied on Denis for confirmation not only

[1] Fouilletourte, according to Avenel, became a councillor of state on 2 Feb. 1617, and died in 1622. Ibid. i, p. 702.

[2] Saint-Simon, as quoted by Gabriel Hanotaux, *Histoire du Cardinal de Richelieu* (Paris, 1896), i, p. 42.

[3] Marie de Médicis to Louis XIII, undated, copy, BN, Collection Baluze 323, fol. 72. 'Les provisions de secretaire d'Estat qu'il vous a pleu m'envoyer pour Bouthillier en la place du feu Sieur d'Oquerre, a faict cognoistre de plus en plus a tout le monde l'affection que vous me portés, et la confiance entiere que vous avés en moy, prenant pour vous servir en une charge importante comme celle-là une personne que vous avés recogneue m'avoir longtemps servie avec toute sorte de fidelité, je m'assure qu'il respondra à la creance que vous avés qu'il ne l'aura pas moindre en cette charge dont vous l'honorés, et que vous n'aurés point de regret de l'avoir pris de ma main, comme je n'en ay point eu de l'avoir pris de celle de Mon Cousin le Cardinal de Richelieu qui me le donna il y a pres de dix ans, me le recommandant particulierement pour la sincerité et fidelité. . . .'

[4] Roland Mousnier, 'Les Règlements du Conseil du roi sous Louis XIII'. *Annuaire-Bulletin de la Société de l'Histoire de France*, 1946–7, p. 198.

of the Queen Mother's actions, but also of her attitudes in every domain.[1] This was especially important when Louis and Richelieu were absent from Paris, leaving Marie to preside over the *Conseil du Roi*. Through reports from the Bouthilliers, Richelieu was able to watch over the government in Paris from a distance.[2]

The Bouthilliers and Richelieu, while occasionally acting in their own interests, continued within the party of the Queen Mother through the court intrigues and plots of the early 1620's. Richelieu was ever gaining in influence in other quarters without breaking with Marie, whose cleverness and love of intrigue made the political observations by the Bouthilliers necessary to Richelieu. Contemporaries and later historians have been astonished by the fact that the cardinal seemed to know all of the court intrigues and plots in advance. The story of his having developed a secret service has been reflected in history and literature. Actually the cardinal needed no secret service in the modern sense of the term; his friends and relatives, situated in key positions and willing to place the interests of Richelieu and the party above their own, were all that was necessary.[3]

[1] See Richelieu to Rancé, 30 Apr. 1629, Avenel, ed. cit., iii. cliv particularly; and clvi and clviii.

[2] Claude le Bouthillier's role in presenting Richelieu's points of view to Marie, or letters written by him to be sent as if written by the king, can be noticed in Richelieu to Bouthillier, ibid. ii. cvi, 20 Oct. 1626; and cix, dated 1 Oct. 1626.

[3] There were also two other Bouthillier brothers who played roles in the Richelieu party. Through the cardinal, Victor (d. 1670) was named Bishop of Boulogne and later coadjutor to the Archbishop of Tours. In both capacities he reported on religious, political, and economic affairs in the two regions (see the 'Commission à M. l'Archevêque Coadjuteur de Tours pour la recherche de quelque Crimes énormes et possession des démons à Chinon', 1640, AG, A[1], 62, fol. 22, and more specifically on a problem concerning royal justice, Richelieu to Sublet, 15 Sept. 1635, Avenel, ed. cit. v. cix; and Victor Bouthillier to Bellièvre, 28 Dec. 1637, BN, MS. 15915, fol. 52). In return for this co-operation Richelieu continued to shower favours on Victor Bouthillier, procuring the position of almoner to Louis's brother, Gaston (Richelieu to Gaston, 6 May 1636, Avenel, ed. cit. v, p. 971). The fourth Bouthillier brother intimately associated with Richelieu was Sebastien, Bishop of Aire and Prieur de la Cochère (d. 1625). In 1619 Sebastien Bouthillier, along with Père Joseph, pressed Marie de Médicis to rescind the orders exiling Richelieu to Avignon. *Mémoires du Cardinal de Richelieu*, ed. Michaud and Poujoulat (Paris, 1857), xxi, part 1, p. 193. He was also sent to Rome as a special envoy to hasten Richelieu's elevation as cardinal, indicating the measure of confidence which he held before his premature death (Avenel,

The genealogies of the *ancien régime*, particularly those in manuscript in the *Cabinet des titres* at the Bibliothèque Nationale, indicate more fully the social history of the Bouthilliers and, for that matter, of all the families of Richelieu's creatures.[1] A detailed analysis indicates that other members of the family—cousins to the third degree and uncles only by marriage—also received offices and pensions with the help of Richelieu and their relatives in the government. Small offices, priories, abbacies, almoneries, and so forth dot the history of the family from the reign of Louis XIII.

Claude le Bouthillier was born in 1581, a *simple gentilhomme;* that is, probably without lands.[2] He married Marie de Bragelonne, daughter of the Seigneur de Caves, near Ponts-sur-Seine. Bouthillier began to enlarge the lands at Ponts-sur-Seine, and in 1608, two years after his marriage, he purchased the port of Caves.[3] Richelieu was fond of Madame Bouthillier; his concern for her health and welfare was the subject of many letters that the cardinal addressed to her throughout his life.[4]

Following the sudden death of Nicolas Potier, Seigneur d'Oquerre, Secretary of State, in September 1628 Louis chose Bouthillier to replace him. This was a great favour to the Queen Mother, who saw in the appointment of her secretary an increase in the influence of her party. Richelieu's influence on the appointment is impossible to determine, owing to his position as a partisan of Marie de Médicis at the time. Louis's decision to appoint Bouthillier was due to the influence of both the Queen Mother and the cardinal. Unfortunately, as was nearly always the case with Louis's decisions concerning appointments, no record of his own views on the subject has survived.

ed. cit. i, p. 571; and letter dxxxiii of 29 Aug. 1620, from Louis to Pope Urban VIII in the same volume).

[1] The modern genealogy of the Bouthillier family is by Louis le Clert, *Notice généalogique sur les Bouthillier de Chavigny, Seigneurs de Ponts-sur-Seine, de Rancé, et de Beaujeu* (Troyes, 1907).

[2] Chevalier and Seigneur de Ponts, Rossigny, Fouilletourte, and a host of other small lands, *Cabinet des titres, dossiers bleus*, 126, 'Bouthillier'.

[3] Le Clert, op. cit., p. 9.

[4] For a detailed though unsound study of Richelieu's relationship with Marie de Bragelonne, see M. Deloche, *Richelieu et les femmes* (Paris, 1931).

Bouthillier, as secretary of state, assumed charge of the department given to Oquerre by the *règlement* of 1626.[1] His accession to the department of foreign affairs did not occur until some time after the death of Raymond Phélypeaux, Seigneur d'Herbault, in May 1629.[2] There was considerable discussion and intrigue before Louis appointed Herbault's successor. A letter addressed to Rancé and his brother, Claude le Bouthillier, provides an insight into the intrigue which preceded office appointments. 'I [Richelieu] still persist in the exclusion of the man you know about for the *charge* of the deceased [Herbault] but what I wrote you about Monsieur de La Vrillière was only undigested and passing thoughts; in parting I beg you not to hurry a resolution on these grounds.'[3] More details are given in the *Mémoires de l'establissement des secrétaires d'Estat*, especially on La Vrillière and the conflict between Marillac and Richelieu; but this does not explain Bouthillier's accession to the department of foreign affairs.[4] It may be that Claude le Bouthillier and La Vrillière struck a bargain, so that in return for Richelieu's and Bouthillier's support, La Vrillière would accept the *charge* without the department of foreign affairs, which was in precedence superior to the others. In any case, almost immediately after La Vrillière's appointment, Bouthillier took up the task of secretary of state for foreign affairs.

With the accumulation of offices and wealth, Bouthillier expanded his landholdings at Ponts-sur-Seine; combined them with the seigniory of Caves, the inheritance of his wife; and constructed a fine house on the property.[5] The

[1] BN, Clairambault 664, fol. 129. This was a department where only internal affairs in certain provinces and the Atlantic navy were under his jurisdiction.

[2] L. Delavaud, 'Quelques collaborateurs de Richelieu—rapports sur l'édition des mémoires du Cardinal de Richelieu', *Société de l'Histoire de France* (Paris, 1915), II, fasc. iv and v, p. 200.

[3] 9 May 1629, Avenel, ed. cit. III. clxi.

[4] BN, MS. 18236, fols. 137 ff. See below, p. 71, for further information on La Vrillière.

[5] Ponts-sur-Seine is near Nogent-sur-Seine (Aube). Of Bouthillier's original château by Le Muet, only the courtyard of the farm remains, with its *abreuvoir* and *pigeonnier* enclosed by an arcade. In the village church (chapel to the right) is a painting of the Bouthilliers as donors; the same portraits on a larger scale are in the château. We wish to thank Madame Sommier of Vaux-le-Vicomte and Ponts-sur-Seine for furnishing these details.

marriage of his only son, Léon, born in 1608, to the only daughter of the Seigneur de Villesavin, a member of the proud and influential Phélypeaux family, is a further indication of the new prosperity and prestige of Bouthillier.[1]

Richelieu showered affection on young Bouthillier, but this was not enough to allay the father's concern for his son's future. This concern is apparent in a letter, unfortunately not dated, written by Bouthillier to Richelieu, after a reference to the deceased Secretary d'Oquerre's widow and children:

When I remember that four years ago upon seeing my son, you paid me the honour of saying to me, 'This boy is coming along well, he will be capable in two years of succeeding you in your *charge*'; that almost two years ago you also paid me the honour of writing to me at Pontoise . . . 'In addition, I have seen your heir, whom I found a grown man, modestly courageous, suitable *ad rem*, in a word, a better man than his father'; that when I arranged his marriage you did not approve at first that I give him a *charge* of *conseiller de la cour*, paying me the honour of saying to me that it was in order to take over mine. . . .[2]

Avenel attempted to find an explanation for Bouthillier's concern for his son by giving the hypothesis that he was having a quarrel with some member of the Richelieu family. The reference to Oquerre's widow and children just previous to this quotation was not considered by Avenel as important enough to be included.[3]

[1] The seigniory of Villesavin is in the Loir-et-Cher; the stately sixteenth-century château with its great slate roofs *à la française* still survives, as do certain relics from the time of the Bouthilliers.

[2] AAE, France, 801, fol. 169; and in part Avenel, ed. cit. iv, p. 330.

[3] According to the anonymous author of the *Mémoires de l'establissement des secrétaires d'Estat*, Bouthillier paid the Oquerre family 200,000 *livres* as recompense for the loss of the office, which would normally have been granted to the heir of Oquerre or, if he were a minor, to an uncle until the heir reached majority. In addition to this, the Queen Mother also gave the Oquerres 100,000 *livres*. But, as in previous cases, in spite of payment for an office, in the event of a ministerial upheaval and the disgrace which followed, a secretary of state who had paid for his office could lose his position as well as his money. In a time when only the always precarious health of the king stood between favour and disgrace for the entire Richelieu party, such a concern for the welfare of his son was a real one. Léon de Bouthillier, his son, was not only in favour with Richelieu but was also later admired and accepted by Gaston d'Orléans. When Bouthillier referred to someone who was plotting to disgrace him (quoted by Avenel), the gravity of the situation seemed to be beyond a family quarrel. Perhaps Châteauneuf, who was to be disgraced in

Whatever the cause of Bouthillier's concern, his hopes were realized in 1632 after the death of the Superintendent of Finance, Effiat. Léon le Bouthillier was granted the office of secretary of state for foreign affairs by survivance when his father, along with Claude de Bullion, became superintendent of finance.

The two Bouthilliers served in these very important positions as creatures of Richelieu until the latter's death broke the ministerial circle which he had created, and by 1642 the Bouthillier family as a whole had become very influential and wealthy. Richelieu's creatures supported him faithfully, but at the same time they did not hesitate to come to the cardinal to ask for favours. Richelieu was constantly sought after to arrange for greater incomes, advantageous marriages, and, above all, offices with pensions for their families.

Claude de Bullion became superintendent of finance jointly with Claude le Bouthillier in 1632. While also a member of the group totally loyal to Richelieu, he held a special place among the creatures because of his greater age and long record of service to the Crown.[1] From a rich and influential family, Bullion began his political career early as a councillor in the Parlement of Paris. His father had held various offices under Henry III, and his mother was a member of the immensely rich and influential Lamoignon family. Thus neither prestige nor fortune was lacking, and he became a master of requests and royal councillor under Henry IV. During the regency of Marie de Médicis, he served in positions that brought him into the royal court; as superintendent of Navarre in 1612, and chancellor to the Queen Mother in 1615, Bullion had opportunity to attend the court and to grow in favour. His position as representative of the Crown at the Assembly of Saumur in 1611 indicates that he had the confidence of Marie de Médicis and her councillors at this early date.[2] According to Hozier, Bullion was married

1633, was seeking to strengthen his position in the government by replacing Bouthillier with a member of the Oquerre family. BN, MS. 18236, fol. 126ᵛ.

[1] The date of his birth is unknown. The old genealogical histories estimated his age as about seventy when he died in 1640. See also BN, MS. 18660, fol. 182ᵛ.

[2] J. H. Mariéjol, *Histoire de France*, ed. E. Lavisse (Paris, 1911), VI, part 2,

in 1612 to Angélique Faure, and was at the time already a councillor in the *Conseil d'État* and in the *Conseil Privé*.[1] In 1617 Bullion is mentioned as the commissioner sent to Rouen to enforce the *arrêts du conseil*.[2]

With the exception of several special missions which kept him away from Paris, Bullion spent the rest of his life serving the Crown on the councils. By the *Règlement sommaire pour le conseil de la direction des finances* of 1619, Bullion was given special duties involving the provincial administration of finances.[3] (Only honoured and already well-experienced councillors received brevets to enter this *conseil*.)[4] Finally, in June 1624, Bullion was given the unconditional privilege of sitting on all the king's councils, a privilege indicating his prestige and importance at the very moment when Richelieu entered the councils.[5]

In the difficult years from 1624 to 1630, when Richelieu's position was unstable because of the party led against him by Michel de Marillac, Keeper of the Seals, Bullion became one of Richelieu's supporters. The first political connexions between Bullion and Richelieu have yet to be discovered, but the cardinal had taken him into his confidence as early as 1628 on such a delicate matter as his quarrel with the Duc de Guise over the direction of the southern navy,[6] and by the crucial year of 1630 Bullion was definitely in Richelieu's party. The cardinal even borrowed money from him.[7] Bullion's position as a creature is certain, for he carefully informed Richelieu of the various court intrigues developing against him two months before the Day of the Dupes in the fall of 1630.[8]

p. 150. See the *Mémoires du Cardinal de Richelieu*, ed. cit., *passim*, for numerous references to Bullion's career at court.

[1] *Cabinet des titres*, D'Hozier, 72, 'Bullion'.

[2] Duc de la Force to Loménie, Secretary of State, 14 Nov. 1617, ed. Duc de la Force, *Le Maréchal de la Force* (Paris, 1950), p. 347.

[3] Mousnier, 'Règlements du Conseil', ed. cit., p. 157.

[4] Roland Mousnier, 'Le Conseil du roi de la mort de Henri IV au gouvernement personnel de Louis XIV', *Études d'Histoire Moderne et Contemporaine*, i (1947), p. 47.

[5] Mousnier, 'Règlements du Conseil', ed. cit., p. 161.

[6] Avenel, ed. cit. iii, p. 173. See also Mariéjol, op. cit., p. 286. The quarrel continued over at least a three-year period.

[7] Richelieu to Bullion, end of April? 1630, ibid. iii. ccclx.

[8] Ibid. iii, p. 845. See also letter xiii of volume iv to Bullion, dated 23 Nov.

Noyers

Throughout this period and into the 1630's Bullion's wealth never ceased to grow. It was reflected in the construction of the lovely château of Wideville, a veritable jewel of simplicity and elegance, situated equidistant from the great forests of Versailles, Saint-Germain, and Marly.[1] In the two-year interval before he was made superintendent of finance along with Bouthillier, Bullion continued to support Richelieu and to advise him on such important problems as the trial of Maréchal Louis de Marillac for treason, and the possibility of a revolt in southern France after the arrest of Montmorency.[2]

The early correspondence between Bullion and Richelieu has a different tone from that of the other creatures. Bullion did not hesitate to give his views to Richelieu; at the same time it is obvious that he knew the king respected him in his own right, and that he had arrived at a high position in the government without Richelieu's help. Only in the last great period of his career was the cardinal's influence predominant. When Bullion became superintendent of finance with Claude le Bouthillier, at the time when Richelieu had just succeeded in crushing Châteauneuf and the last faction among the ministers ever to rise against him (1632), Claude de Bullion's many years of experience in the Parlement and *conseils*, as a diplomat, and as an *intrigueur*, were very valuable to Richelieu. As Bullion worked frantically to pay the heavy expenses of the war, his devotion to Richelieu was unwavering; but he did not hesitate about neglecting or even brushing aside the cardinal's orders.

Just as Bullion became Richelieu's trusted aide on financial questions, so Sublet de Noyers held a similar position for the administration of the army. François Sublet, Chevalier and Seigneur de Noyers, like many of Richelieu's other creatures, came from a family which had held minor offices in the government over several generations. Born about 1588, the son of Jean Sublet, a councillor of the king and a

1630, where Richelieu confided his desperation and anxiety about the Queen Mother's actions.
    [1] See Marquis de Galard, *Monographie du château de Wideville* (Paris, 1879), *passim*.
    [2] Avenel, ed. cit. iv, pp. 241 and 365, after extracts of Bullion's letters to Richelieu.

minor official in the *chambre des comptes*, young Noyers began his political career with the help of his mother's family.[1] Magdalaine Bochart, Sublet's mother, was descended from a long line of office holders in the Parlement; her brother, Jean de Champigny, was an important political figure in the 1620's, who became superintendent of finance and comptroller general in 1624.[2] Champigny asked his young nephew to become his clerk; and as the former increased in favour— becoming first president of the Parlement of Paris in 1628— Sublet de Noyers became an intendant of finance.[3]

Much has been written on the intendants in general, but there is little information on the complex problem of the different kinds of intendants—army, finance, justice.[4] The position of the intendant of finance is particularly mysterious. In the last years of the reign of Louis XIII there were generally four intendants of finance, all important members of the councils who, like the secretaries of state, had certain regions under their responsibility; but they differed in that the intendant of finance used the *généralité* instead of the province as a basis for geographical divisions. In addition, certain revenues—the farms, salt taxes, and so forth— were distributed among the four, as were the sovereign courts.[5] They also alternated for three-month terms in the position of comptroller general, another office not yet clearly defined for the reign of Louis XIII.[6]

Sublet's duties in Picardy were considerable when Louis and Richelieu were attempting to rebuild fortifications and raise troops in the area.[7] The intendants of finance were

[1] Fauvelet-du-Toc, *Histoire des secrétaires d'Estat contenant l'origine, le progrès, et l'establissement de leurs charges* (Paris, 1668), p. 291.
[2] Mousnier, 'Règlements du Conseil', ed. cit., p. 199.
[3] Fauvelet-du-Toc, op. cit., p. 291.
[4] For the latest statement on the intendants, see R. Mousnier, 'Etat et Commissaire, recherches sur la création des intendants des provinces (1634–1648)', *Forschungen zu Staat und Verfassung, Festgabe für Fritz Hartung* (Berlin, 1958).
[5] Two of these divisions, one for 31 Dec. 1642, and the other for shortly after, are in the Bibliothèque de l'Arsenal, MS. 4058, fol. 291; and MS. 3783, fol. 208.
[6] Bibliothèque de l'Arsenal, MS. 4058, fol. 291.
[7] C. Schmidt, 'Le Rôle et les attributions d'un intendant des finances aux armées, Sublet de Noyers, de 1632 à 1636', *Revue d'Histoire Moderne et Contemporaine* (Paris, 1901) is unobjective but useful for the preparations at Corbie before 1635.

often called upon to carry out special missions; Particelli, Seigneur d'Hémery (or Emery) and Intendant of Finance, made numerous trips to Savoy, where he attempted to build up the armies, restore financial order, and gain friends for France among the dissident factions of Savoyard nobles.[1] Yet neither the special missions of Sublet nor those of Hémery have a real connexion with the financial jurisdictions established for their offices. There is only one small clue to the problem. On 31 January 1633 Sublet addressed a letter to the *Trésoriers de France au Bureau des Finances de Lyon* to inform them that henceforth they should address their correspondence to Hémery, as it was he who was succeeding Sublet 'dans le gouvernement de leur généralité'.[2] Was it then the duty of the intendants of finance to receive the correspondence of the lower financial administration for the *Conseil du Roi*? Further research in the financial papers of the departmental archives might well clarify the duties of this important office.[3] Sublet de Noyers no doubt learned much about military and fortification problems in Picardy, and he also was probably very familiar with the intricate financial structure of the royal government in the provinces.

Sublet may also have carried out certain reforms in the monetary system as intendant of finance. It was probably in 1634 that he wrote a treatise on money in which he discussed the international problems of money, the flow of gold and silver from Spain, the poverty of France in these metals; and in which he proposed a programme for ameliorating the condition by changing metal ratios in the coinage and by erecting strict monetary barriers on the borders.[4] In January 1634 Sublet wrote to Richelieu that he was anxiously awaiting the results of the *épreuves*, gold or silver ratio calculations and experiments, which he was directing at the

---

[1] See his correspondence with the court at the AAE, Sardaigne, 27, *passim.*

[2] *Catalogue Charavay*, Alavoine 42-(11)-101, Thiercelin, no. 58 *bis.*

[3] For example, see the *Estat de l'estimation des vivres . . . qui ont esté trouvé dans les magasins de la citadelle de Ré suivant la preuve verbale qui en a esté faite par Monsieur de la Thuillerie, Intendant de la Justice à la Rochelle*, 16 Dec. 1628. The document, with many marginal notes by Sublet, was presented *en conseil* in 1631 and 'Fait et arresté au Conseil du Roi tenu pour ses finances à Paris, le 8 fevrier, 1631', and signed by de l'Aubespine, Keeper of the Seals; Effiat, Superintendent of Finance; and Sublet, AN, K. 113, fol. 59; see also fol. 60.

[4] BN, MS. 18504, fol. 82; AAE, France, 810, fol. 271 ff.

mint.[1] Thus Sublet attacked the problem of money reforms, not only on the theoretical level but also on the practical one. Was this done in his capacity as intendant of finance?

Sublet's entrance into Richelieu's circle occurred in the last years of the decade; that is, before 1630, although no letter from the cardinal to Sublet expressing his affection for him has survived. Even so, Richelieu was already well in command of most of the office appointments by the time Sublet became intendant; and since officers in the central government appointed through Marillac's efforts were disgraced after 1630, it seems safe to assume that Sublet belonged to Richelieu's party by 1628. According to the anonymous author of the *Mémoires de l'establissement des secrétaires d'Estat*, Sublet was first presented to Richelieu through the good offices of his influential friend, the future Maréchal de Feuquières, an intimate friend and relative of Père Joseph.[2] The cardinal might have felt some affection for Sublet because of his Bochart descent, for Richelieu's maternal grandfather was a Bochart of the same branch as Sublet's mother.[3]

In the early 1630's Richelieu began to rely on Sublet as an intendant with various armies, under Estrées, Effiat, and La Force, in north-eastern France and Lorraine. As Sublet supervised the rebuilding of the frontier fortifications, it became his responsibility, in the name of the king, to hasten the work and to gain the co-operation of townsmen, governors, and army officers.[4] In his correspondence with Richelieu, he described construction problems, espionage, budgetary difficulties, and administrative or governmental ineffectiveness. The direct relationship between the intendant—in this case Sublet—and the principal minister does not, however, explain the rise of the intendants in the broad sense. Sublet worked constantly with the keeper of the seals, with other councillors, and with the secretary of state for the region.

[1] Sublet to Richelieu, 28 Jan. 1634, AAE, France, 810, fol. 67; Séguier to Richelieu, n.d., in the same volume, fol. 325.

[2] BN, Cinq Cents Colbert, MS. 136. fol. 508ᵛ; BN, Collection Cangé, MS. 68, fol. 139.   [3] L. Moreri, *Grand Dictionnaire historique* (Paris, 1759), 'Bochart'.

[4] See the many letters in the AAE, France, 811, fol. 38 and *passim*; and in the correspondence of Séguier in the BN.

His work in the field with armies and towns gave Sublet a good background for the new task.[1] The intimate relationship between Richelieu and Sublet began only in 1636, after the latter became secretary of state. His rise in favour quickly followed.

The ministers just described, with Séguier and Richelieu himself, formed the group which, together with the king, formulated and executed policy. Within the group some found more favour than others. Bullion, for example, requested Chavigny to ask Richelieu for an office for his son's tutor.[2] When jealousies arose among the creatures, the cardinal ironically calmed the offended one and appealed, 'In God's name, please agree with what I am telling you so that the great affairs [of state] do not suffer from the jealousies that you are manifesting. . . .'[3] Such differences usually were only momentary; Richelieu did not tolerate them within his party.

The party, allegiance to Richelieu, and friendship generally determined appointments and favours. Chavigny frankly wrote that he had decided to employ a certain gentleman, not for his qualifications but simply because he was a friend of Charnacé, the ambassador to Holland, who was in favour with the group.[4] The creatures saw to it that Richelieu also benefited from all of the favours which were in their power to command. Chavigny wrote to Maréchal d'Estrées: 'Since I wrote this letter the Sieur Gobert has given me the *mémoire* included. He is the almoner of Monseigneur the Cardinal, which is sufficient to tell you and oblige you to gratify him with the canonry of Saint-Malo that he requests.'[5]

There were occasional exceptions to the general rules of

[1] His correspondence has survived in surprising quantity, but his businesslike manner kept him from writing about himself or his family, as some of the other creatures did. An exception is Sublet to Guébriant, 13 Oct. 1641, BN, Cinq Cents Colbert, MS. 108, fol. 91.
[2] Bullion to Chavigny (in correspondence of the secretary and Richelieu, and internal evidence assures one that it was not addressed to the cardinal), AAE, France, 820, fol. 143, Feb. 1636?
[3] Richelieu to Claude le Bouthillier, 30 Apr. 1639, Avenel, ed. cit. vi. clxxxviii.
[4] Chavigny to Charnacé, 8? Aug. 1636, BN, MS. 17946, fol. 57.
[5] Chavigny to Coeuvres, Ambassador to Rome, 12 Jan. 1638, BN, MS. 4071, fol. 165 (copy).

appointment by favouritism. Richelieu himself chose a candidate for office because of his honesty, even though he was from the opposing party, and had married a niece of Marillac.[1] Once Richelieu had selected a candidate for an office, he requested a secretary to present his name to the king. This became the normal way for the cardinal to influence patronage when he and Louis were separated.

[1] To Chavigny, 4 Oct. 1635 : 'Je jette les yeux pour mettre en la place de Cahusac sur son frère. Je sçay bien qu'il a esté du party contraire, et a espousé une des nièces de Marillac, mais sa probité est par-dessus tout cela, à mon advis. Cependant, comme je ne veux rien faire sans sçavoir la volonté du roy, je vous pris d'en parler à Sa Majesté. . . .' Avenel, ed. cit. v. cxxx.

III

The Secretaries of State

LITTLE of real value has been written about the secretaries of state for the first half of the seventeenth century. For the last years of the reign of Louis XIII the Duc de La Force sketches their position *vis-à-vis* Richelieu, but he fails to trace their development.[1] In the nineteenth century the Comte de Luçay wrote the only modern history of the secretaries, but he treats the entire sixteenth century and the reigns of Henry IV and Louis XIII in one introductory chapter.[2] Vicomte d'Avenel was more careless than Luçay, but his few pages on the secretaries, though full of errors, show a better capacity for searching out what is significant in administrative history.[3] Other nineteenth-century administrative historians, notably Caillet and Chéruel, only touched on the secretaries and, like their contemporaries, attempted to describe the office from the *règlements* without posing the problem of whether the secretaries really functioned in that way.[4] The views of modern French historians, as found in manuals and general histories, hardly surpass this level for the whole period 1559–1643.[5]

Of all the descriptions of the secretaries, Vicomte d'Avenel's is in many ways the most illustrative of how scholars have approached the secretaries for the reign of Louis XIII. He concluded that the power of the secretaries

[1] Duc de La Force, *Histoire du Cardinal de Richelieu* (Paris, 1933), particularly vols. v and vi.

[2] Comte de Luçay, *Les Secrétaires d'État depuis leur institution jusqu'à la mort de Louis XV* (Paris, 1881).

[3] Vicomte d'Avenel, *Richelieu et la monarchie absolue* (Paris, 1884), vol. i.

[4] J. Caillet, *L'Administration en France sous le ministère du Cardinal de Richelieu* (Paris, 1863); A. Chéruel, *Histoire de l'administration monarchique* (Paris, 1855).

[5] H. Sée, A. Rebeillon, and E. Préclin, *Le XVIᵉ Siècle* (Paris, 1950); E. Préclin and V. Tapié, *Le XVIIᵉ Siècle* (Paris, 1955); G. Zeller, *Les Institutions en France au XVIᵉ Siècle* (Paris, 1940).

had never been great, and that it declined under Richelieu;[1] but in a footnote he described Sublet de Noyers, Secretary of State for War, as an officer wielding great powers in military affairs.[2] Such contradictions develop when history is written from the legislative bones of the *ancien régime*; descriptions from the *règlements*, without a thorough study of the personalities holding the office, are not only inaccurate but sterile. For the secretaries of state the *règlements* reflect the development of the office, and provide an opportunity to sketch the position of the office in the government; but only the working correspondence of the secretaries and of the other ministers, in addition to the *règlements*, give a picture of the office as it actually functioned. Such a task for the entire reign would be enormous; therefore only the *règlements* and secondary materials for the background to 1635 are used. Administrative correspondence will be the chief source for the last years of the reign.

The contrast between the ministers of Louis XIII, except Richelieu, and those of Louis XIV failed to lead historians, with the exception of Louis André, to search for the secretary-ministers of the *Roi soleil* fifty years earlier. André, in his *Michel Le Tellier et l'organisation de l'armée monarchique*, widened the frontiers of administrative history by analysing in detail one aspect of the central administration and its relationship to the lower echelons of the military administration; but in the introduction the impression gained is that Le Tellier began, amid administrative chaos, to form the *armée française* with new and daring ideas, while in the conclusion it seems that Le Tellier only carried on the work of his predecessors, notably Sublet de Noyers.[3]

The contrast between the ministers of the two great reigns of the seventeenth century, however, remains. Colbert, Lionne, Pomponne, Louvois, and others were powerful ministers heading effective bureaucratic organiza-

---

[1] D'Avenel, op. cit. i, p. 65.

[2] Ibid., p. 69.

[3] Louis André, *Michel Le Tellier et l'organisation de l'armée monarchique* (Paris, 1906). André thought that Richelieu left the task of reorganizing the army unfinished, and he called Sublet 'competent', p. 24. He concluded that under Le Tellier the secretary of state for war became a minister, in the more modern sense of the term, p. 651.

tions, while the ministers of Louis XIII, as described by scholars in the nineteenth century, seem to have been only royal clerks executing the orders of a proud and sickly ecclesiastic and ignoring a weak-willed king.

To understand the secretaries of state, the records of the sixteenth century must be searched to find the first secretaries to bear the name.[1] The real origins, however, are as old as the monarchy itself. The kings of France had always maintained some clerks to aid them with their letter-writing. The rise in influence, and ultimately in power, of the office caused historians, even in the mid-seventeenth century, to attempt to explain how this occurred. Their utility is limited, however, because they stopped their work in the sixteenth century, assuming that their readers knew the contemporary scene.[2] In the last quarter of the century, when Colbert was forming his library, several short histories of the secretaries were included, but their value is again chiefly for other periods.[3]

In the eighteenth century Moreau, or one of his secretaries who had carefully read the manuscript histories written in the minority of Louis XIV, rose above genealogical and

[1] One finds *secrétaire d'état et des commandements*, which was still frequently used under Louis XIII, and also *secrétaire d'état et des finances*. These were used synonymously by the reign of Louis XIII, but there may have been a distinction in the sixteenth century. By 1635 only two secretaries had the power to sign financial legislation, but there was no distinction of title given to reflect this, either in their brevets or in the salutations used in correspondence. See Appendix B.

[2] Few of the manuscript histories give anything beyond biographical details for the reign of Louis XIII. The most important of these is the *Mémoires de l'establissement des secrétaires d'Estat*, which stops in 1647. See above, p. 30, for a description of this most important source. Several copies of the *Mémoire curieux sur l'origine et la succession des secrétaires d'État jusqu'au règne de Louis XIV* have survived partially or under different titles. The most complete copy is perhaps the one prepared by Godefroy or one of his clerks, which is now in the Bibliothèque de l'Institut, Collection Godefroy, MS. 310, fols. 182 ff. For the reign of Louis XIII it does not go beyond the *Mémoires de l'establissement . . .* in content or period.

[3] See the *Mémoires sur Messieurs les secrétaires d'Estat*, 'written for Colbert in 1668', BN, Collection Clairambault, MS. 664, fols. 49 ff.; and the *Recueil de diverses matières de secrétaires d'État fait pour les renseignements du Ministre Colbert ou de son fils*, by a Monsieur Foucault, Secrétaire du Conseil, Bibliothèque de l'Arsenal, MS. 5298. These were written from earlier histories, perhaps those cited in footnote 2. The second manuscript is particularly interesting for a study of the *Conseil* under Louis XIV, and for the letter-formulas used by the secretaries in the same reign.

other details to give his explanation of the development of offices in the *ancien régime*:

The majority of the best *charges* of the kingdom had very mediocre beginnings and were only made illustrious by favourable circumstances of the times, and by birth, merit, or the *faveur* of those who possessed them. Those of the secretary of state are of that nature; and although their origin has nothing illustrious about it, since it is in the household of, and near the person of the king where all positions are honourable, one cannot deny that [they] have made marvellous progress. . . . Everything that can be said about them up to the reign of Henry II is so intermingled with the secretaries of the king in general that there is almost nothing specific; but nevertheless the kings before Henry II always chose a few of them to serve near their person and in their most secret affairs, and it is this choice which finally caused the establishment of the *charge* of secretary of state.[1]

A plan to describe the rise of the secretaries by emphasizing personalities as an explanation for administrative development has therefore been proposed.

Doucet noted quite accurately that Henry III attempted to diminish the powers of the secretaries in his *règlement* of 1588.[2] Four of the royal secretaries, entitled secretaries of state and commandments, were to receive their office by commission, which made the *charge* revocable. Their principal labour was to read his correspondence to the king. They were also to prepare replies after his dictation and to keep extracts of the letters.[3] Direct relations with the king in a clerk's capacity might well describe their position, and it was from this humble beginning that the secretaries of state developed. The royal letters of the period carry the signature of the king or regent after the body of the letter, and bear a secretary's counter-signature below it. At least in the

[1] BN, Collection Moreau, MS. 1090, fol. 362. See also the *Préface* to the *Inventaire des manuscrits de la collection Moreau*, by H. Omont (Paris, 1891), for an analysis of the problems of authorship in the collection. More typical and less valuable is Briquet, *De l'origine et du progrès des charges de secrétaires d'État* (The Hague, 1747), who states: 'il seroit inutile . . . de détailler tous les changemens qui peuvent être arrivés depuis Henri II . . .' and moves on to Louis XIV, p. 58.

[2] R. Doucet, *Les Institutions de la France au XVIe siècle* (Paris, 1948), i, p. 159.

[3] 'Règlement des secrétaires d'Estat' of 1588, pub. by Guillard, *Histoire du Conseil du roi* (Paris, 1718), pp. 126 ff.

reign of Louis XIII, however, royal letters were, in certain cases, valid only when a secretary of state countersigned them.[1]

The separation of royal correspondence by country and province to form geographical departments of the secretaries provided administrative organization in the sixteenth century. Under Francis II they were a measure for prestige in the court; for departments at that time were given to the secretaries on the basis of seniority, while in the *règlement* of 1588 Henry III reserved the right to rotate them every year.[2] The departmental rotation and the royal prohibition of any governmental correspondence with ambassadors or provincial officials by the secretaries without the king's knowledge were measures to break political friendships and restrict the power of the secretaries.[3] By inference one may conclude that correspondence of political importance between secretaries and royal officials existed during Henry III's reign, or even earlier. An analysis of this correspondence would be very useful in determining the political position of the secretaries at this early date. The organization of the departments was quite obviously geared to the system of couriers, in the administration of which the secretaries, at least under Louis XIII, had some part.[4]

Even in the early sixteenth century the secretary having the greatest prestige—which under Francis II was the one with the longest service record—specialized at the expense of his colleagues. War affairs and the royal household, in

[1] 'Règlement des Finances' of 5 Feb. 1611, pub. by Roland Mousnier, *Annuaire-Bulletin de la Société de l'Histoire de France*, 1946–7, p. 128.

[2] For a short anonymous history of the secretaries under Francis II, see BN, MS. 15519, fol. 153, from the library of the Harlays.

[3] *Règlement* of 1588, Guillard, op. cit., pp. 128 f.

[4] From the manuscript history of the secretaries, mentioned in footnote 2, the departments under Francis II were:

1. The Levant (Constantinople, Italy, Piedmont, and Savoy) as well as Provence, Languedoc, Dauphiné, Lyonnais, the forest of Beaujolais, Bourbonnais, and Auvergne.
2. The Spains, the Low Countries, as well as Guyenne, Saintonge, Poitou, Limousin, and Picardy.
3. Poland, the German Empire, Switzerland, the Grisons, Lorraine, as well as Burgundy, Champagne, and Brie.
4. England, Scotland, Sweden, Denmark, as well as Normandy, Brittany, Paris, Île de France, Anjou, Touraine, Maine, Orléans, and the Chartres country (*Pays Chartrain*). BN, MS. 15519, fol. 153.

addition to a geographical department, came under the
direction of one secretary by the reign of Francis II, although
this specialization is not mentioned in either the *règlement* of
1578 or that of 1588.[1] Only a detailed study of the secretaries in the sixteenth century can determine whether the
secretary of state had some power in the army administration
and in the royal household. The absence of provisions
regarding these future secretarial departments in the *règlement*
of 1588 is significant, but it does not enable one to determine the exact situation at the moment. Secretarial powers
had fluctuated in the sixteenth century; with each new king
changes in the procedure and influence occurred which
were only partly reflected in the *règlements*. Also, while
appearing to describe every aspect of an office, the *règlements*
frequently did not do so for departments or procedures
functioning as the Crown saw fit. It is impossible to determine by the *règlements* whether the departments of war
and the royal household existing under Louis XIII had a
continuous history even in a very limited form from
the mid-sixteenth century.

The numerous details about the working day and the
manner in which the secretaries had to conduct themselves
at court do not directly help in determining their political
influence, but they reflect the social position and prestige of
the secretaries.

The secretaries will go every morning to the ante-chamber or
chamber of His Majesty at five o'clock where they will wait for
his decisions . . . having entered into His Majesty's presence, the
parcels of letters will be distributed to them by the king; they will
open them when he orders them to do so, and in his presence and
not otherwise, and will read him the letters in their turn as he calls
upon them . . . however, if His Majesty does not wish that one of
them read his letters aloud, none of the others will approach His
Majesty if he is not summoned. His Majesty having directed them,
they will bring these and other dispatches to him the following
morning, at the latest, to have them signed. . . .[2]

If the *règlement* of 1588 is in any way a reflection of the posi-

[1] BN, MS. 15519, fol. 153; the *règlements* in the BN, nouvelles acquisitions,
MS. 32; and Guillard, op. cit., pp. 126 ff. Doucet thought that this specialization began in 1570, op. cit. i, p. 161ᵛ.
[2] BN, MS. n.a. 32, fol. 364.

tion of the secretaries, one must conclude that their work was largely manual and that politically the office possessed only opportunities. These, of course, were very real; daily contact with the king was in itself important, as was the duty of the secretary of state *en mois* to attend council meetings.[1]

Throughout the sixteenth century the secretaries of state continued to follow the many customs of the old corps of royal secretaries, the ancient group from which they were originally chosen. The practice of passing the office from father to son remained strong, owing to the venality of the older *charges* in the old corps, of which every secretary of state was still obliged to be a member.[2] This provided a continuity of personnel in the L'Aubespine, Bochetel, and Neuville families which dominated the secretariat during much of the sixteenth century. For example, under Henry IV, Villeroy (Nicolas de Neuville) added prestige and precedents to the office, through his personal favour with the king. The correspondence with foreign countries was temporarily united, as Villeroy dealt with foreign ambassadors in an official capacity as representative of the king.[3] There was thus a powerful secretary of state in a period when, only a few years before, the *règlement* of 1588 portrayed those officers as no more than specialized clerks. Personalities with influence on the Crown and a voice in the royal councils began early to establish precedents for the minister-secretaries of Louis XIV.

Finally, the continuity of administration was provided by the hereditary traditions of all the royal secretaries. Family archives and secretarial archives continued to be one and the same throughout the seventeenth century; family libraries were handed down from father to son, and as a result the position of the new secretary was not ordinarily as chaotic as some historians depict it.[4] Richelieu's plaintive request to ambassadors and other royal correspondents for copies of

---

[1] *Règlement* of 1588, Guillard, op. cit., p. 131.

[2] Pierre Robin, *La Compagnie des secrétaires du roi* (Paris, 1933), p. 6.

[3] J. H. Mariéjol, *Histoire de France*, ed. by E. Lavisse (Paris, 1911), vi, part 2, p. 27.

[4] A. de Boislisle, *Correspondance des Contrôleurs Généraux* (Paris, 1874), 'avant propos', where he also cites Avenel, ed. cit. i, lxvii.

their letters previously sent to the Crown is partly explained by the practices of the time. He was the first secretary of state in the du Plessis family; in accordance with custom, his predecessors in the office had not turned their archives over to him.[1]

Under Louis XIII, after much trial and error, two secretaries of state became effective branches in the royal administration. The secretaries for war and for foreign affairs became heads of bureaucratic machinery; and, more important, certain customs obliging the ministerial government as a whole to consult them and to administer through them existed at the end of the reign.

The tendency of the Crown to establish direct relationships with all levels of the royal government provided the necessary climate for the rise of the secretaries. More than ever, direct action on even minor details of the administration came from the king and his councils. The two organs of government nearest the king—the secretaries of state and the councils—both closely united and functioning together, broadened their powers greatly at the expense of the old sovereign courts, the provincial courts, and the governors.

Political events, especially the war which broke out in earnest in 1635, hastened a process which was already well under way. In the last decade of the reign traditional conceptions of offices and councils continued to exist and be influential; but amid all of the flexibility of jurisdictions characterizing government in the *ancien régime*, a new and more powerful form of government made a momentary appearance. New lines of administration were traced, if not clearly drawn, as the reign progressed; they were reflected in the *règlements* of the secretaries of state published here for the first time.[2] Despite this slow but steady change, the old administration based on geographical boundaries never completely gave way; but by the end of the reign the

[1] The library of the Loménie family, the Counts of Brienne, is a fine surviving example of the working archives of a secretary of state under Louis XIII. L. Delisle, *Le Cabinet des manuscrits de la Bibliothèque Nationale* (Paris, 1868), pp. 215 ff.
[2] See Appendix A.

departments of war and of foreign affairs were firmly established and continued to exist in the personal reign of Louis XIV, where they became the foundation for real ministerial departments.

It will not be necessary to summarize the changes in the secretaryships from the *règlements*, as the latter are full of details which only a thorough analysis could make meaningful. Some general comments, however, are necessary to place the departments of war and of foreign affairs in perspective. The first *règlement* under Louis XIII was made on 21 June 1617, at Fontainebleau; it dealt strictly with the administration of petitions to the Crown for ecclesiastical offices and pensions, seigniorial rights of the Crown, and royal pensions. The *règlement* is plainly for the secretary *en mois*, whose duty it was to reply to the petitions in the name of the king. Secretaries were already taking monthly shifts in the king's council early in the sixteenth century so that they could report council deliberations to the king when he himself did not attend.[1] Royal appointments, especially in the Church, also presented an enormous administrative task; the *règlement* of 1617 defined the duties of the secretary of state in this domain.

The very limited functions of the secretary of the war department and the provinces under his jurisdiction are clearly outlined in the *règlement* of 29 April 1619, made at Saint-Germain-en-Laye. The loose, sprawling organization not only of the central government but also of the whole military administration is readily apparent. The secretary of state for war was to write commissions and royal orders only to the 'first and principal army', the cavalry, infantry, and artillery, while other armies and garrisoned troops were to be under the jurisdiction of the other secretaries according to their geographical location. The most striking example of the decentralization, however, involved army movements: if an army crossed the geographical jurisdictions of the secretaries, that is to say, from one province to another, it must be the duty of the secretaries to decide who should write the king's orders to the officers in command!

Numerous quarrels occurred between the secretaries. The

[1] *Règlement* of 1588, Guillard, op. cit., p. 131; Doucet, op. cit. i, p. 159.

danger of failure on the part of the central government in communicating the king's orders effectively also continued, but in the last years of the reign several measures were taken to unify and secure stability in the military administration. The scales weighing the old geographical jurisdictions and the new ones based on military and foreign affairs had not yet tipped in favour of the latter.

In the 1620's the problem of tracing the department of war by texts establishing the duties of the secretaries becomes more difficult, but also more interesting. There is a text in the Bibliothèque Nationale entitled, *Pour Régler les Fonctions des Charges de Messieurs les Secrétaires d'Etat sur les différendz qui pourroyent arriver entre celluy qui a la charge de la Guerre et les autres qui ont le département des Provinces.*[1] On the reverse side of the folio it is stated: 'Mémoire Résolu et Concerté, Octobre 1621, Monsieur de Villeroy', and another name which is lost in the binding. On folio 176 of the same volume there is another text entitled, *Pour faire cesser les Différendz qui sont entre Messieurs les Secrétaires d'Estat touchant la Fonction de celuy qui a le département de la guerre et les dépesches que les autres ont à faire en provinces dont ils ont la charge.* There are no identification statements, but the internal evidence leads one to believe that it is from the same period as the document cited just above.

Neither document is a *règlement*, but perhaps they influenced or reflected the growth of the new war department just as much as royal legislation. The secretaries themselves may have come to an agreement, written down the procedural changes which they had made in the form of a *mémoire résolu et concerté*, and acted accordingly.[2] There might also have been a dispute between the secretaries over their powers to dispatch royal letters. To solve the problem one need only examine the documents to see if they are an extension or merely an elaboration of powers described in previous legislation. Obviously, the *règlement* of 1619 had not removed the possibility of quarrels; conflicting jurisdiction and the resulting differences of opinion caused the two documents

---

[1] BN, MS. 15519, fol. 172, from the Harlay family library.

[2] There is also some evidence for the 1630's to show that secretaries made agreements among themselves regarding their duties and personnel. See the letter from Jean de La Barde to Bouthillier, 3 Jan. 1630, AAE, France, 798, fol. 10.

under discussion to be written. No important changes in the position of the secretary of state for war are described in the documents, but there was a real effort to describe the duties listed in the *règlement* of 1619 in more detail. From the *Mémoire Résolu et Concerté* it is clear that the war secretary was at least part of the financial machinery of the military administration.[1]

The last general *règlement* for the secretaries of state under Louis XIII was made on 11 March 1626 in Paris. The departments of foreign affairs and war were for the first time to have permanent jurisdictional forms. Furthermore, the office of secretary of state for war as described in 1619 was reaffirmed and even carried new responsibilities.[2] All correspondence with armies outside of the realm was to be under his control.

Even more important, the *règlement* of 1626 brought all foreign correspondence into one departmental jurisdiction, and under one secretary. This may be considered as a definite break with the past. Henceforth the departments of war and foreign affairs were to be free of the old geographical divisions. Some minor exceptions to the complete union of war and foreign-affairs correspondence under two heads still remained, but the scales had tipped in their favour.

The importance of the new departments, the personalities in them, and the international crises of the moment were all reflected in the last *règlement* of the reign, made in September 1633. It was written 'in anticipation of inconveniences and differences of opinion which might develop between the secretaries of state having the departments of war and foreign affairs'.[3] The administrative problems arising from armies in the field outside the realm, the jurisdictions over conquered territories, and the extraordinary diplomatic activities which occurred in periods of war or diplomatic tension were the major points discussed. After 1633 there were no other *règlements* for the secretaries, even though it was the period of their greatest growth in the reign. The supposition that Richelieu's plans for reforming the central government

[1] BN, MS. 15519, fol. 172. [2] See Appendix A, p. 189.
[3] See Appendix A, p. 192.

were never completed, because of full war beginning in 1635 and because of his success in restoring order in the realm, only partly explains the absence of other *règlements*.[1] Instead of drawing up other *règlements*, Richelieu relied on the men whom he had chosen to direct the councils and the king's correspondence. Instead of further institutional reforms, he depended upon the obedience and efficiency of his creatures in the key places of the central government.[2]

The importance and growth of the office of secretary of state was largely the result of his key position between provincial officials, the royal councils, and the king himself. Letters and personal relationships with governors, intendants, ecclesiastics, *baillis*, and all other provincial officials enabled the secretaries to accumulate, more than anyone else in the central government, administrative details and knowledge of the particular conditions in each province. Whether letters were addressed directly to the king or to a secretary, the latter was informed of their contents as he read them to the king, or if the king were absent from the court, as the secretary received an order to prepare the royal replies.

The secretaries of state were royal councillors as well; in the last years of the reign all four secretaries held brevets for various councils.[3] Their position, especially on the essentially administrative councils such as the council of state, enabled the secretaries to inform the other councillors about provincial conditions. At the same time the secretaries

[1] Roland Mousnier, *Les Règlements du Conseil du roi sous Louis XIII* (Paris, 1949), p. 39.

[2] Both Richelieu and Louis undoubtedly changed the administrative procedure of the secretaries; an interesting example is the minute for a letter addressed by Sublet to the three other secretaries of state, modifying the procedure of the secretary of state *en mois*, 5 Jan. 1638, AG, A[1], 43, fol. 32. This type of document, all too rare, is as important as the *règlements* in writing the history of the secretaries of state. See Appendix A.

[3] See the pension list of 1635, where all four received 5,000 *livres* as *gages* as councillors. They also received 20,000 *livres* each as secretaries, AAE, France, 819, fol. 154. For the *appointements extraordinaires*, they were to receive 600 *livres* a month, *règlement* of 1630, Roland Mousnier, 'Les Règlements du Conseil du roi sous Louis XIII', *Annuaire-Bulletin de la Société de l'Histoire de France*, 1946–7, p. 194. (This article should not be confused with Mousnier's short publication with the same title cited in footnote 1).

learned of budgetary and legal possibilities for action open to the Crown.

Lastly, direct contact with the king, the source of government in the realm, permitted the secretaries to exercise powers which, while they do not have legal expression, most certainly existed. The first of these might well be called the 'power of suggestion'. Secretaries of state, well informed on provincial problems as well as on attitudes of the royal councils, were often asked to recommend policies or actions in the king's cabinet at times when the monarch saw no course of action. It was partly through the 'power of suggestion' that Richelieu directed the affairs of state, for he frequently relied on the secretaries to be faithful to his ideas when they were working with Louis XIII.

The long history of direct correspondence of powerful nobles and ecclesiastics with the king did not come to an end under Louis XIII, but its character gradually changed. Louis XIII was the real initiator of the process whereby the royal administration came between the king and his subjects regarding governmental matters, a phenomenon which never ceased to grow in succeeding reigns. The letters personally addressed to the king tended to become only long statements of praise and fidelity, while for political matters the correspondence addressed to the secretaries increased in importance.

A wide diversity of subjects was included in the secretarial correspondence. It represented the entire range of action that was the government of the time; no subject was too insignificant to be brought to the attention of the king through his secretaries. Owing to the ever-growing bureaucracy of secretaries, provincial administrators who wrote to the king received answers with surprising speed, all of which tended to diminish the prestige and influence of other royal institutions to which the multitude of small officers had customarily turned for direction.

The efforts of the secretaries to oblige royal correspondents to address their letters to them did not extend to channelling all royal letters through their hands. These efforts were rather a part of the complicated protocol of politeness and rank existing in the *ancien régime*. The secretaries were offended if someone of low rank wrote directly to the king or the cardinal.[1] However, the secretaries never succeeded in establishing themselves as the only receivers of mail addressed to the central government. This was impossible so long as the councils also represented the king and took action in his name.[2] Finally, Richelieu himself continued to receive petitions which involved direct governmental action. Personalities, friendship, and family relationships still frequently determined where and to whom a request should be made.

Aside from problems of protocol, the secretaries requested that the royal correspondence pass through them so that they might be informed. Claude le Bouthillier wrote to Hémery:[3]

I think it is very suitable that you close all the dispatches which you make to Monseigneur the Cardinal, and that you no longer send them to me open, for my clerks, having neither your seal nor your silk [letters were bound with silk strands and sealed with a wax seal bearing the coat of arms of the sender] cannot close them as you wish; and then it is necessary in the king's affairs to keep a continuity which is formed by dispatches of ambassadors, who should never fail to make them very ample, to Monsieur the Secretary of State who has the department of foreign affairs. It is therefore up to you to draw up your dispatches for my son or me as it is convenient, or to send us a copy of those which you write to His Eminence. . . .[4]

Cardinal Richelieu insisted that the secretaries be informed of everything. On one occasion he wrote:

Messieurs le Bouthillier and Servien, to whom all the dispatches from foreign countries and armies are addressed, ought to know

[1] Chavigny was offended when the French ambassador to Holland wrote directly to Richelieu instead of to him. La Vrillière wrote to the Ambassador, La Thuillerie: 'J'ay un extreme desplaisir d'avoir appris par Monsieur de Chavigny qu'il ayt suivi de blasmer la conduitte que vous tenez en l'addresse de vos depesches; sa plainte est ce me semble bien juste et fondée sur la derniere que vous avez directement envoyée à Son Eminence sans qu'elle ayt passé par ses mains ainsy qu'il se pratique par tous ceux qui sont dans un employ pareil au vostre. . . .' 6 Aug. 1641, AN, K 114B, fol. 75.

[2] The correspondence of Séguier at the Bibliothèque Nationale contains numerous letters about food problems in towns where troops were garrisoned, hay, horses, financial problems, &c. See the useful but outdated, R. Kerviler, Le Chancelier Séguier (Paris, 1874), passim, and E. Girard and Joly, Trois Livres des offices de France (Paris, 1638), i and ii, passim.

[3] Intendant of Finance, on a diplomatic mission to Savoy.

[4] 11 Oct. 1635, AAE, Sardaigne, 23, fol. 348.

better than anyone the present state of affairs in Germany; and nevertheless it is considered opportune that they meet this evening with Père Joseph and the Sieur de Charnacé, who is well informed in this type of affair, in order to decide together what they deem most appropriate. . . .[1]

Such small meetings occurred frequently, not only among ministers but also between one secretary and provincial officers. A 'Résultat de la Conférence faicte par Monsieur Servien avec les Sieurs d'Argencourt et Plessis-Besançon' has survived, giving a description of fortification problems on the coast of Provence in 1635.[2] The role of Secretary Servien is partly indicated by the title of the document; it was the secretary who directed the inquest in which the provincial official participated.

As the roles of the provincial intendant and the commission for special problems developed, the secretaries grew in importance. They were not the only ones from the central government to communicate with the intendants, but the pressing problems brought on by the open war after 1635 marked a greater use of the intendants, and generally put them into a close administrative liaison with the secretary of state for war. The minutes of the letters of Sublet de Noyers addressed to all the intendants—army, provincial, and financial—conserved at the Archives de la Guerre, are the greatest single source for this early period of the history of the intendants. In fact one might say they are one of the most remarkable and as yet virgin sources for the France of Louis XIII as a whole.

Once again the old system of jurisdictions suffered at the hands of the administrators, who saw internal problems in the context of the war effort. But the whole administration of the intendants remained disunified under Louis XIII, leaving the impression that when the intendants and the

[1] 23 Apr. 1635, Richelieu, *Lettres, instructions diplomatiques et papiers d'État*, ed. by M. Avenel (Paris, 1853–77), IV. ccclxxxv.

[2] AAE, France, 1703, fol. 23. Geographical jurisdictions over fortifications were maintained for secretaries; but in times of crisis the Crown sent intendants directly into the field to supervise the construction. Hence fortification dispatches were addressed either to the council, Richelieu, or the secretary of state for war, although the secretary with the particular geographical department involved still played a role. It was he who prepared and sent royal letters and *provisions* involved.

secretaries intervened directly in provincial affairs, such action was extraordinary and was prompted by the war.[1]

On the provincial level the secretaries were constantly occupied with ecclesiastical problems, rebellious parlements, famines, peasant revolts, hunting and wood rights, pensions, and so forth.

The activities of the secretaries of state in the royal councils were important and complex. By the *règlement du Conseil* of 1624, after having been granted the right to attend the *Conseil de la direction des finances, Conseil d'État,* and the *Conseil privé,* the secretaries were given rank and precedence according to the date upon which they had taken the oath as secretary.[2] It would seem that their appointment gave them no special prestige with the other councillors. André Lefèvre d'Ormesson, who compiled a list of the councillors for 24 December 1640, placed the secretaries apart along with the intendants of finance, all of whom were *ordinaires du conseil,* indicating that they served on the councils all the year round.[3]

In addition to being *ordinaires,* the secretaries attended the councils in rotation as reporters, so that the king and the other secretaries could be informed of the decisions made in the more administrative councils, particularly those mentioned above. The *mémoire* published by Pagès as emanating from the *Conseil des dépêches* was probably a communication from one of the secretaries *en mois,* whose clerk had jotted down letters to be prepared by the other secretaries.[4]

[1] Roland Mousnier, 'État et Commissaire, Recherches sur la création des Intendants de Province (1634–1648)', *Forschungen zu Staat und Verfassung, Festgabe für Fritz Hartung* (Berlin, 1958), pp. 325 ff.

[2] Mousnier, 'Le Conseil du roi sous Louis XIII', loc. cit., p. 162.

[3] *Mémoires d'André Lefèvre d'Ormesson,* Bibliothèque de Rouen, Manuscrits Léber, 5767, fol. 136. Although Chéruel published parts of these memoirs in the *documents inédits* series, there is still much unpublished information on the personnel and operation of the government of Louis XIII in the manuscript.

[4] Georges Pagès, 'Le Conseil du roi sous Louis XIII', *Revue d'Histoire Moderne,* 1937, p. 309, where he published the *mémoire* found in AAE, France, 255, fol. 6. See also the *règlement* of 1630, Mousnier, 'Les Règlements du Conseil du roi sous Louis XIII', loc. cit., p. 191. The most accurate text of this *règlement* is in the *Mémoires d'André Lefèvre d'Ormesson,* where the phrase *collationé par moy* and the signature of Cornuel make it almost an original, for it was he who as *secrétaire du Conseil* had countersigned the *règlement.* A. Chéruel neglected to note this when he published the document in his *Histoire de l'administration monarchique,* op. cit., I, app. ii, p. 377.

According to the *règlement* of 1630, the councils were to be held regularly with clear delineation as to subjects discussed in each one.[1] Except for the secretary of war, who was to help with the preparation of the military budget,[2] the secretaries were given no special duties beyond the stipulation that all four men were to sign the pension list.[3]

Membership in the more elusive advisory council, the *Conseil d'en haut*, as Mousnier rightly prefers to call it, was again on the basis of secretary *en mois*, although no references have been found to substantiate what had earlier been established by *règlement*.[4] Sublet de Noyers and Chavigny enjoyed constant access to this most important council, along with the chancellor and superintendents of finance. Normally such an honour was reserved for the great officers of the Crown and for the *ministres d'état*. Neither Sublet nor Chavigny held such honours; Chavigny became minister only after the death of Richelieu, when Louis XIII formed the Council of the Regency.[5] The two secretaries needed only the confidence and affection of the king to be invited by the Crown to attend the *Conseil d'en haut*, and while this was not recognized by brevet, it was reflected in the formulas of politeness of the time.[6]

When Richelieu was not present at Louis's councils with military officers, Chavigny wrote him detailed reports of the participation of the various governors and generals, as well as of his own.[7]

If the secretaries were limited to the relatively unimportant role of reporters who were rotated monthly in the councils, there would be little need to analyse them, but this

---

[1] Mousnier, 'Les Règlements du Conseil du roi sous Louis XIII', loc. cit., pp. 183 ff.

[2] Ibid., p. 193.　　　　　　　　　　　　　　[3] Ibid., p. 193.

[4] Roland Mousnier, 'Le Conseil du roi de la mort de Henri IV au governement personnel de Louis XIV,' *Études d'Histoire Moderne et Contemporaine*, 1947, pp. 38 and 42.

[5] E. Lavisse, *Histoire de France*, ed. by E. Lavisse (Paris, 1906), vii, part 1, p. 2.

[6] Chavigny once received a letter where he was addressed 'Conseiller du Roy dans tous Ses Conseils', from the Maréchal de Brézé, 1 June 1635, AAE, Allemagne, 15, fol. 165.

[7] 23 Sept. 1636, AAE, France, 821, fol. 315.

was not so. The secretaries intervened and actively participated in the deliberations according to the customs of
precedence governing the councils. A striking example was
the participation of Servien, Secretary of State for War in
1635, in the council when he wrote to Richelieu: 'We have
worked all morning in the council on the dispatches for
the *arrière-ban*.'[1] When Bullion wrote to Richelieu: 'We had
been told on behalf of Monseigneur the Chancellor that
Monsieur Servien is supposed to speak about the affairs
of Provence tomorrow . . . ', was he referring to a report
scheduled to be made before the council?[2] The fact that the
chancellor and a superintendent of finance, both *chefs du
conseil*, referred to the scheduled report would lead one to
believe so. Provence was indeed in Servien's department;
and furthermore, Bullion continued:

If that is so [that Servien is to present a report] we will do everything possible on the matter. . . . We are obliged to tell Your
Eminence that in the last six weeks or two months we have decreed
diverse financial contracts made in the past six months about
which we have no hopes for the service of the king, in spite of
their having been sealed and formulated in the council. . . . We
are very sorry to weary Your Eminence with such discourses, but
the extreme necessity forces us to do so, foresight being powerless
when affairs have been decided and someone prevents the execution of them. . . .[3]

From this it would seem definite that the secretary of state
for war worked with the other ministers in the council to
prepare dispatches.

In addition to transmitting legislation of the council to
the provinces, the secretaries also presented projects for
laws to be sealed and signed. Sublet wrote to Cornuel, a
councillor and intendant of finance:

[1] 9 July 1635, AAE, France, 814, fol. 255.
[2] Jan.? 1636, AAE, France, 820, fol. 91[v].
[3] Ibid., fol. 91[v]. Bullion, along with several other ministers, sought to
disgrace Servien in the last months of 1635, and the wily old superintendent
did not conceal his displeasure with Servien in his letters to Richelieu. The
accusation of non-enforcement of council decrees is particularly interesting.
Were the powers of the secretaries of state already so great that the Crown
held them responsible for the enforcement of laws? Hardly so. Bullion was
probably complaining about Servien's failure to transmit the council decrees
to the appropriate officials in the provincial administration.

The enclosed decrees for Lyon, for Auvergne, for Tours, and for [*illegible*] are urgently requested by the commissioners whom we have in those quarters for the maintenance of the troops; they declare that they are not able to draw a *sol* [from the treasurers] without them and reply that they have diverse urgent disbursements on their hands. I am sending you the documents upon which [the decree] was drawn up which concerns the imprisonment of the clerk in the [*illegible*] of provisions in the *généralité* of Tours who is in flight and who escaped to Orléans. You will please, Monsieur, examine these decrees and have them signed and sent as soon as possible.[1]

Numerous other references to the preparation of council decrees or the minutes for them could be given from the correspondence of both Chavigny and Sublet. Proposed decrees were sometimes modified by the secretaries, who personally added or crossed out words, indicating the high degree of precision required for such legislation.[2]

In times of war or crisis, when the king was obliged to be away from Paris for weeks or months, special powers to sign in his name were occasionally given to the secretaries. In the summer months of 1642, when Louis, Richelieu, Sublet, and Chavigny were all in southern France on military campaigns, the Comte de Brienne, one of the secretaries whose role in the government had considerably declined, was given special powers in the *Conseil d'État* to dispatch royal orders as though the king himself had signed and sealed them.[3]

The constant movement of the secretaries from Paris to Rueil, provincial towns, royal palaces, and so forth necessitated flexible institutions. The council was just that, and while it possessed a schedule according to the *règlements*, it was often modified by the circumstances of the moment. The handful of anecdotes and specific references to actual council sessions in the whole ministerial correspondence from

[1] 14 Mar. 1638, AG, A¹, 44, fol. 242.
[2] AG, A¹, 62 and 66 contain numerous examples as well as problems centring on the relationship between the secretaries of the *conseil* and the clerks of the secretaries of state.
[3] 'Commission à Monsieur Loménie de Brienne pour signer en l'Absence du Roy estant au Voyage de Languedoc, toutes les expéditions d'État', 26 Jan. 1642, BN, MS. 18243, fol. 118 (copy). See also the proposed commission for Servien, AG, A¹, 26, fol. 83.

1635 to 1642 makes it impossible to be specific about this most important institution. Why this penury of anything but one-word references? When Claude le Bouthillier wrote: 'His Majesty is at Versailles from where he will come after dinner to hold a *conseil* at Ruel; Monseigneur the Cardinal arrived there yesterday. . . ', it was not necessary for him to explain further to his correspondent the nature or membership of the meeting.[1]

In Rueil (or Ruel), Richelieu's favourite residence, meetings of ministers, personal secretaries, and favourites were often held. Political problems were frequently debated, dispatches were read to the group, and governmental decisions were made in an atmosphere of cordiality and informality. Sublet de Noyers described one of these sessions in a letter to Mazarin, who was on a diplomatic mission to Savoy:

Monsieur de Bullion, being present at the reading of your dispatch, paid you a great compliment, and His Eminence, jesting with him and wishing to do you a good turn with him said to him, 'I see clearly now that Monsieur Mazarin *fait l'amour* to Monsieur de Bullion and that he would like to pick his pockets' —upon which there was abundant laughter. It was resolved at once that Madame [the Duchess of Savoy, for whom Mazarin was seeking a pension] would be helped by a sum of money, about which Monsieur de Chavigny will give you an account. . . .[2]

The text is significant for at least two reasons. First, the persons present were numerous and important: Richelieu, Bullion, Sublet de Noyers, and perhaps Chavigny, who, if he was not present, was soon informed about the session so that he could write to Mazarin. While these were not properly meetings of the *conseil* with all the formalities, they continued governmental action in an informal framework.

---

[1] Bouthillier to Césy, Ambassador to the Levant, 25 Nov. 1636, BN, MS. 16157, fol. 269.

[2] 17 Dec. 1640, AAE, Sardaigne, 31, fol. 662. Another time Sublet wrote to Richelieu: 'Hier au matin je travaillay avec Messieurs du Houssay [intendant of finance] et Gobelin [maître des requêtes de l'Hôtel] et tiray d'eux tout se qui se peut de lumiere, sur le fait des bleds de Lorraine et de Champagne. Apres disner, Messieurs les Surintendans avec le R. P. Joseph, employerent tres-utilement quatre bonnes heures à l'expedition des affaires projettées. . . .' 25 Apr. 1636, Aubery, *Mémoires pour l'histoire du Cardinal Duc de Richelieu* (Cologne, 1667), iii, p. 60.

Second, the position of the secretary of state in these meetings was probably more important than in the regular *conseil*.

In these sessions the secretaries described political situations communicated to them by the provincial administration; on frequent occasions political decisions were a joint effort, as when Sublet wrote to the French ambassador in Holland: 'Having had the honour to attend the resolution of the dispatches that Monsieur de Chavigny is sending you. . . .'[1] While Sublet corresponded only for military affairs and the affairs of his provinces, he attended sessions where French foreign policy was deliberated, and where diplomatic and military problems were discussed for the same region. Often the ambassador or official received two letters, one from each secretary, covering what had been decided in a council or informal meeting of the ministers.[2]

But the importance of group resolution and the necessity for harmony and co-operation among the ministers can only be appreciated when one recalls that *conseils* were the greater part of the daily routine for all of the ministers. Policies were changed quickly; on one occasion a secretary was ordered to stop the preparation of a dispatch because new information required consultation. The cardinal wrote to Servien: 'Monsieur Servien will please come here before making up the dispatches which were resolved yesterday for the relief of Schlestat . . . because I have just received a dispatch that it is necessary for you to see. . . .'[3]

Richelieu dominated the organization established for making policy decisions. This was not done by reason of his titles as cardinal and principal minister, but because of his favour with the king and the other ministers. When he wished the ministers to co-operate and arrive at decisions, he generally gave them specific orders. He wrote to Servien:

You will do me the pleasure, as soon as you receive this, to communicate about it with Père Joseph and the Sieur de Vignoles, who is coming from Germany; and in case you all agree that I am right, as I believe I am, dispatch the Sieur de Vignoles to

[1] To Charnacé, 31 May 1636, AAE, Hollande, 18, fol. 590.
[2] See Sublet to Charnacé, 31 May 1636, ibid., fol. 382.
[3] 22 Dec. 1635, AAE, France, 816, fol. 187; Avenel, ed. cit. v, p. 959.

Monseigneur the Cardinal de La Valette . . . to explain to them the thoughts of the king.[1]

If circumstances and additional information required it, Richelieu carefully used the other ministers to review his decisions and to modify them.

Whenever it was convenient, the secretaries of state participated in the ceremonies of the court, such as the *levée* of the king.[2] Louis almost always had one secretary with him at all times, and it was often the latter's task to transmit the king's orders to his colleagues according to the various departments. The general practice of sending memoranda full of details of day-to-day government enabled Louis to accomplish the role which he saw fit to play; that is, to review all governmental action and modify it where he saw fit.

The functions of the secretaries in the *Cabinet du roi* were simple, centring on the reading of dispatches to the king and the preparation of replies. Chavigny wrote to Charnacé, the ambassador in Holland:

I reported what you wrote to me about Monsieur de Beringhen to the king and Monseigneur the Cardinal, and I did not omit a single thing which you informed me in his favour. I was very pleased to be of service on this occasion, but I found His Majesty rather little disposed to listen to the reasons.[3]

The secretaries, who were informed on provincial problems, often suggested men for offices or means to enforce a royal decision. Servien wrote to his cousin Audiger, President in the Parlement of Grenoble:

I should wish that the *intendance* of which you speak were of that nature. I assure you that I would do everything possible to make it fall into your hands, but since the king has not yet made a resolution concerning the manner in which he wants to administer justice in Pignerol, and since I see that His Majesty wishes to choose by himself the one whom he will make the head of it. . . .[4]

Servien was clearly ready to help his cousin to acquire the

1 8 July 1635, Avenel, ed. cit. v. l.
2 Richelieu to Chavigny, 10 Dec. 1637, ibid., v, p. 1068.
3 18 May 1636, AAE, Hollande, 19, fol. 33.
4 22 Jan. 1635, AG, A¹, 24, fol. 44.

office, but he was quite certain there would be little chance for him to influence the appointment.

It was through the secretaries that Richelieu controlled patronage. The Crown was frequently informed by the secretary of the death of some far-away ecclesiastic or royal officer; and to be sure that the cardinal could exercise his influence on the appointment of a successor, the secretaries spoke to the king in such a way that the decision was held up temporarily. Chavigny wrote to Richelieu: 'On the news that we have had of the death of Monsieur de Rhodes, Monsieur de Noyers and I have spoken to the king about his *charges* so that no one [will have them?]; he will not grant them until Monseigneur has returned. . . .'[1]

The frequent letters of gratitude indicate the importance of the secretaries themselves in the appointments by the Crown. No specific references to 'gifts' in return are extant, but there are thank-you letters suggesting a feeling of real obligation on the part of the office seeker. Montbrun de Roubac wrote to Claude le Bouthillier: 'The indebtedness that I have to your brother . . . by whom I have just received through you a commission from the king for a company of light horse, could only have come from the *bons offices* that it has pleased you to do for me . . . .'[2] Again the importance of the different secretaries varied greatly and depended upon their favour with the king and the cardinal, but the main duty of the secretaries was to transmit royal orders and to act as a liaison between the king, the ministers, and the councils. Chavigny wrote to Richelieu:

The king has commanded me to write a letter to Monsieur de La Meilleraie in accordance with the *mémoire* that he himself drew up, and also to send a copy of it to His Eminence as something which he himself thinks. I am sending His Eminence an extract of Monsieur d'Angoulesme's letters; I know very well that it will not please him, but I am obliged to inform him of all that is happening. . . .[3]

The secretaries felt it their duty to inform, and it was also at this level that the deliberate administrative confusion

[1] 15 Aug. 1642, AAE, France, 845, fol. 235.
[2] 7 Feb. 1635, AAE, France, 1546, fol. 263.
[3] 10 Oct. 1635, AAE, France, 815, fol. 325.

between the acts of the king and of the cardinal occurred. Richelieu did not hesitate to give the secretaries memoranda for letters to be prepared and sent as though they were from the king himself. He wrote to Chavigny: 'I am sending you the *mémoires* for [the letters to] Messieurs the Maréchaux and the Sieur de Feuquières. You will prepare, if you please, the dispatch promptly, and have the courier who bears it leave by tomorrow evening. . . .'[1] Unity of action between the king and the cardinal was assured and put into legal form by the secretaries.

At the end of the reign, with the personality of Richelieu dominating the entire ministerial government, his favour more than traditional rights enabled certain officers to increase their powers at the expense of others. The four secretaries of state are a good example, for while they were in theory equal in powers and rights, only two of them played active roles in the government.

Henri-Auguste de Loménie, Seigneur de La Ville-aux-Clercs, and Louis Phélypeaux, Seigneur de La Vrillière, continued to prepare dispatches for their particular provinces; but because of the growing jurisdiction of the department of war and the unification of the departments of the *maison du roi* and foreign affairs, these two secretaries were far less influential then Sublet and Chavigny.[2]

The Loménie family, particularly Antoine, Comte de Brienne, furnished secretaries of state under Henry IV, Louis XIII, and Louis XIV. Brienne, according to Fauvelet-du-Toc, was the son of a royal secretary who was assassinated on St. Bartholomew's Day 1572.[3] In 1606 Henry IV granted Brienne the right of succession to the office of secretary of state held by Ruzé, under whom Brienne had served as first clerk.[4]

Henri-Auguste de Loménie, son of Antoine, received the

[1] 24 Mar. 1635, AAE, France, 813, fol. 192; Avenel, ed. cit. iv, p. 793.
[2] A letter from Richelieu transmitting orders to the secretaries of state through Sublet, 5 July 1636, Avenel, ed. cit. v. ccliv, is a fine example of how the geographical departments continued to be respected, as is proved by the marginalia.
[3] Fauvelet-du-Toc, *Histoire des secrétaires d'État contenant l'origine, le progrès, et l'establissement de leurs charges* (Paris, 1668), p. 195. See also, *Mémoires de l'establissement des secrétaires d'Estat*, BN, MS. 18236, fol. 92.
[4] Ibid., pp. 195 f.

droit de survivance to the position of his father in 1615, and both men continued to work together as secretary almost up to the death of the father at the age of eighty-two in January 1638.[1] The influence of Loménie and his son in the central government was not very great; the correspondence of Richelieu contains very few references to them.[2] While the bulk of their correspondence for the period has not survived, their library, which is preserved at the Bibliothèque Nationale, Cabinet des Manuscrits, still exists.

Henri-Auguste wrote his *Mémoires* to instruct his son in the office of secretary of state.[3] The fact that Loménie scarcely spoke of the great diplomatic and military problems of the reign is proof that he was of minor importance to the government of Louis XIII. Hostility toward Richelieu and his creatures is the latent theme in the work; it is couched in the traditional framework of repugnance for royal favouritism, which is not surprising from a courtier who was never really in favour. Nevertheless, the loyalty of the Loménies was never questioned. They continued to attend the king in court and to advise him occasionally.

The few personal letters of Phélypeaux are solemn and business-like in tone.[4] With the aid of the creatures, Richelieu probably deliberately kept him from being influential in affairs of state. Even so, he rendered services as one of the 'king's men' in the Parlement which none of the creatures could perform. As *conseiller d'honneur* in the Parlement he made a speech defending the Crown in early 1636, when opposition to the increased sale of offices was very great.[5]

Though not in favour, Loménie continued to play politics; when the *conciergerie* of Fontainebleau became vacant, he proposed candidates; and in the event that the king did not

---

[1] Ibid., p. 196.

[2] For the period 1635–42, Avenel, in editing the letters of Richelieu, found none addressed to the Loménies.

[3] *Mémoires du Comte de Brienne*, ed. by Michaud et Poujoulat, séries 3 (Paris, 1838). They were written after the cardinal's death which, according to Loménie, brought great happiness to Louis XIII, p. 75.

[4] See the correspondence of Louis de Nicolay, President of the *Chambre des Comptes*, AN, 3AP, particularly fol. 23.

[5] 'Discours fait au Parlement de Monsieur de La Ville-aux-Clercs', AAE, France, 820, fol. 17; see also the *Extrait des Registres du Parlement* at his entry in 1632, BN, MS. 18243, fol. 115 (copy).

like them, Loménie requested that Chavigny propose his own name![1] At the same time, however, to avoid the stigma of ministerial domination, Richelieu kept Loménie in the government despite the latter's desire to resign.

The reason for this refusal and the disgrace of the Sieur de La Ville-aux-Clercs arose from the fact that the Cardinal de Richelieu, having made himself absolute master of the king's mind, wanted all those who approached his person to be his creatures and to promise to obey him without reservation. Since Monsieur de La Ville-aux-Clercs never wanted to do so nor to allow himself to be won over by the advantages which he could have had for himself by being friendly with the cardinal, [the latter] resolved to push him aside in the affairs of government and took away one of the principal functions of his department, which was to draw up the list of pensions, and had it given to Monsieur de Chavigny, the secretary of state who had the department of foreign affairs. Chavigny made up the list by his order, then sent it to Monsieur de La Ville-aux-Clercs to sign it without looking it over first. Monsieur de La Ville-aux-Clercs, not having agreed to do so, Monsieur de Chavigny signed it and afterwards took this job away from him completely, annexing it to his own department. This refusal, and the resolution which Monsieur de La Ville-aux-Clercs had made to lose his position rather than to bend and submit or do anything cowardly, inclined the cardinal even more to put him in the wrong with the king, who—being susceptible to all the impressions which his favourites gave him—considerably cooled the affection which he had had for Monsieur de La Ville-aux-Clercs, as a result of the belief that he had been given that [La Ville-aux-Clercs] found fault with everything he did.

This coolness on the part of the king and the cardinal's spite led Monsieur de La Ville-aux-Clercs to ask the king for permission to resign from his *charge*, which Monsieur the Cardinal caused to be absolutely refused him so that posterity would not reproach him for having arbitrarily removed from his position, without any reason other than malice, a person who had for thirty-five years continued carefully the services which his ancestors had rendered to the state.[2]

Richelieu's part in the development of the secretaries of state for foreign affairs and for war was greater than he

---

[1] Bullion to Chavigny, 11 Sept. 1636, AAE, France, 821, fol. 282. Sublet received the *charge*, thanks to Richelieu.

[2] *Mémoires de l'establissement des secrétaires d'Estat*, BN, MS. 18236, fol. 115ᵛ.

realized. The combined forces of his disapproval of two secretaries and his great favour for the two men already possessing expanding powers served to change permanently the traditional framework.

Louis Phélypeaux, also the son of a secretary of state, was the member of a very old and influential family with a long history of service to the Crown.[1] The appointment of secretary of state was revocable, and the right of succession was eagerly sought after by secretaries for their sons or nephews. When he died in 1629, Raymond Phélypeaux had not obtained this right for his son La Vrillière, and Louis XIII seemed little inclined to grant the office to him. If the king had actually failed to accept him, it would have meant both a great loss of prestige and a financial catastrophe for the family.[2] Claude le Bouthillier ardently supported La Vrillière, but this was not enough. Yet when Marillac, leader of the faction opposed to Richelieu, proposed a candidate to Louis XIII, Richelieu came to the aid of La Vrillière by influencing the king to accept him.[3] This left La Vrillière under an obligation to Richelieu and his creatures, particularly Claude le Bouthillier. Throughout the period Richelieu occasionally gave La Vrillière small assignments in addition to his regular duties as secretary of state.[4] In 1640 he was occupied with revolts in Languedoc, one of his provinces.[5] Like La Ville-aux-Clercs, he was given the right to sign dispatches away from the king when he accompanied Chancellor Séguier to Normandy to quell the revolt of the *Va-nu-pieds* in 1639.[6] Normandy was in his department.

---

[1] *Cabinet des titres: Hozier, dossiers bleus; pièces originales.* See also Avenel, ed. cit. ii, p. 72.

[2] The loss would not have been complete, for it was the custom for the successor to reimburse the former secretary or his family. See Roland Mousnier, *La Vénalité des offices sous Henri IV* (Rouen, 1946), p. 337, for the values of the *charge* of secretary of state at different times in the reign.

[3] *Mémoires de l'establissement des secrétaires d'Estat*, BN, MS. 18236, fol. 139ᵛ.

[4] It was probably greater than that played by Loménie, however, especially after the marriage alliance with the Particelli family headed by Hémery, a favourite of Richelieu.

[5] See the 'Mémoire pour Monsieur de La Vrillière' by the Bishop of Nîmes, 14 Aug. 1640, AAE, France, 837, fol. 184.

[6] Verthamont, *Relation du voyage du Chancelier Séguier dans la Normandie en 1640*, ed. by Floquet (Rouen, 1842), *passim*; Fauvelet-du-Toc, op. cit., pp. 265 f.

The geographical and departmental jurisdictions noted in the sixteenth century were still very real in the last years of the reign of Louis XIII.[1] After having prepared a royal letter, the secretaries followed the formality of having the proper secretary countersign it, even if it meant a delay of several days.[2] Occasionally secretaries signed for each other, but permission was necessary. Servien wrote to La Vrilliére, who was with the king : 'If you please, sign what letters there are for my department, and believe that I look upon it as a great favour.'[3] Even when a problem had already been taken up by one secretary, the jurisdictions were respected for the king's reply :

Monseigneur, I add this letter to my preceding one in order to assure you that when they put the troops into garrison, I will take care that your companies of light horse are sent to Burgundy; and regarding the noblemen whom Monsieur the Abbé de Coursan proposed that you arrest, it is something about which I have no knowledge, and I have not yet learned the king's intentions, but I will speak to him about it at the first opportunity, and because it does not concern the war, you will be able to learn [the king's] decision from Monsieur de La Vrillière.[4]

Evidence to show that the secretaries rigidly respected the departments is profuse. Departmental jurisdictions were sometimes deliberately violated by a secretary.[5]

---

[1] The departments of the secretaries in 1635 were : (1) La Ville-aux-Clercs : royal household, Île de France, Orléannais and Chartres country; (2) Bouthillier : foreign countries, Atlantic navy, Champagne and Brie, Brittany; (3) La Vrillière : Languedoc, Guyenne, Aunis, Burgundy, Bourbonnais, Nivernais, Normandy, Picardy, Touraine, Anjou, Maine, Perche, Auvergne; (4) Servien : war, Lyonnais, Dauphiné, Provence, Poitou, Angoumois, from Limousin to Marche, Mediterranean navy. Bibliothèque de l'Institut, Collection Godefroy, MS. 310, fol. 206. For an earlier organization of departments, see above, p. 49.

[2] Servien to Bouthillier, 30 Aug. 1635, AG, A¹, 25, fol. 260.

[3] 25 Sept. 1635, ibid., fol. 398.

[4] Servien to Condé, 21 Nov. 1635, AG, A¹, 25, fol. 539.

[5] One of the Loménies, either the father or the son, co-operated with Richelieu and the Bouthilliers by preparing and signing dispatches which were destined to go to Servien's department. The aim of the whole affair is not explained, but the good humour of Loménie does not hide the importance and seriousness of the violation which he undertook. 'Monsieur, J'ay une telle haste(?) de vous obeir que je ne scay sy je doibs signer les depesches que vous m'avez envoyées, ou bien [*illegible*] commandé. En cet estat je prens party et signe de la main droite, et j'escris celle-cy de la gauche ce que vous

More frequently political friendships caused the secretaries to correspond with officials and subjects in other departments. Servien, after having mentioned in a previous letter that the affair in question was in Chavigny's department, wrote to the Comte de Joyeuse:

As for the letters which Monseigneur de Rheims is asking for, I believe that his position merits passing over formalities, but you know that the power of the secretaries of state does not extend that far, especially on an occasion such as this. Therefore, it is a question of his being content with the letters addressed to an established regular court. . . .[1]

Servien's participation in the ecclesiastical politics of a province in Chavigny's department may well have been one small incident among many which caused Chavigny to lead his group to disgrace Servien in 1636.

Once Louis XIII himself disregarded departmental jurisdictions, and was sharply informed about it by Richelieu, who wrote to him:

The company of Bussy de Vere has been very inopportunely cut to pieces in Auvergne owing to a contradiction in orders, something which can cause much harm. They were established in the garrison which Your Majesty had approved by Monsieur de Noyers' order; another order signed by Phélypeaux with a *département* [quartering orders] of Descures [*Maître des Logis*] made them leave that position and sent them to another place which did not wish to receive them, not seeing an order from the Secretary of War. Thus they were forced to scour the country, which aroused this disorder. The service of Your Majesty requires that you forbid every other secretary of state except Monsieur de Noyers to interfere with war orders.[2]

The responsibility for this confusion is unknown. The important factor is that in many ways the reign of Louis XIII

cognoistrez assez en la voyant sy mal escrite, et qui pis (?) est, j'ay esprit tres troublé ayant sceu que Monsieur Servien se trouve offensé que j'aye entrepris sur sa charge, mais j'ay un bon guarand puisque c'est par ordre de Monseigneur le Cardinal; je vous supplie de vous tenir pret de me servir de second sy l'affaire va plus avant. . . .' 14 Sept. 1634, AAE, France, 811, fol. 19. It was addressed to one of the Bouthilliers by internal evidence and because it is in the correspondence of Chavigny in the AAE. It is difficult to read.
[1] 3 Mar. 1635, AG, A¹, 24, fol. 121; see also fols. 39 f.
[2] 10 Mar. 1637, Avenel, ed. cit. v. cdxxvi.
821443   F

was decisive in tracing the new jurisdictions for the future secretary-ministers. Richelieu, not the king, provided the discipline to institutionalize them.

Having described the relationships of the secretaries with the provincial administration, councils, and king, we will consider briefly their relations with the other ministers. Co-operation with the keeper of the seals or chancellor existed in the framework of the councils and also in the preparation of the dispatches.[1] After the *lettres patentes* and certain other documents had been prepared by the secretary, they were sent to the chancery to be sealed; Chavigny wrote to Séguier: .

> You will be presented with two procurations [*pouvoirs*] sent in the name of Monsieur the Maréchal de Brézé; one to administer on behalf of the king, as His Majesty's procurator, the oath which the Counts of Barcelona have been accustomed to make in person in these areas before performing any act of sovereignty in Catalonia; the other is to exercise the *charge* of viceroy. They are both in the Latin language, as the Catalans wished. . . . It will please Monseigneur [Séguier] to seal them both so that they can be delivered to Monsieur the Maréchal de Brézé, who must leave as soon as possible.[2]

In addition to the mechanics of administration, the secretaries and the chancellor co-operated with the intendants. Villarceaux, an intendant in Bar and a frequent correspondent with Séguier, wrote:

> I am going to Pont de Joins(?) at Verdun to consider the means of bringing wheat into the city. For the ordinary provisions of the garrison, I will take wheat from all of the King's reserves. . . . I

---

[1] This excerpt of a letter from Servien to Richelieu, 27 July 1634, furnished many details on how the ministers co-operated in preparing legislation. 'Le Garde des Sceaux [Séguier] a communiqué à Messieurs les Surintendants, les mémoires qu'il a pleu à Son Eminence luy envoyer et par leur advis on a dressé trois arrests en faveur des ecclesiastiques, de la noblesse et des villes frontieres qui pourvoyent ainsy que l'on peult desirer aux plainctes que l'on a faictes de l'execution de la declaration. Monsieur Bouthillier a les arrests entre les mains — sytost qu'ils seront mis en parchemin le garde des sceaux les scellera pour les envoyer par des courriers expres dans les généralités, ce qui sera demain au plus tard, cependant on donnera ordre que l'arrest de la noblesse soit dans la gazette [*Gazette de France*].' AAE, France, 810, fol. 371.
[2] 25 Sept. 1641, BN, MS. 17373, fol. 82.

shall also look over the accounts of the bursar of the bishopric. Monsieur de Feuquières has been [*illegible*] me for a long time to go to Verdun for these two matters. I am writing to Messieurs the secretaries of state that if they send me the money, or if they give me an order to receive some there, I would work to make the rivers navigable as far as Blamont. . . .[1]

This example is typical, as it shows the administrative division and the necessity for a provincial official to communicate with several ministers at the same time.

The chancellor and the secretaries also co-operated in the appointments of intendants, especially the intendants of justice. Sublet wrote to Séguier: 'Monsieur the Duc de Ventadour [Governor of the Limousin] has recently written that he hopes to hold his government in obedience, but that he needs an intendant of justice who is mild and prudent. If you please, ask these gentlemen for someone, and I will deliver the commission to him.'[2] Here the secretary of state does not seem to be only a favoured clerk of the king; the frankness and easy co-operation between the chancellor and the secretary, one whose office had been the most powerful in the realm for centuries and the other a new-comer, dramatize the change in the position of the secretaries.

The secretaries of state probably worked most closely with the superintendents of finance. Activity between these ministers was intense on all issues, particularly between Bullion, Sublet, and Chavigny. Sublet wrote: 'I sometimes wrote as often as six times a day to Monsieur de Bullion about troublesome and vexatious affairs. . . .'[3] When they met together, they frequently advised Richelieu by letters which all of them signed. Bullion and Servien wrote to the cardinal: 'We have conferred together, Monsieur Servien and I, about the affair concerning the Maréchal de Vitry, and we have thought, with the good pleasure of Your Eminence, that you would approve if we accord him 15,000 *livres* for the royal guards. . . .'[4]

Their co-operation with the superintendents and the

[1] 25 Oct. 1636, BN, MS. 17370, fol. 34.
[2] 8 July 1637, BN, MS. 17373, fol. 164.
[3] Sublet to Claude le Bouthillier, 26 June 1641, AAE, France, 838, fol. 285.
[4] 21 Mar. 1635, AAE, France, 813, fol. 181.

chancellor is a good measure of the progressive change in their positions. Although the secretaries were not equal in rank and precedence to the great officers of the realm, they enjoyed broad administrative powers, making them an integral part of the administration at the highest level.

IV

Léon le Bouthillier, Comte de Chavigny, Secretary of State with the Department of Foreign Affairs

LÉON LE BOUTHILLIER, thanks to the favour of Richelieu, climbed to a high station during the reign of Louis
XIII. Becoming secretary of state in 1632 at only twenty-
four years of age, he faithfully served the cardinal through
the dark days of war with Spain and the plots to disgrace
the principal minister, until Richelieu died in 1642. He was
a haughty and sensitive young man with plenty of wit and
charm, yet not all in the court of Louis XIII shared the
pleasure of his company with as great a satisfaction as Richelieu. The English ambassador wrote:

... for he is as hard to be found as a mouse in a barne; he lyes
sometimes at bathing houses and sometimes in other places, and
is so much a man of pleasure, as it is a wonder to many, that the
great Apollo of this State will put so many and so great businesses
into his hand; yesterday and no sooner Mr Augier found him at
the last where he was at dinner with Bullion, Senneterre, and
others at a privat-man's house, for they being in their debauche,
he could not speake with any of them, for by my faith they say
they drinke hard here now some time. . . .[1]

But there was much more than this to young Bouthillier.
Richelieu showered a particular affection on the son of
Claude and Marie le Bouthillier, both of whom he loved as
if they were members of his own family.[2] The cardinal
watched over the health of young Bouthillier, cautioned him
to follow the doctor's orders when he was ill; and when
affairs of state or special missions for Richelieu obliged

[1] Leicester to Coke, 2 Oct./22 Sept. 1637, PRO, State Papers, series 78, vol. 104, fol. 212.
[2] See above, p. 34. I wish to thank the editor of the *Revue d'Histoire Diplomatique* for permission to reprint portions of this Chapter which appeared earlier in an article in the *Revue*.

Bouthillier to leave the familiar quarters of Paris and Rueil, the cardinal always expressed regret at his departure.

This memorandum is to say good-bye to you and to express to you the regret I feel at your departure. Absent or present will always be the same thing in my regard. You will believe this, I am sure, and will recognize it at all times.[1]

This affection was not simply the result of pure favouritism. The cardinal learned that he could trust Bouthillier with the most important secrets upon which perhaps not only his position as principal minister but even his life sometimes depended. Often the two of them conducted secret negotiations or formed policies which remained secret from all other ministers, and even from Louis XIII himself.[2]

Léon le Bouthillier cannot be described simply as the secretary of state for foreign affairs. His importance in this domain was really not very great, but as a personal liaison between the cardinal, the king, and Gaston d'Orléans, Chavigny—as he began to call himself in 1635[3]—played a role in the government of France not far below that of his illustrious master. Richelieu's confidence in Chavigny's ability to deal effectively with the king and his brother caused him to organize the secretary's life. Orders to go to Blois, to hurry back as soon as possible, to be at the *levée* of the king, to be at a given place at a given moment to see the cardinal are characteristic of Richelieu's correspondence with Chavigny.[4] Chavigny was almost constantly touring

---

[1] Richelieu to Chavigny, 18 Mar. 1635, Richelieu, *Lettres, instructions diplomatiques, et papiers d'Etat*, ed. M. Avenel (Paris, 1853–77), iv. ccclvii. Richelieu cautioned Bouthillier to look after his health on 21 July 1637, p. 1044 of vol. v.

[2] This was especially true in handling the delicate problem of Gaston d'Orléans.

[3] Léon le Bouthillier, with the wealth from his new office and his father's aid, bought the manor of Chavigny. He wrote to Richelieu: 'J'advoue Monseigneur que Chavigni m'a extremement pleu et que si mon pere y fait la despense que vous m'avez fait l'honneur de me dire plusieurs fois qu'il fault qu'il face, ce sera une tres agreable maison. Je trouve qu'une de ses grandes beautés est de n'estre que trois lieues de Richelieu. . . .' 28 May 1635, AAE, France, 814, fol. 125. Even before adopting the title Comte de Chavigny, Bouthillier was affectionately called *Monsieur le Jeune* to avoid confusing him with his father, the superintendent of finance.

[4] Characteristic of these orders is Richelieu's letter to Chavigny of 10 Dec. 1637: 'Ce mot est pour avertir Monsieur de Chavigny qu'il est nécessaire

battlefields, hunting-grounds, or rebellious provinces with
Louis. When the king personally led his armies, the correspondence between Chavigny and Richelieu was full of
military details: the condition and number of troops,
strategy, and problems of moving and feeding the armies.[1]
The secretary was always careful to keep Richelieu informed.

Louis was accustomed to receive the suggestions of his
principal minister through Chavigny; it was their normal
way of concerting their action and formulating the policies
of state. Richelieu wrote to Louis: 'The king will see by the
dispatch which I prepared tonight for Monsieur de Chavigny
that his servitors do not let his thoughts fall to the ground.'[2]

The king was also fully aware of Chavigny's position as
a creature of Richelieu. He well knew that his moods, angers,
orders, in short every aspect of his character, were being
transmitted by Chavigny to Richelieu whenever the king
and the principal minister were apart. Generally, Louis and
Richelieu were separated, though not by great distances,
and a means of communication between them was necessary,
not only for affairs of state but also for the assurance that
a new favourite was not gaining royal affection. Chavigny,
and to a lesser extent Sublet de Noyers, faithfully maintained not only the administrative liaison between the king
and the cardinal, but the personal one as well.

Chavigny was responsible for literally managing the king.
He received orders from Richelieu, and it was his duty to
present them to Louis, to convince him that they were in the
best interest of the State, and ultimately to communicate
the king's decision to the other ministers, so that it could be
officially transmitted to the realm as the royal law or will.
Richelieu often sent long *mémoires* to be presented to Louis
by Chavigny; often administrative details were handled

qu'il vienne aujourd'huy coucher icy, à quelque heure que ce soit, pour estre
demain à 7 heures et demie à Saint-Germain pour le sujet qu'il sçait. Monsieur
de Noyers y a esté aujourd'huy à la mesme heure, et n'y a pas esté trop tost,
Sa Majesté estant desjà levée et en son prier Dieu. . . .' Avenel, ed. cit. v,
p. 1068.

[1] Richelieu's letters to Chavigny, dated 20 and 21 Sept. 1636, show how
the cardinal co-ordinated the military operations of several armies. On this
occasion Chavigny was with Gaston d'Orléans, brother of the king and
commander of an army. Ibid. v. cccxix and cccxx.

[2] 22 Sept. 1636, ibid. v. ccxxiii.

quickly and efficiently by letters, where either Chavigny or the king himself wrote his decision in the margin.[1]

When there were differences of opinion between the king and the cardinal, Chavigny did not hesitate to defend Richelieu. On these occasions, both Louis and Richelieu became particularly difficult. If one is to take the accounts of the times at face value, both men became emotionally unstable and physically ill. Once, when Richelieu had displeased Louis over a decision on the number of guards which Louis was to have as an escort, the latter became childishly angry and fell into *mauvaises humeurs*. Chavigny wrote to the king about the affair, saying: 'But I think once again of assuring Your Majesty that he [Richelieu] has been very greatly displeased regarding what they have done, since he would prefer to die a thousand times rather than to displease you in the smallest way. . . .'[2] The *mauvaises humeurs* of Louis were always carefully described by Chavigny; and with this information Richelieu could determine how he himself should act before the king. These reports were indispensable to Richelieu, who always hastened to write to Chavigny to do everything possible to alleviate the king's illness and moroseness.[3]

Normally, however, Chavigny had no difficulty in getting Louis's approval for Richelieu's propositions. The following letter to the cardinal describes the typical relationship between Louis, Richelieu, and Chavigny:

Yesterday evening I saw Monsieur de Bullion, who is still agreed to have the nine thousand *livres* given to Monsieur de Mauroy. . . . This morning we will finish this matter and will immediately send the Sieur Foucault to Monsieur de Bordeaux, who will be able to reach the naval forces before the eighth, which is absolutely necessary.

The king is answering the Archbishop of Bordeaux in his own hand (by Monsieur Lucas nevertheless) to express to him the

---

[1] A fine example of this form of government in action is the *mémoire* addressed to Chavigny by Richelieu, 22 Oct. 1636, ibid. v. cccxlv.

[2] Chavigny to Louis, 15 June 1635, AAE, France, 813, fol. 29.

[3] Richelieu to Chavigny, 1 Oct. 1635: 'Vous ne sçauriés mieux servir le roy ny plus m'obliger qu'en faisant tout ce que vous pourrés pour dissiper les mélancolies qui prennent souvent Sa Majesté, et le délivrer de ses inquiétudes. . . .' Avenel, ed. cit. v. cxxvi.

pleasure which he had from the services rendered him at their last meeting.

His Majesty is writing the two letters which Monseigneur judged opportune. The gentleman who bears the first to Monsieur de Chastillon knows nothing about the second one, which His Eminence will send him or will give him in passing as he sees fit. There was no difficulty in deciding His Majesty to give this order to the Marshal, having considered to what point his shortcomings have prejudiced the welfare of [the king's] affairs this year, and the harm that they could still receive in the future without this remedy. His idea had been to give the same order to Monsieur d'Arpajon, and he ordered me to write it to Monseigneur. It isn't that His Majesty has made up his mind to do so, but it is to notify Monseigneur about the frame of mind he is in, in case he judged that it should be done. The king approves of Monsieur de Noyers' writing the necessary letter to Monsieur de La Force to command the army alone.

If the king continues to keep his disposition in the plate where it now is, His Eminence should have no difficulty in proposing whatever he pleases to him, for His Majesty will not make any opposition to following his advice, and I see that at this moment he is out of that distrustful mood which he expressed in the past.

The disorders which exist in the king's armies are unimaginable, and it seems to me that they are led by children. Monsieur de Meilleraie showed that he had much prudence in refusing the military command which the king wanted to give him this year.

What Monseigneur writes concerning the one whom the Queen Mother might send here and the way in which Monsieur de Bellièvre will have to act towards her will be carried out point by point. I don't believe it is necessary for Varenne to go to visit her when he goes to England, it being sufficient that His Majesty's ambassador has paid her this courtesy.

I've learned nothing new since yesterday evening about the king's illness; however short it be, I don't know if it will be wise for His Majesty to make the Picardy trip, as many accidents can happen. If it lasts ever so little, Monseigneur will permit me to tell him, with the respect that I hold for him and the passion that I have for his service, that it is absolutely necessary that he come here in order to watch the course of the market.

For the last two days the king has been sometimes good, sometimes bad with the creature, and it is certain that there is a vast intrigue at court to destroy him. I have presented him to the king on diverse occasions in order to show him the advantages which he will gain from the decision he has made.

The king will decide nothing for Monsieur de Saint-Denis until His Eminence is near him.

I have sent the account of the battle won by Monsieur de Bordeaux to Renaudot, and will have the map [*plan*] printed as Monseigneur orders me.

I am going at once to Monsieur de Bullion's and am bringing along the Sieurs Mauroy and Foucault in order to send him [Foucault] off at the same time; and I will immediately return to Saint-Germain, having nothing else on my mind but the care to please Monseigneur, and the passion to show him by all my actions that I am his very humble, very obedient, very faithful, and very obliged creature,

Chavigny.[1]

The key position of the secretary, as between Louis and Richelieu, is clearly visible in the phrases: 'there was no difficulty in deciding His Majesty to give this order . . . ', and 'His Eminence should have no difficulty in proposing whatever he pleases to him'. Chavigny constantly helped Richelieu in his relations with Louis. In an age without modern communications, and with Richelieu and Louis often separated, such information enabled Richelieu to exercise with great freedom and assurance the broad powers given to him as a result of the king's favour.[2]

A fascinating source for Chavigny's complicated relationship with Louis XIII is his correspondence with the Cardinal de La Valette, where in code he admits: '. . . Chavigny is

---

[1] Chavigny to Richelieu, Paris, 3 Sept. 1638, BN, MS. 9354, fol. 259. This letter is exemplary for other reasons. It indicates that while Louis made the final decision on army appointments, he was closely advised by Richelieu. The importance of sending two letters to Chastillon, one from the king and probably one from the king with a note from the cardinal, is unexplained. The account of the victory of the Archbishop of Bordeaux (Sourdis) to be given to Renaudot, the editor of the *Gazette de France*, is one more example of how this paper was used by the government to inform the public as it saw fit. Several things are unclear in the text. What does 'watch the course of the market' refer to? Was Louis to watch over produce sales, or the sale of offices or *rentes*? Or was Chavigny using the press of governmental affairs as an excuse for keeping the king in Paris? The fourth paragraph from the bottom about the 'creature' is also mysterious. Is the 'creature' Cinq-Mars, who was introduced into Louis's court by Richelieu?

[2] When Chavigny could not succeed in manœuvring Louis, he quickly reported it to Richelieu. See the letter dated 9 Oct. 1635, AAE, France, 815, fol. 324.

still on bad terms with the King, but he is on good terms with Monseigneur the Cardinal, near whom he remains assiduously. . . . '[1] When Chavigny's favour with Louis became dangerously low, the cardinal spoke to the king in his favour.[2]

Louis's affection for Chavigny depended on his moods and also on the latter's efficiency. Louis wrote to Richelieu: 'I am very satisfied with *le Jeune*, and I can assure you that he helps me very much and works day and night.'[3] But when Chavigny did not inform him of diplomatic developments, the king did not conceal his dissatisfaction; he wrote to Richelieu: 'I forgot to tell you today that I am giving audience tomorrow to the English ambassadors. I pray you to communicate to me what I should reply to them. . . . If Monsieur de Chavigny were doing his duty I should not have bothered you.'[4] Even if it did not always go well between Chavigny and Louis, his success with the king made the cardinal very dependent upon him. Consequently, gifts and offices were given to the secretary, enabling him to rise in power and to gain great prestige in only a few years.[5]

Chavigny was governor of the château of Vincennes, an important military installation and prison.[6] When the Abbé de Saint-Cyran was imprisoned there for his Jansenist views, the *châtelain* wrote to Chavigny that 'he is lodged in the lower chamber which you gave him. He requests that we install a wooden floor and that we put an iron plate in the fireplace. . . .'[7] The position of governor was inconsiderable,

[1] Chavigny to La Valette, 2 July 1637, BN, MS. 6648, fol. 122. This correspondence extends from MS. 6647 to MS. 6649; the simple code is: Chavigny = Ajax, 40, 41; Louis XIII = Nix, 12, 13; and Richelieu = Nestor, 18, 20, 29. On 10? July 1637 Chavigny wrote that Richelieu had intervened to put him on good terms with the king; MS. 6648, fol. 163.

[2] Chavigny to La Valette: 'Monseigneur le Cardinal a fait mon raccommodement avec le Roy, je suis aussi bien avec Sa Majesté que j'ay jamais esté. . . .' 10? July 1637, BN, MS. 6648, fol. 163.

[3] 22 Sept. 1635, AAE, France, 244, fol. 146.

[4] 27 Dec. 1637, ibid., fol. 280.

[5] De Vic, a French correspondent to the English government, recounted that Chavigny, who had just bought the mansion named Hôtel Saint-Paul, was aspiring to be duke and peer of France. 2 Aug. 1635, PRO, State Papers, series 78, vol. 98, fol. 163.

[6] The correspondence of Chavigny relative to the administration of Vincennes is largely in the AAE, France, 590.

[7] Moulinet to Chavigny, 10 July 1641, ibid., fol. 301.

but Chavigny was nevertheless consulted on matters of detail, and his permission had to be obtained before other royal officials could order troops to leave the château or before prisoners could be removed.[1]

Chavigny may also have wanted to take over the administration of the royal postal system. Several copies of a 'Proposition pour l'union de la charge de général des postes à celle de premier secrétaire d'Estat' exist in the various manuscript collections; but while the evidence would indicate that it remained only a 'proposition', Chavigny's desire to enhance his *charge* in the name of efficiency probably made him propose the union of the two offices.[2]

More honorary, but also more lucrative, was Chavigny's position in the king's orders. He frequently participated in the ceremonies of the *Ordre du Saint Esprit*, having been granted the *survivance* of his father's office of grand treasurer of the king's orders.[3]

As councillor, secretary of state, secretary of the king *ordinaire*, notary, governor of the château of Vincennes and of Antibes, Chavigny's revenues were considerable. His pensions were also very substantial.[4] Since gifts for political

---

[1] See the letter from Louis XIII to Chavigny, 12 Sept. 1641, countersigned by Sublet de Noyers, for the release of Saint-Aubin from the château of Vincennes, AAE, France, 286, fol. 92. Chavigny was also governor of the city and fortress of Antibes; Fauvelet-du-Toc, *Histoire de secrétaires d'Etat* (Paris, 1668), pp. 283 f.

[2] A copy in the hand of one of Chavigny's secretaries is in the AAE, France, 844, fol. 202; and at the BN, Collection Cangé, MS. 69, fol. 91, there is a fine eighteenth-century copy. There are essentially two ideas in the document: the union of the two *charges* of secretary of state (with the department of foreign affairs) and that of *Maistre des Courriers pour les affaires étrangères* would not increase expenses for the Crown and would facilitate the discovery of foreign plots. If the proposal were accepted the secrets of state would be handled only by the secretary of state for foreign affairs and the first clerk, while at the moment 'Cinq ou six personnes de basse condition' were in charge of the task. The proposition was probably made in 1635; see the letter of H. de Vic to Coke, 16/26 Jan. 1635, 'Nous apprenons de bon lieu qu'il [Chavigny] a quelque dessein de rembourser les trois officiers de Maistre des Courriers estrangers, et de les prendre en ses mains pour les faire dépendre de sa charge de Secrétaire d'Estat pour le dehors. . . .' PRO, State Papers, series 78, vol. 97, fol. 17.

[3] Louis Moreri, *Le Grand Dictionnaire historique* (Paris, 1699), i, p. 546.

[4] As councillor and secretary he was given a pension of 2,500 *livres tournois* in 1635, 'Gages, Estats, Apointements et Pensions', AAE, France, 819, fol. 167ᵛ.

favours were probably equal to if not a more important source of income than his royal revenues, it would be difficult to estimate his total income. Even so, with his great land purchases and the construction of a château at Chavigny, he was probably very much in debt.[1]

In some ways Chavigny's task of managing Gaston d'Orléans, the brother of Louis XIII, was even more delicate than his relationship with the king.[2] Richelieu's personal prestige with Louis was very great; when Chavigny failed to overcome hostilities in Louis, the cardinal himself, to the very end, could always come to terms with the king. But this was not true for Gaston. Neither Louis nor Richelieu had any faith in the promises of affection from this indecisive man, who was full of deceit and who, with good intentions or not, rocked the kingdom with endless revolts and plots. In a period when only the king's uncertain health kept Gaston from the throne (before 1638) and Richelieu from disgrace and perhaps death, it was frequently Chavigny's task to observe and control Gaston as best he could when the latter seemed to be plotting.

Chavigny cleverly gained the sincere affection of Gaston. At the same time he seems to have been, at least to some degree, truly sympathetic with Gaston. Perhaps Chavigny saw only too clearly the political consequences of the king's lack of an heir and of his ill health, and he wanted to be on the winning side. Chavigny and the Sieurs d'Elbène and, to some extent, de La Rivière gained Gaston's confidence, while at the same time they remained the agents of Richelieu. Chavigny was clearly the leader; and in the critical months of late 1634 and early 1635, before the open declaration of war with Spain, and under Richelieu's orders, he carefully

---

[1] This was due partly to his practice of borrowing in his own name for the king. See *Avis* from Augier, 10/20 Dec. 1635. '. . . Mr de Chavigni se voiant à la veille d'estre fait Duc et Pair tasche à se deffaire de sa charge de Chancelier de Monsieur, laquelle ne luy a rien cousté et dont il refuse pourtant 80 m. escus. Mond. S^r est en extreme necessité d'argent. Il doibt plus de 1800 m. livres et n'a pas un denier pour les payer, plusieurs croyent qu'on pretend se servir de sa necessité pour le faire ployer à ce qu'on desirera de luy. . . .' PRO, State Papers, series 78, vol. 99, fol. 250.

[2] For a thorough account of Gaston and an excellent introduction to his times, see Georges Dethan, *Gaston d'Orléans, conspirateur et Prince Charmant* (Paris, 1959).

purged Gaston of his favourites and also of his rebellious ideas. Indeed, Richelieu, while waiting for the diplomatic situation to ripen, may have hesitated to declare war until he was sure that Gaston was politically isolated.

Chavigny wrote to Richelieu long reports from Blois, the residence of Gaston, concerning the Prince's moods and views in general. But Richelieu, while having confidence in his creature, acted strongly and brutally to have the assurance that Gaston could do him no harm. On 17 October 1634 Chavigny wrote a rosy description of Gaston's relations with his favourite, Puylaurens, whose friendship Richelieu had tried to win by giving him a niece in marriage, while the king had given him a peerage. The letter makes it clear that Chavigny not only observed Gaston and his favourites, but that he also negotiated with him and tried to bring him to terms regarding nullification of the prince's previous marriage.[1] Four months later Puylaurens was arrested.

In August 1635 Chavigny became chancellor to Gaston, a position which he held throughout the period under study.[2] Several documents prove that Chavigny actively administered Gaston's demesne, especially on legal contentions between Gaston and the Crown.[3] But while Chavigny dealt sincerely with Gaston, his loyalty to Richelieu kept him a creature of the cardinal and out of the prince's plots. When Gaston unexpectedly made a move, or even came to Paris without a warning, Chavigny was immediately alerted to ascertain his purpose. On one such occasion Richelieu wrote to Chavigny:

The arrival of Monsieur is as unexpected as the reason for his journey seems trifling. Few people will believe that no other matter brought him to Paris; and I will confess that if I didn't know his

[1] Chavigny to Richelieu, AAE, France, 811, fol. 97. (Avenel gave fol. 259.) For the entire affair see Avenel, ed. cit. iv, p. 624. The general dispatch announcing the arrest of Puylaurens has survived in great numbers. A good example is Louis XIII to Césy, 15 Feb. 1635, BN, MS. 16157, fol. 199.

[2] See the genealogies of the *ancien régime*; and the interesting letter written by Claude le Bouthillier to Césy, 21? Aug. 1635, BN, MS. 16157, fol. 218.

[3] See the interesting document about the *rentes* on the gabelles for the College of Blois, AAE, France, 826, fol. 130; and the correspondence of Goulas, Gaston's secretary, to Chavigny (who was obliged to handle many details for Gaston), see a *mémoire* by Goulas to Chavigny in 1637, AAE, France, 828, fol. 226.

restless moods, I would have difficulty in being persuaded myself. Those who are near the object always see more clearly; this is why I refer to you for your judgment.[1]

Louis XIII was fully aware of Chavigny's special missions to see Gaston; he once wrote to Richelieu: 'I am so happy about the return of Monsieur de Chavigny so that I can learn in what disposition my brother is. . . . '[2]

In spite of all this, Gaston trusted Chavigny, who was his only real confidant in the inner circle of the king. The secretary's influence over Gaston enables one to see something of the character of the rebellious brother. Gaston depended on Chavigny to help him in his relations with Louis XIII. Monsieur wrote to Chavigny:

Monsieur de Chavigny, yesterday evening I saw Monseigneur, who told me that the king was at Saint-Germain and that Monsieur the Dauphin was sick. Tell me if I should go this evening to Saint-Germain or if I must simply send a note, or if I should ignore his illness. He also told me that Monseigneur the Cardinal is still a little ill, and that they thought that the ceremony for the Jesuits was postponed. Tell me about all of that, so that if there is something to change, I can change the disposition of my conduct.[3]

Richelieu had great confidence in Chavigny's ability to 'bring Monsieur to reason' during these frequent crises. This and Chavigny's precarious position in the king's cabinet, where he explained and gained approval for the cardinal's policies, constitute his only real political importance.[4]

Chavigny worked constantly with Sublet de Noyers,

[1] 13 Mar. 1635, Avenel, ed. cit. IV. cccliii.

[2] 28 Apr. 1636, AAE, France, 244, fol. 203. Richelieu, on one occasion, wrote to Gaston but requested that Chavigny decide if it was appropriate to give the letter to Gaston. See Richelieu to Chavigny, 27 Dec. 1636, Avenel, ed. cit. V. cdiv. Even so, Louis did not leave the control of his brother entirely to Richelieu and Chavigny. By a letter countersigned by Phélypeaux de La Vrillière, Louis ordered Chavigny to leave his brother immediately and return to the court, 31 Dec. 1636, AAE, France, 822, fol. 400.

[3] May 1641 ? (in different hand and ink), AAE, France, 286, fol. 87.

[4] Chavigny was also the link between the cardinal and the guardians of the imprisoned and disgraced Châteauneuf; see his correspondence with Amont. A good example of their relationship and the importance of Chavigny as the spokesman of the Crown is Amont to Chavigny, 4 Jan. 1635, AAE, France, 1475, fol. 327.

Secretary of State for War, but their correspondence rarely included items beyond governmental problems common to both. Aside from their almost daily communication of orders from the king or the cardinal, their letters have only one factor in common: devotion to Richelieu and Louis XIII. Occasionally they worked together to exert pressure on the king in order to strengthen his affection for Richelieu, especially in moments of crisis such as in 1642, when Louis's affection for Cinq-Mars threatened the cardinal and his creatures with disgrace.[1]

In addition to gaining Louis's assent to policies proposed by Richelieu, Sublet and Chavigny also presented friends' requests to the king. They worked together in an effort to induce Louis to send Turenne to Italy under the command of Cardinal de La Valette; and in the same context Chavigny wrote to La Valette: 'I also made an attempt for Monsieur de Thou, but it is certain that the king has conceived such a real aversion toward him that it is impossible to dissipate it; nevertheless, I will lose no occasion to try to give him the employment that you desire for him near you, Monseigneur.'[2]

Though they worked together, Chavigny and Sublet did not always remain on good terms. Chavigny became increasingly jealous of Sublet when the *petit bonhomme*, as Louis called him, continued to grow in favour and importance not only with Richelieu but also with the king. When Sublet was given the office of *concierge* of Fontainebleau immediately after having been made superintendent of buildings, Chavigny wrote to La Valette: 'I can assure you that he [Sublet de Noyers] is not in a bad way at Ruel.'[3] The influence of Richelieu, therefore, in procuring offices and favours for Sublet de Noyers was obvious—to the dismay

---

[1] When, in the autumn of 1642, Richelieu was very ill and near death at Narbonne, Chavigny and Sublet de Noyers worked constantly to maintain Louis's affection for Richelieu by coldly pointing out the faults of Cinq-Mars, his slights, ambitions, and fits of passion. To neglect the menace of Cinq-Mars to Richelieu and his creatures by saying that their position in the government was assured by Louis's *raison d'état* is to neglect the tone of the letters written in the period. The sense of urgency and desperation on the part of Richelieu, Chavigny, and Sublet would indicate the gravity of the whole affair.

[2] 4 June 1638, AAE, Sardaigne, 26, fol. 295.

[3] Rueil was the country house of Richelieu; 26 Oct. 1638, ibid., fol. 572.

of Chavigny. When Richelieu sent Chavigny on a diplomatic mission to Italy in 1639, the latter became childishly furious with Sublet over the ordonnance which Sublet had sent him providing money for the trip. Chavigny politely accused Sublet of trying to humiliate him, and in the end openly described his own position, as more humiliating, than that of Abel Servien, a secretary of state who had been disgraced by the creatures of Richelieu.[1]

Chavigny's relations with the other two secretaries, Brienne and La Vrillière, continue to be a mystery. The absence of their letters in his correspondence—except for occasional references to La Vrillière in the letters of Particelli, Seigneur d'Hémery, Intendant of Finance and father-in-law of La Vrillière—indicates that La Vrillière and Brienne probably did not share Chavigny's confidence. Chavigny did not enjoy La Vrillière's company when the latter was with Louis. Once he even implied that La Vrillière was responsible for making the king nervously ill.[2]

In relations with Bullion, the particularly powerful position which the superintendent of finance held in the council as well as his greater age among the creatures of Richelieu, frequently made him a formidable obstacle to both Chavigny and Sublet. Even the difficult task of gaining Bullion's approval and financial support for new troops was left to Chavigny. This was in every way a troublesome duty, considering Bullion's personality and stubborn nature.[3]

Chavigny attached great importance to his good relations with Bullion. When his friend, the Cardinal de La Valette, threatened to act in a way which certainly would have displeased the superintendent, Chavigny cautioned moderation and advised him to come to terms with Bullion.[4] Like many

[1] Chavigny to Sublet de Noyers, and Sublet de Noyers to Chavigny, both dated 21 Apr. 1639, AAE, Sardaigne, 28, fols. 230 and 232.
[2] Chavigny to Richelieu, Sept. 1635, 'Cette nouvelle [a letter from Vaubecourt] a changé la melancholie de Sa Majesté en laquelle Vrilliere l'avoit mise. . . .' AAE, France, 815, fol. 228.
[3] Chavigny to Richelieu, 6 May 1635: 'J'ay insinué les nouvelles levées pour Italie à Monsieur de Bullion en sorte que cela a heureusement reussi ainsy que vous le voiez. . . .' AAE, France, 814, fol. 20.
[4] Chavigny to La Valette, 13 Sept. 1638?: 'J'advous que je ne sçait que luy dire quand il [Bullion] me parle de cette sorte car vous cognoissiés bien son humeur mais cependant les affaires reussissent. Vous avez grande raison,

other correspondents of the ministers, La Valette was kept closely informed of his tenuous position at court. When officers, ambassadors, or provincials acted in a way that displeased the king, the cardinal, or even the other ministers, the secretaries informed the men in their friendly correspondence. The absence of such advice from the secretaries no doubt hastened or even caused the disgrace of officials under Louis XIII. Groups or parties, based on friendship or political and family alliances, provided the *cadre* for personal action. Individuals in the government were limited in action, not only by traditional but also by partisan and group pressures.

Chavigny also remained on good terms with Père Joseph, either because of sincere affection for this austere monk or because of the latter's great favour with Richelieu. The cardinal observed Père Joseph's affection for Chavigny, and mentioned it to his young creature.[1] Until his death in 1638, the influence of Père Joseph on French foreign policy, especially with regard to the Holy Roman Empire, is clearly observable through references and comments in his hand and also in his letters to ambassadors which have been preserved at the Archives des Affaires Etrangères. Chavigny and Père Joseph worked together under the supervision of the cardinal. Richelieu once wrote to Chavigny: 'I think that it would be good if you, Père Joseph, Messieurs Servien and Charnacé would meet today to confer together about the information you will have received from Germany, to see what is to be done.'[2]

When Mazarin began to rise in favour with Richelieu, Chavigny was quick to recognize it and to seek his friendship. As early as 1636 Chavigny wrote to him: 'I spoke to Monseigneur the Cardinal about the Abbey of Saint-Auold. His Eminence has agreed that you are to have it, and I have

Monseigneur, de ne pas vous vouloir brouiller avec luy. . . .' AAE, Sardaigne, 26, fol. 487.
   [1] Richelieu to Chavigny, 20 Apr. 1633: 'Je croy que le Père Joseph et vous estes inséparables, car il ne se parle point de luy en ce païs que quand vostre santé vous permet d'y faire sçavoir de vos nouvelles. Il est, à mon advis, comme Monsieur Mulot, qui prend souvent plaisir à estre avec des jeunes gens de vostre humeur et de vostre sagesse.' Avenel, ed. cit. IV. ccxxxvii.
   [2] 23 Apr. 1635, ibid. IV. ccclxxxiv.

taken it upon myself to write to Monsieur le Prince [Condé] to have his consent. As soon as I have a reply, I will inform you. . . .'[1] Chavigny's intercession to procure a benefice for Mazarin is proof that the secretary sought his friendship. By 1640 mutual trust and political friendship existed between the two men, to the point where Chavigny even discussed his personal relations with Richelieu in letters to Mazarin.[2] This confidence and friendship did not last long, however, for after Richelieu's death Mazarin and Chavigny soon began to quarrel.

There were essentially two aspects to Chavigny's administrative role. The first and most important was his supervision of all the royal correspondence between governments and their ambassadors; and the second aspect was his influence on the day-to-day diplomatic decisions which determined French foreign policy.

Under Louis XIII the secretary for foreign affairs directed the preparations for treaties, dispatches, and diplomatic instructions for departing ambassadors. These documents, long and formalized, required much time and care in preparation, because of the traditions determining whether they were to be on parchment or paper, or whether they were to be prepared for the great seal or to be *lettres de cachet*. Chavigny helped his clerks, especially Jean de La Barde, with the delicate wording of the treaties.[3] Often he and his clerks were limited to the secondary but important task of putting general points into the diplomatic language of the period, for the contents of the treaties were usually established *en conseil*.[4]

[1] Chavigny to Mazarin, 25 July 1636, AAE, France, 821, fol. 106.

[2] Chavigny to Mazarin, 6 Nov. 1640: 'Je suis mieux que jamais avec Monseigneur le Cardinal. Je ne me souviens point qu'il m'ait parlé avec plus de confiance et de tendresse qu'il fait. . . .' AAE, Sardaigne, 31, fol. 328. See also fol. 592 of the same manuscript.

[3] Jean de La Barde was Chavigny's cousin. See C. Piccioni, *Les Premiers Commis des Affaires Etrangères aux XVIIᵉ et XVIIIᵉ siècles* (Paris, 1928); de La Barde's own *Matrolarum ad Sequanam marchionis de Rebus Gallicis historiarum libri decem, ab anno 1643 ad annum 1652* (Paris, 1671); and E. Griselle, *Les Tribulations d'un ambassadeur en Suisse, Jean de La Barde* (Paris, 1920).

[4] The rough drafts for treaties, dispatches, and instructions in the hands of Chavigny and La Barde survive in large numbers at the AAE in all of the foreign series. Richelieu frequently reviewed the labours of the secretary and his clerks, and it might have been after doing so that he good-naturedly

Chavigny, again with the aid of his clerks, prepared hundreds of dispatches—both special ones and the *ordinaires* sent to all of the countries with which the king had diplomatic relations. These dispatches were royal letters signed by the king, countersigned by the secretaries, and sealed with the simple red seals bearing the lilies of France and called *cachets*. There were two principal reasons for the dispatches. First, French ambassadors in foreign capitals received their instructions through royal letters prepared by Chavigny; and second, these dispatches informed ambassadors of the general diplomatic and political scene as viewed by the government. Sometimes Chavigny or his clerks, either through haste or carelessness, neglected the second aspect. Richelieu wrote to his brother, the Cardinal de Lyon:

You well know that the crushing weight of affairs does not permit me to do in every way the tasks of the secretaries of state, who should inform those who are in foreign countries of everything which happens. I charge them to do as much . . . if they do not do it, I become more angry than I should know how to describe to you. I am always quite sure of their fidelity, but not of their diligence.[1]

The practice of sending by all diplomatic posts weekly letters describing the political and diplomatic events was well established under Louis XIII. These letters were called *ordinaires*, because they were prepared and sent on a regular schedule. Fortunately, a copy of the schedule has survived, although it dates from the minority of Louis XIV, when the Comte de Brienne had the department of foreign affairs.[2] Chavigny wrote to Estrades, ambassador to Holland, that his letter had arrived just as the *ordinaire* to him was to leave. As a result the answer to the newly arrived letter would have to be postponed until he, Chavigny, had seen Richelieu.[3]

wrote: 'Je vous envoye les articles du traitté d'Angleterre que j'ay leus et veus; je ne sçay si celuy qui les a mis en françois est bon latin, mais je sçay bien qu'il est mauvais François.' Richelieu to Chavigny, 24 Apr. 1639, Avenel, ed. cit. v. cdxxxv.

[1] Jan. 1636, ibid. v. clxxxv.

[2] BN, MS. 18243, fols. 130 ff., beginning with a very valuable formulary for the secretaries giving the names of their correspondents at the end of the reign of Louis XIII.

[3] 17 Mar. 1640, BN, Collection Clairambault, 572, fol. 341.

Frequently a personal letter from one or more of the secretaries was included with the more official dispatch. These letters were in many ways as important as the official messages, for—depending on the confidence which a secretary had in a particular correspondent—elaboration of royal policy or further explanation of diplomatic objectives were included.

The great mass of letters which Chavigny himself received has been partly preserved with the papers of Richelieu in the *Mémoires et documents, France*, at the Archives des Affaires Etrangères. Provincial problems, famines, religious affairs, office appointments, pensions, diplomacy, finances, fortress construction, army and navy problems were discussed. There are numerous letters of request, usually for offices,[1] indicating that Chavigny's influence over the king and the cardinal in this domain was eagerly sought. Administrative requests were also frequent; Chavigny wrote to La Valette: 'I spoke to Monseigneur the Cardinal about the money which they promised you for the army and garrison in Italy. . . .'[2] Even when their affairs were out of his department, Chavigny did not hesitate to speak for his friends.[3]

In turning to the second function of Chavigny as secretary of state for foreign affairs, one must remember that his part in the preparation of the correspondence which he put in final form was limited. The formation of French diplomacy under Louis XIII was the work of several ministers; the predominance of Richelieu is only part of the story. Bullion, Bouthillier, Sublet de Noyers, Père Joseph, and later Mazarin, were all influential. Normally the *Conseil d'en haut* was the forum for major decisions; no documents enabling one to

[1] Even Marie de Médicis sought Chavigny's help. In one instance it was about a commission for her almoner. Marie de Médicis to Chavigny, 13 Mar. 1641, AAE, Angleterre, 48, fol. 285.

[2] 7 Jan. 1639, AAE, Sardaigne, 28, fol. 10.

[3] The many volumes of Chavigny's correspondence, letters often written in his own hand, are scattered; but the bulk of them are preserved at the Archives des Affaires Etrangères and the Bibliothèque Nationale. In the former the correspondence is arranged by diplomatic post—England, Spain, and so forth—and minutes of the letters written by Chavigny and his clerks are combined with dispatches from ambassadors in foreign countries. While the correspondence is thus divided into internal and foreign affairs, the letters themselves follow no such pattern. Chavigny often discussed internal affairs with his ambassadorial friends in foreign countries.

measure the importance of Chavigny in this most powerful council have survived.

The document entitled 'Observations du Père Joseph sur le traicté proposé par la France et l'Angleterre' is significant, especially with this most important comment in the hand of Sublet de Noyers:

> Père Joseph is of the opinion that, in view of the conditions listed above, we can negotiate with England in no other way, Ruel, vii February, 1635—the entire Council is in agreement, and after a new reading of the treaty it was necessary to make an agreement with the English at once about the positions which the king may attack along the coast of Flanders.[1]

Foreign-policy decisions were made by several ministers *en conseil*. Richelieu, Père Joseph, and Sublet were all clearly informed of these negotiations, and the phrase, 'the entire Council is in agreement' indicates that other ministers were also consulted. Surely Chavigny influenced French foreign policy also; Sublet wrote to him: 'You will see by His Eminence's letter, as well as by the one which the king is addressing to you, that they have entirely followed your views on the resolution of Italian affairs. . . .'[2] This note is dramatic evidence of Chavigny's important role as a royal councillor in foreign affairs.

Though he was head of the department of foreign affairs, Chavigny enjoyed no greater powers or prestige in the council when diplomatic questions were discussed. He spoke, however, in the royal councils, probably not because he was secretary, but because he held a brevet as councillor. Once, when he and not Richelieu was with the king *en conseil*, the secretary wrote: 'I proposed this morning in the council . . .'[3] as he described the day's political events at court to Richelieu. Specialization in foreign and military affairs did not circumscribe the ministers; major decisions were made by the king and the ministers as a whole.

Likewise, Chavigny did not exclusively see foreign ambassadors in the name of the Crown. For England, it was

---

[1] AAE, Angleterre, 47, fol. 45.
[2] 11 Nov. 1640, AAE, France, 836, fol. 155.
[3] 23 Sept. 1636, AAE, France, 821, fol. 315. Louis was in Picardy supervising preparations for the recapture of Corbie.

normally Bullion who received them. But the English ambassadors, and they were not extraordinary, made a habit of
calling on all the ministers.[1] Chavigny, however, usually
served as the chief negotiator with foreign ambassadors in
Paris. Occasionally these visits became *causes célèbres*, such as
the tempestuous interview between Chavigny and the papal
nuncio Scotti in 1639, which was a significant event indicating the persistence of the Gallican–ultramontanist
controversy in the reign of Louis XIII.[2]

Chavigny had few exclusive privileges in diplomatic
affairs. The only right which he truly possessed was that of
preparing and countersigning all royal correspondence with
other nations. Consequently it became his duty to control
information arriving from foreign countries and in turn to
present it accurately in its diplomatic background to Louis,
Richelieu, and the other ministers. Chavigny frequently read
or summarized newly arrived dispatches to Louis or Richelieu.[3] It was a time when it was still customary to read dispatches aloud before sovereigns and others of high station.
This is reflected in the letters of the period by the long and
sonorous phrases of politeness and the dramatic tone.

The letters of Richelieu to Chavigny are a long series of
requests for royal letters. Frequently the cardinal took the
trouble to give in detail the content if not the form of the
letter. Richelieu did not seem to trust anyone administratively. He was constantly reminding the other ministers of
minor details. For example, he wrote to Chavigny:

You must not send Monsieur de Senneterre a copy of the treaty,
of which certain articles will be displeasing to England. He may
be permitted to say that, in order to have peace, the king has

---

[1] Leicester to Coke, 3/13 June 1636: 'My visites to the other ministers
I will dispatch with as much diligence as I can that (?) I may be readie to
demand another audience, for I conceive that this King will assigne some of
his ministers to treate with me and it is not hard to ghesse who they will
be. . . .' PRO, State Papers, series 78, vol. 101, fol. 111.

[2] See the 'Relation sur l'entrevue de Monsieur de Chavigny avec Monsieur
le Nonce Scotti', *Mémoires d'Omer Talon*, ed. by Michaud et Poujoulat, séries
3, vi, p. 71.

[3] Chavigny to La Valette, 29 Sept. 1637: 'J'ai rendu conte au Roy et à
Monseigneur le Cardinal de tout ce que vous m'aviez commandé. . . .' BN,
MS. 6649, fol. 121.

resolved to break with Spain, but he must not talk at all about the projected partition. . . .[1]

Richelieu, however, respected Chavigny's views and kept him informed of the entire diplomatic scene when the latter was away from court. Chavigny did likewise when the cardinal was absent. Richelieu once wrote to him: 'I have seen the papers which you had sent me concerning England; I do not see how one can hope for a conclusion. However, I find the reply to be good, because it does not commit the king and continues negotiations with persons with whom it is always necessary to negotiate.'[2]

Richelieu supervised the writing of dispatches, and once informed Chavigny that one which he had prepared would have to be rewritten before it could be sent.[3] The haste with which Richelieu changed foreign policy to conform with new factors might well explain the need for such a request. Also, the custom of writing dispatches after sketchy *mémoires* prepared by the cardinal may well have caused divergences between Richelieu's thoughts and Chavigny's dispatches. With the approval of Louis, Richelieu often made direct orders which Chavigny converted into royal letters to be signed either by the king or by a clerk who imitated the king's signature. Neither Louis nor Richelieu felt that Chavigny must be consulted when they prepared dispatches. Chavigny wrote to Charnacé, ambassador to Holland: 'This dispatch was composed during a little trip which I made to Fontainebleau. I found the *mémoires* all prepared for it when I returned.'[4] On the other hand, the king and the cardinal were dependent on the secretary for specific

---

[1] Apr. 1635, Avenel, ed. cit. viii, p. 280. A typical example of the precision and detail of the letters of Richelieu to Chavigny. A more dramatic and better-known example concerns the Latin terms to be used in the alliance with Sweden against the German emperor in the negotiations conducted by Chavigny with Oxenstierna in Apr. 1635, Avenel, ed. cit. iv. cccxcviii.

[2] 4 Sept. 1636, ibid. v, p. 989.

[3] 8 May 1637, ibid. v, p. 1028. On one occasion involving the conspiracies of Marie de Médicis, Richelieu, after describing in a *mémoire* what he wished to be written in a royal letter, added some points for Chavigny to write in a personal letter to the correspondent: 'Monsieur de Chavigni dira, comme de luy-mesme, . . . que la reyne ne doit pas s'enivrer en cela d'une fausse générosité. . . .' 23 Mar. 1641, ibid. vi. ccclxxxiii.

[4] June 1636, AAE, Hollande, 19, fol. 41.

information and documents; Richelieu wrote to Chavigny:
'I need the first three treaties that the king made with
Monsieur [the Duke] de Lorraine; that is why I pray you to
have them looked up and sent to me promptly.'[1]

But if Chavigny was not more important than the other
ministers and far less important than the principal minister
in determining foreign policy, his personal influence with
the king and the cardinal gave him stature *vis-à-vis* the ambassadors, both French and foreign. He exercised powers
difficult to measure. Even if his letters were not instructions from the king, the ambassadors took careful note of
them. Chavigny wrote to Cœuvres (Maréchal d'Estrées),
ambassador to Rome, that his dispatches had not yet been
shown to the king or the cardinal. Then Chavigny gave his
sentiments (political opinions) on the questions discussed in
Cœuvres's dispatch. Only in a succeeding letter did Chavigny
send an official reply in the form of a royal letter.[2] Thus
ambassadors, eager to please the ministers in Paris, accepted
advice from Chavigny, who also wrote to Cœuvres that he
should modify his dispatches. The secretary gave careful
instructions so that the ambassador might better please Père
Joseph.[3] Needless to say, he did not perform this valuable
service for ambassadors who were not in his favour.

Through the royal letter, the most important diplomatic
medium of communication, the legal fiction that the king
was responsible for all decisions again makes it impossible
to think in terms of ministerial responsibility. In this greatest of sources for diplomatic history, the roles of the king,
Richelieu, Chavigny, and all the other ministers become in-
distinguishable and unified.

To his duties in the department of foreign affairs and in
supervising correspondence for certain provinces, Chavigny
added the department of the royal household, to the detriment of La Ville-aux-Clercs.[4] Perhaps the latter kept some
of the duties, probably the right to prepare dispatches for
the king's guards, but Chavigny took over the entire task of

[1] 19 Dec. 1635, Avenel, ed. cit. v, p. 958.
[2] Feb. 1638, BN, MS. 4071, fols. 169 and 172.
[3] 9 Oct. 1638, ibid., fol. 317.
[4] See above, p. 70.

supervising royal pensions. The numerous pension lists in both his and Richelieu's correspondence enable one to measure the political importance and immensity of the task.[1] Chavigny and Richelieu were the only ministers to conduct and establish pensions for Rome.[2]

When Louis XIII accorded a pension and Chavigny was not present, the other secretaries of state were obliged to inform him of the decision rather than prepare the documents themselves.[3] Occasionally legal difficulties arose over pensions, and Chavigny was obliged to consult Chancellor Séguier about the legality of a pension that the king wished to grant.[4]

The administration of the navy under Louis XIII has never been clearly described.[5] In the divisions of the secretaries by provinces made while Servien was still secretary, between 1630 and 1636, the royal fleets were still under two secretaries: Bouthillier for the Atlantic, and Servien for the Mediterranean.[6] In the pension list for 1637, however, Chavigny was listed as 'councillor of the king in his councils and secretary of the commandments of His Majesty, having the department of the navy for his pension'.[7] The pension granted was on the list of navy pensions, hence there is the question of an administrative reality or simply a favour from Richelieu. As grand admiral, the cardinal might have been authorized to give a pension from the navy without consulting the king.

In 1640, in the minutes surviving from the letters prepared by Sublet de Noyers, there are brevets for naval officers, commissions to cut wood for ship construction, and

[1] For example, 'Gages, Estats, Apointements et Pensions que le Roy veut estre payez par le trésorier de l'Espargne. . . .' 1635, AAE, France, 819, beginning on fol. 154. For 1638, see AAE, France, 832, fol. 148.

[2] Richelieu to Estrées, Avenel, ed. cit. v, cdxxxviii, 9 May 1637.

[3] Sublet to Chavigny, 30 Apr. 1638, AAE, France, 830, fol. 127, is a typical example of a pension notice sent to Chavigny.

[4] Chavigny to Séguier, 4 Nov. 1636, BN, nouvelles aquisitions, MS. 6210, fol. 20. A thorough study of the patronage and pension practices under Louis XIII would be valuable, for only in that way could its political importance be measured.

[5] Ellul thinks there were already navy and colonial departments; J. Ellul, *Histoire des institutions* (Paris, 1956), vol. i.

[6] See above, p. 72.

[7] 'Estats des Pensions', 1637, AAE, France, 829, fol. 246ᵛ.

even letters patent granting Loménie de Brienne fishing rights on the high seas.[1] Indeed, letters pertaining to naval affairs left traces throughout the correspondence of the war secretary right up to the death of Richelieu. This would seem to indicate that no modification in favour of a navy department was made under Louis XIII.

There was still much to be done before the departments would appear in the personal reign of Louis XIV.[2] For foreign affairs, however, the boundaries of action were already fixed in the reign of Louis XIII. The king's correspondence with foreign powers was in the hands of one secretary who, at the head of a small but effective bureau, not only listened but also spoke in the *Conseil du roi*.

In carrying out his duties, Chavigny, like all the creatures save Bullion, appears two-sided and unpleasantly slippery. His servility to Louis and Richelieu is a shocking contrast to the haughty disdain obvious in his letters to lower officials. His dependence upon Richelieu was so great that with the death of the cardinal Chavigny's star began to fall. Counting on his influence over Gaston in the turmoil of the regency of Louis XIV, Chavigny was stripped of his powers and disgraced, dying in 1652 at the age of forty-four, just when it looked as though favour were returning.

[1] AG, A¹, 62, *passim*.
[2] An indication of the frontier between the jurisdictions of the admiralty and of the secretaries of state is given in a letter from Bullion to Chavigny, 20 Jan. 1635, France, 813, fol. 41.

V

François Sublet de Noyers, Secretary of State for War

IN 1635 Abel Servien, *homme de robe* from the Dauphiné, was secretary of state for war. Appointed with the cardinal's help in 1630, Servien supervised the great efforts made to prepare the French armies for open war. In spite of the military disasters which plagued France in 1635, Servien kept at his post, working constantly and closely with Louis XIII and Richelieu. However, in the winter of 1635–6, when the military and economic situation was at the breaking-point, Richelieu was obliged to dismiss Servien because of jealousies and administrative quarrels among the creatures.[1]

This left the position open for François Sublet, Seigneur de Noyers, and Baron de Dangu.[2] He was a little man, an indefatigable worker of forty-eight when he became secretary on 17 February 1636.[3] In the seven brief years next preceding the death of Richelieu, Sublet supervised the preparation of some 18,000 letters and dispatches which have

[1] The 'affaire Servien' has already been described by several historians who emphasized the jealousy of Chavigny, who supposedly influenced Richelieu to dismiss Servien. The quarrel between Bullion and Servien over military expenditures has been overlooked.

[2] Dangu is situated near Gisors in the department of Eure. According to Louis Moreri, *Grand Dictionnaire historique* (Paris, 1699), 'Sublet', the barony was given to Sublet by Louis XIII when he became secretary. *Mémoires de l'establissement des Secrétaires d'Estat* state in addition that the king first purchased Dangu from Madame de Luxembourg for 300,000 *livres*. BN, Cinq Cents Colbert, MS. 136, fol. 509ᵛ.

[3] See the 'Don de la charge de secrétaire d'Etat' for Sublet de Noyers. BN, MS. 18243, fol. 116 (copy); BN, Collection Cangé, MS. 68, fol. 138 (copy). 'Nous [the king] avons donné et octroyé, donnons et octroyons par cᵉs patentes signées de notre main la charge et office de notre Conseiller en nos conseils et Secrétaire de nos commandements et finances . . . et en vertu de iceluy, signer et expedier toutes les depesches dependantes de ladite charge et en jouir et user aux honneurs, autorized, prerogatives, pre-eminences, franchises et libertez, gages, pensions, et appointements. . . .' The *provisions* of the secretaries were very formalized and did not reflect the changes in the office.

MESS.^{re} FRANCOIS SVBLET Che. Baron de Dangu Seig.^r de Noyers, la Boi
ſſiere et aues lieux,Con.^{er} du Roy en ſes co ſeils dEſtat et priue Secret.^{re} de ſes comandeñ:
Surintend.^t des baſtim.^{ts} et manufactures de France Cap.^{ne} et concierge de Fontainebelleau, fils de Maitre Iean. Sublet Con.^{er} du Roy et M.^e ord.^{re} en ſa châbre des comptes à Paris. Apres auoir eſté employé
pluſieurs anneés aux affaires plus importātes de lEſtat et sen eſtre aquité auec ſoing probité et
ſuſiſance, tant en ſa charge dIntédant des finances que ſurintendāt des fortificaōns de Frā-
cé fut honoré de célle des ſecr.^{re} dEſtat lan 1636, quil exerça durant 7 anneés, et parmy les aff
aÿres de la guerre dont il auoit ladminiſtraōn fit regner les arts de la paix en France, par les
beaux ouurages de Peinture,Graueure,Architecture,et dImprimerie quil y entretenoit: se retir.
a de la Cour en 1643 fuyant les attaintes de lEnuie, mourut en 1645, et fut enterré dans lEsoliſe du
Noniciat des Ieſuites du faubourg St Germain quil auoit fait baſtir.

A Paris chez Daret auecpriuil. du Roy 1652.

survived as minutes in the Archives de la Guerre. From these and other letters one may reconstruct his bustling administration. He wrote once to an army commander:

Perhaps you will be astonished to see in one single day so many messengers, almost all bearers of changing orders. But the good pilot changes his sails as many times as the wind changes, without being blamed for fickleness. Likewise, those who serve the king ... must seek new advice as many times as the enemy movements force them to.[1]

In addition to an ambitious vigilance over the king's affairs, Sublet was deeply religious. His piety, combined with his administrative energy, gave his character crusader proportions. He wrote to Chavigny: 'You will never find changes in me, because, as I have told you before, it is easy for a man who has neither ambition nor avarice to stick to his duties. Now, God has done me the favour of keeping me on those terms up to the present . . . .'[2]

Unlike Chavigny, Sublet played an administrative role far more important than his duties as a political favourite. He was well prepared for the duties of secretary of state for war. As intendant of finance, Sublet had become familiar with and had participated in the *Conseil du roi*. He was already working on army affairs, as is shown by an *arrêt* to purchase 6,000 pairs of shoes for the armies in Germany, signed by Sublet, the keeper of the seals and the superintendents *en conseil* in 1635.[3] As intendant of the army, he

[1] 3 June 1639, BN, MS. 3762, fol. 30; Aubery, *Mémoires pour l'histoire du Cardinal Duc de Richelieu* (Cologne, 1667), iv, p. 105.

[2] 29 July 1639, AAE, France, 833, fol. 250. It was customary in the seventeenth century to give a religious tone to letters. This was done in all sincerity by Sublet de Noyers, upon whose religious zeal Richelieu even commented. The cardinal wrote to Claude le Bouthillier: 'Ce billet est pour prier Monsieur le Surintendant d'avoir foy en certains saincts qui sont de longtemps en son memento, c'est-à-dire de croire en ce que luy mande Monsieur de Noyers (qui se béatifie tous les jours) sur le sujet des vaisseaux et des galères du Levant.' 9 Sept. 1641, Richelieu, *Lettres, instructions diplomatiques et papiers d'Etat*, ed. M. Avenel (Paris, 1853–77), VI. ccccxxxiv. This letter caused Avenel to comment on the extraordinary religious tone of Sublet's letters. It was also strongly suspected that he was secretly a Jesuit; see *Mémoires du Cardinal de Retz* (Paris, 1870), i, pp. 206 f.; and also the interesting character sketch by E. Sue, editor of the *Correspondance de Henri d'Escoubleau de Sourdis, Archevêque de Bordeaux*, Collection des Documents Inédits (Paris, 1839), i. xlv.

[3] 'Fait au conseil d'Etat du Roy tenu pour les finances, à Paris, le premier jour de janvier, 1635', AN, K114ᴬ, dossier 1, fol. 3.

carefully observed military installations and inspected troops, munitions, and food supplies in Picardy and Champagne in 1634–5. At the same time he worked as a councillor on military problems.

Traditionally, like the three other secretaries, Sublet was responsible for receiving all the royal correspondence from certain provinces, and in turn preparing and sending the replies of the king.[1] Like Chavigny, Sublet prepared letters relating to all aspects of the royal government. A random selection concerning religious affairs includes authority for the Archbishop of Paris to name a preacher in Notre Dame for Lent, permission for nuns to wall up or close a street in order to enlarge a convent, the gift of a Protestant church to some monks, the gift of the right of *franc salé* to a convent; statutes for the formation of a school for girls, a brevet granting 'fruits and revenues' of a bishopric to an individual, and a commission to re-establish a religious order in an abbey.[2]

In army affairs, however, the variety is even more interesting. Military affairs were interpreted broadly. Sublet probably contributed to this aspect of his *charge*, and in so doing increased his powers. In the volume mentioned above, one finds commissions to estimate funds necessary for new fortifications at Grenoble, for a captaincy of a regiment of light horse, for the command of a château, for an intendant; brevets for pensions, for a captaincy in the cavalry; orders for Swiss guard payments, for a retired officer to keep his rank, for a Jesuit to direct military hospitals in Flanders and Burgundy, for the exchange of Spanish and French prisoners; and so the list goes on. A long tradition determined the nature of the document, commission, letter, brevet, order, proclamation, and so forth, for each governmental action.

In addition to religious and military letters, Sublet prepared letters which fit neither category: revocations of a

[1] Sublet's provinces were probably the same as those of Servien: the Lyonnais, Dauphiné, Provence, Poitou, Angoumois, Limousin; see above, p. 72.
[2] This random sample was taken from AG, A¹, 62. The letter to the Archbishop of Paris is a further example of the action of the secretary of state *en mois*. It was generally the right of Loménie to send letters for the Île de France, which included Paris.

survivance of a finance officer, a passport to import Flemish tapestries, an *arrêt* to cut down green wood near Périgueux to sell for the king's benefit, the transfer of the sovereign court and bureau of finance of Provence because of an epidemic, an order to send all vagabonds to the galleys, and a brevet for the establishment of a college and royal academy in the city of Richelieu.[1]

Subject though he was to the constant pressure of affairs of this nature, Sublet also prepared the royal letters directing the armies and strategy in the field. He generally added a personal letter to each major officer, giving him special orders, encouragement, court gossip, and, in some cases, even sympathy. The heavy weight of correspondence sometimes caused him to be late with his replies, but more often made him terse and formal. While he kept the king and the cardinal informed on military movements, &c., from the dispatches that he received, he assured officers and provincial administrators that the contents of their letters were being communicated to the king.[2]

In the actual organization of the armies Sublet's duties were varied and many. With the coming of open war in 1635, the department expanded, and new clerks were added to handle the extra business of war. Even before Sublet, Servien wrote to Bullion:

I am forced to bother you with something which I forgot to talk to you about before leaving Paris, that is, that the duties of my *charge* having increased by the addition of large numbers of soldiers . . . I have been obliged to take several people to work with me, and since the appointments of the first clerks have been [*illegible*] and the other revenues reduced, I assure you, Sir, [*illegible*] is not sufficient for their upkeep. . . .[3]

The need for money was obvious, providing evidence indicating the expansion of the department of war in the last years of the reign.

[1] All of these examples have been chosen from AG, A¹, 62.

[2] Sublet wrote to Saint-Germain Beaupré, 3 July 1636: '. . . Je me promets que vous excuserés une personne chargée des depesches de cinq ou six armées d'où il arrive tous les jours divers courriers, et que vous vous contenterés d'estre asseuré que je ne manque point de faire sçavoir à Sa Majesté les soins que vous prenez de l'execution des ordres qu'elle vous envoye. . . .' AG, A¹, 28, fol. 200 *bis*.

[3] Minute, n.d. but probably May 1635, AG, A¹, 24, fol. 285.

The secretary of state for war, along with his clerks, established the *contrôles*, or muster rolls, of the army. It was the duty of the army officers, working with the *commissaires*, to inform the secretary of the size of the army under their command by regiment. When officers failed to send their *contrôles* at the proper time, Sublet sent them polite but firm letters of reminder.[1] On the basis of these *contrôles*, the secretary calculated the provisions of food and munitions needed with the munitioners, as well as the amount of money to be paid to the officers, who in turn paid the troops.[2]

From these separate muster lists elaborate *états* were made to establish the strength of the entire French army. Several of these have survived; the most interesting examples have corrections or additions made by Sublet and Richelieu.[3] Once the general muster lists were completed, the secretary presented them to the king and the cardinal, either *en conseil* or more informally. Sublet wrote to Chavigny, who was with the king:

I am sending you a muster list of the armies to be given to the king, as he commanded me through you. I request that you show His Majesty the ordonnance that he ordered me [to prepare] at the last council concerning the re-formation of the militia men, so that he will be able to approve it before anyone else sees it, if he wishes. Also [show him] the letter that I am writing in His Majesty's name to our whole cavalry, and another ordonnance to require officers to return to the armies, I mean to their troops, since their absence is causing disorders of which all France is complaining. When I show the *état* of the troops to His Majesty at Versailles, I will tell him that the commissioner who has returned

---

[1] See the correspondence of Sublet and the Maréchal de Chastillon, published in Aubery, ed. cit., *passim*.

[2] Chastillon wrote to Sublet, 17 Sept. 1640: 'Ce courrier vous porte les extraits de la reveuë generalle que j'ay fait faire à toutes les troupes que nous avons icy; dont, en attendant le detail, je vous ay mandé la force en gros par ma derniere. Ce sera, s'il vous plaist, sur ce pied-là que Monsieur de Bullion aura ordre de faire le fonds pour la seconde montre [muster payment].' Ibid. iv, p. 715; AAE, France, 1679, fol. 263.

[3] See AAE, France, 828, fol. 288ᵛ, for a change by Sublet and the more complete 'controlle général des troupes tant d'infanterie que de cavallerie et des lieux de leur garnison', for 1637, in the same volume, beginning on fol. 293. For Richelieu, see the numerous examples published by Avenel, of which the abridged version of the *controolle général* of May, 1635, is typical, ed. cit. v, pp. 3 ff.

from Aumale and Abbeville complained greatly of the weakness and bad conduct of the companies. . . .[1]

In addition to supervising the musters of existing armies, the secretary also made detailed plans for raising future armies. Under Louis XIII this task included the choice of officers who were to hire and form regiments, estimates of costs and maintenance, and finally the choice of areas where the new regiments could be most advantageously formed. Before beginning open war in 1635, Richelieu requested Servien to prepare plans for raising a new army of 25,000 men.[2]

Like the other functions of government, military planning was an inter-ministerial effort. The secretary saw the superintendents, treasurers, munitioners, intendants, and other officers daily.[3] The superintendents of finance, who reviewed the muster lists, eagerly sought ways to cut army expenditures. The secretary was consequently placed in a middle position administratively between the army officers, who were constantly demanding more money, and the finance ministers, who sought ways to avoid payment. The power of the secretary to settle disputes himself or by appealing to the king or cardinal made him an important figure in financial affairs. He influenced both parties—neither of which trusted the other, and rightly so. Sublet was for ever struggling with Bullion to extract promises of payment for armies in the field. He wrote to Chavigny:

I am going to Paris to struggle with *Messieurs des Finances* and to win by the authority of my master [either Louis or Richelieu]

[1] 15 Mar. 1637, AAE, France, 826, fol. 213.
[2] Servien to Richelieu, 10 Jan. 1635: 'Je vous envoye un project des armées en la forme que vous me l'avez commandé pourveu qu'il vous plaise vous contenter de vingt-cinq mil hommes. . . .' AAE, France, 813, fol. 15. See also, 'Estat du Fonds auquel il fault pourveoir pour les nouvelles levées tant pour leur levée et armement que pour leur subsistance dans les Routes jusque l'armée, par Estimation.' At the end, 'le présent Estat est de trois cens vingt compagnies et montre quatre cens cinquante mil livres mais il faut remarquer qu'il n'est fait que par Estimation'. AAE, France, 816, fol. 159.
[3] This normally took place *en conseil*. In one of the notes summarizing letters to be prepared by Servien, one finds: 'Lettres à Monsieur de Roze [a munitioner and food supplier] de servir et fournir les vivres à l'armée du Roy commandée par Monsieur le Mareschal de La Force suivant resolution prise au Conseil par Messeigneurs les Garde des Sceaux, Bullion, Servien et de La Vrillière aujourd'huy. . . .' n.d. (July 1635?), AG, A[1], 25, fol. 62.

that which reason obtains with great difficulty, not because of their will [the superintendents'], which is always ready to do what service requires, but of their necessity, which often stops their zeal and ours also. . . .[1]

As Sublet wisely commented, the intransigence of the superintendents was not due to their personal whim, but often to the sheer lack of funds.

When ministers clashed over paying the troops, the detailed projects and estimates were quickly modified. Working with the superintendents, the secretary juggled payment schedules, much to the anger of the officers. Yet ministers kept in mind that it was their duty to maintain as many troops equipped and in the field as possible.[2] Despite such difficulties, they continued to make estimates and to attempt to follow them. Army budgets included the number and type of troops and officers. The ministers also determined *en conseil* what funds were destined for the different armies, a particularly important task, since royal revenues differed in real value according to the nature of the source.[3]

From the army officers Sublet received long and angry letters, describing their armies in revolt or deserting for want of pay and bread. Many times this was no exaggeration, and Sublet and the other ministers knew it. The correspondence of Chaulnes and Chastillon, both marshals and joint-commanders of an army, is published in great part by Aubery and is descriptive of officer-secretary relations. No more striking evidence exists to indicate the greater powers of the secretary of state for war than his obvious responsibility for money payments by army commanders.[4]

Besides working with the superintendents, Sublet also

---

[1] 11 Nov. 1640, AAE, France, 836, fol. 155.
[2] See Sublet to Guébriant, 6 Aug. 1642, BN, Collection Cinq Cents Colbert, MS. 108, fol. 112.
[3] See the *contrôles* in the AAE, France, 820.
[4] For example, Chastillon wrote to Sublet: 'Outre la grande Lettre que nous vous avons escrite en commun, je me suis chargé de quelques articles, que nous avons obmis. Le premier est, pour respondre à la négative absoluë que vous faites, de fournir aucun pain à la Cavalerie: neantmoins nous osons vous representer que la necessité est telle de luy en departir pour quelques jours, qu'autrement il est impossible qu'elle subsiste. . . .' 22 June 1640, Aubery, ed. cit. iv, pp. 565 f.

worked with the war treasurers on financial problems. On one occasion he wrote to them:

Messieurs de l'extraordinaire de la guerre will inform me, if it pleases them, for what reason the funds for Cazal are not yet sent according to the *état* that I signed. Monsieur de Bullion has informed me that the funds designated by the *état* are ready; I beseech them, considering the importance of the place, to send all that is destined there immediately.[1]

Sublet exhorted haste in every direction; and characteristically, even after the approval of the superintendents, he followed his directions through to the lower echelons to see that they were carried out. In this way the secretary for war increased his influence in the administration of finances as well as in the administration of the army itself. The old independent branches of artillery and infantry were not unified, but as the secretary took over duties of former independent administrators, greater unification occurred. A good example was the artillery treasurers who, by the middle of the century and while they still continued to exist, saw their duties assumed by the secretary.[2]

The administration of the *taillon*—a special tax originally established, like the *taille*, to meet military expenses—is an even more concrete example of how new administrative jurisdictions developed little by little, and in some cases quite by chance. After 1614 the secretary of state for war had the privilege of verifying certain tax rolls and preparing royal letters for disbursements.[3] Under Servien, who complained

[1] No date, part of the minute was crossed out and rewritten. AG, A¹, 60, fol. 488.

[2] 'Mémoire des Finances de France et de leur administration, tant pour la Recepte que pour la Despense', British Museum, MS. additions 9291, fol. 58, 'Les thrésoriers de l'artillerie vérifoient leurs estats devant le grand maistre qui se raportoient au Conseil et à la Chambre des Comptes avec tous les autres acquits et pieces justificatives pour la rédition de leurs comptes. C'est l'ordre qui estoit cy-devant establi pour l'artillerie mais à present les trésoriers sont sans fonction aussy bien les controlleurs, Monsieur le secretaire d'etat qui a le département de la guerre donnant les ordres pour toutes ces dépenses . . . .' n.d. The handwriting would seem to indicate that it was written in the minority of Louis XIV.

[3] See the *lettres patentes* granted to Puisieux, Secretary of State for War, dated 30 Jan. 1614, countersigned by Neuville, BN, MS. 15519, fol. 162 (copy).

to the king about it, Bullion attempted to take over the direction of the *taillon,* adding it to the office of superintendent of finance. Sublet, who as an intendant of finance had supported Bullion's action, did not claim the rights of his office when he became secretary, and Bullion assumed the *taillon* in 1638.[1] As a result, purely administrative powers to supervise taxation were lost by the secretary, making military and financial jurisdictions clearer.

Sublet, working with the other ministers, negotiated contracts for munitions, weapons, clothing, and food.[2] Sabathier and Rose were two of the most important munitioners in the last years of Louis XIII. Their names crop up periodically in the correspondence of all the ministers, although little is known about them personally.[3] Sublet wrote to Chavigny: 'Monsieur Sabathier has negotiated to furnish war munitions in conformity with the *mémoires,* and he gave me his word personally that nothing will be lacking. . . .'[4]

The secretary obviously sought aid from the munitioners

[1] As a result of a dispute between the marshals and the ministers over the administration of the *taillon* in 1654, a short history of the problem was written. 'Il est constant qu'en l'année 1634 lorsque Monsieur de Bullion, Surintendant, eût commencé de signer (ce qui n'avoit point esté fait auparavant) le projet de la recepte et despense du taillon. . . . Monsieur Servien, lors Secretaire des Commandemens ayant le departement de la guerre, s'en pleignit au feu Roy [Louis XIII], et Sa Majesté ordonna que ce projet ainsi signé seroit rapporté: de sorte que les Estats de la Recepte et Despence du Taillon, continuerent de se faire et expedier en la forme accoustumée, c'est-à-dire, sans que Messieurs des Finances signassent aucune minutte jusques en l'année 1638 que Monsieur de Noyers ayant esté fait Secretaire d'Estat, receut ce projet en forme de minutte signé de Messieurs Bullion et Bouthillier Surintendans, ce que ledit sieur de Noyers souffrit, au prejudice de la charge de Secrétaire des Commandemens; pour ce qu'estant Intendant des Finances dans les années precedentes, il s'estoit joint avec Monsieur de Bullion, pour tascher d'introduire cette nouvelle forme; et il eust eu honte du montrer d'avoir changé d'advis en changeant de charge.' BN, Collection Cinq Cents Colbert, MS. 136, fol. 103.

[2] Several documents relative to these contracts have survived, supplementing our knowledge of this practice as widely found in the *arrêts du conseil* at the Archives Nationales.

[3] Their correspondence has not been found. If extant, it would be a veritable lode for military and financial history of the reign. See the numerous references to Sabathier and Rose in the correspondence of Richelieu, edited by Avenel, who thought that Sabathier was a *trésorier des parties casuelles.* Ed. cit. viii, p. 493.

[4] 14 May 1639, AAE, Sardaigne, 28, fol. 345.

and was on friendly terms with them. Often his position for bargaining with them on goods and prices was weakened by lack of funds and by the immediate necessities of the armies. Once Sublet informed Sabathier of financial manœuvres of the government which endangered the position of the munitioner, and at the same time he bargained with him for needed supplies.[1] On other occasions, Sublet requested Mauroy, an intendant of finance, to negotiate for musket purchases.[2]

Richelieu was kept carefully informed of these negotiations by short summaries prepared by the secretary. The 'Dernier Traité du Sieur Sabathier pour les pouldres et munitions de 1637', in Sublet's hand, was probably addressed to Richelieu.[3] The cardinal, too, sometimes negotiated for army needs. Scudamore, the English ambassador, wrote home: 'Cardinal Richelieu hath caused a bargain to be made with the horse coursers to furnish him 8,000 horse for service and 500 for artillerie at 40 crowns a horse in the month of April.'[4] The administration of the army, like the other branches of the ministry, was obviously not the duty of one minister alone.

The calling up of the nobility by the feudal *ban* and *arrière-ban* was still practised in the seventeenth century; and unlike most aspects of the army administration, the task was still done according to the geographical departments of the four secretaries of state. In July 1635 the secretaries worked feverishly to raise the nobility. Servien wrote to Superintendent Bouthillier, who was preparing dispatches in the absence of Chavigny, La Ville-aux-Clercs, and La Vrillière:

I have been ordered to tell you that the king wishes you to write in his name to the provincial governors, or in their absence to the lieutenant generals of your department, that they are to send His Majesty as soon as possible a list of those who have come to them and are prepared to serve in the *arrière-ban*; and that they

[1] Sublet to Sabathier, minute, 8 June 1640, AG, A¹, 59, fol. 306.
[2] In the minute addressed from Sublet to Mauroy, the secretary specified, 'Il les [the muskets] fault prendre à St. Martin', Aug. 1639, AG, A¹, 53, fol. 486.   [3] AAE, France, 828, fol. 360.
[4] Scudamore to Coke, 28/8 Jan. 1639/8, PRO, State Papers, series 78, vol. 107, fol. 15. The ambassador went on to describe negotiations with the 'upholsters' for tents.

[the governors] are to order the *baillis* and other judges very explicitly to take proceedings against defaulters by seizure of their fiefs and by other customary means in accordance with the severity of the ordonnances.[1]

Even though the execution of the *arrière-ban* was done traditionally, it is significant to note that it was the secretary of state for war who informed his colleagues of the king's will.[2]

The calling up of the nobility, or the payment of a tax in lieu of military service, continued throughout the period. Sublet wrote to his first clerk in 1638: 'Monsieur Le Roy will remember to prepare a declaration or an ordonnance for the publication of the *arrière-ban* for next December. . . .'[3] In 1639 the secretary of state for war again wrote to his colleagues, Chavigny, La Vrillière, and La Ville-aux-Clercs, to tell them that the king was ordering the *convocation de l'arrière-ban*.[4]

The secretary often personally intervened when armies were not going well. On one occasion when money was lacking, Sublet himself set out to bring it to the troops.[5] Again, in 1636, he wrote to Chavigny that he was ordering 'bread, a bridge, and boards from Amiens'.[6] He overlooked no detail in his long letters to the officers in command. He wrote to Chastillon to 'give orders, if you please, to have them fasten down a cover to hold [the bread]; otherwise, all will go wrong, as the least little rain would spoil it.'[7]

---

[1] 3 July 1635, minute, AG, A¹, 25, fol. 13. See also the 'Roolle des Bailliages de l'Isle de France', of 31 Dec. 1635, where each *bailliage* is listed thus: 'Noyon: Sur la plus grande partie des fiefs dudit bailliage est possedé par personnes qui sont actuellement dans le service du Roy en ses armées et que ceulx qui restent dans leur maison aimeront beaucoup mieux fournir en argent la somme à laquelle ils seront taxés que de donner des soldats.' AG, A¹, 25, fol. 652.

[2] On 4 July, one day after Servien's letter, Richelieu wrote to him: 'Faire une dépesche puissante et pressante pour faire avancer l'arrière ban; mandant à tous les sénéchaux et autres officiers des provinces, de contraindre la noblesse de marcher actuellement, en quelque estat qu'elle se trouve.' Avenel, ed. cit. v. xlv.   [3] 17 Sept. 1638, AG, A¹, 49, fol. 173 *bis*.

[4] 30 Jan. 1639, AG, A¹, 50, fol. 290. See also 'Arrière-ban de Bloys', signed by Bouthillier, 26 Sept. 1641, AN, K114B, fol. 45.

[5] 15 Aug. 1640, Richelieu wrote to the generals in command: 'Vous savés trop l'estime que je fais de sa personne et l'affection que je luy porte pour manquer à envoyer l'escorte. . . .' Avenel, ed. cit., vii, p. 266.

[6] 28? Sept. 1636, AAE, France, 821, fol. 332.

[7] 27 Aug. 1640, Aubery, ed. cit. iv, pp. 671 f.

Sublet was frequently occupied with plans for fortifications, and even plans for bridges.[1] He wrote to Chaulnes
and Chastillon in great detail concerning the reconstruction
of some moats, walls, and ramparts.[2] Likewise, Sublet did
not hide his impatience when sieges went badly or slowly;
he wrote to Chastillon:

> Why, Monsieur, here it is the twenty-eighth day that you have
> given the besieged to prepare themselves to receive you well, and
> for the enemies outside to help those inside. . . . I do not dare tell
> you how much these long-drawn-out proceedings are badly
> received, and how many occasions are lost in other places as a
> result, because we do not dare engage any other of our armies
> while you have two of them at your siege.[3]

Like the king, Sublet found no detail too small for his
attention. After the siege of Corbie, Richelieu wrote about
sending flour, cheese, and other supplies along with 'Monsieur de Noyer's mills'.[4] After writing to La Valette that his
dispatches were so completely answered by Chavigny and
Sublet that he had nothing to say, the cardinal assured him
that 'Monsieur de Noyers has sent all of the necessary orders
for the pikes that you have requested'.[5] Sublet even changed
military installations when they did not suit him.[6]

In his political role, it is impossible to measure the influence
of Sublet de Noyers on Louis XIII. The personal correspondence of the secretary has not, to our knowledge, survived.

---

[1] Sublet wrote to Séguier in 1636?: 'Je n'ay encores le plan des forts et ne
manquerai pas de vous envoier aussy tost que je l'aurai pour la munition.
Je n'y voi point d'autre remede que de faire provision de bleds ainsy qu'il
vous pleust me dire hier et je vais despescher à Calais pour en faire venir. . . .'
BN, MS. 17370, fol. 179.

[2] 24 Aug. 1640: 'Aussi-tost que la massonnerie de la breche sera refaite, il
se faut souvenir d'abaisser le cavalier, qui est élevé au dessus de ladite breche,
jettant partie des terres du costé de la ville, pour eslargir le rampart, partie du
costé de la breche. . . . Il faut faire une visite bien exacte de tous les moulins,
qu'il y a dans la ville et cité. . . .' Aubery, ed. cit. iv, p. 666.

[3] 25 June 1638, ibid. iii, p. 677.

[4] Richelieu to Louis, 19 Nov. 1636, Avenel, ed. cit. v. ccclxxvi.

[5] 29 May 1638, ibid. vi. xxxi.

[6] 'Monsieur de Noyers vient d'ouvrir une invention de planter tout du long
de l'abatis, du costé de Gassion, des pieux, et, avec des branches des arbres
qu'on coupera, clayonner tout du long à la hauteur d'un mousquetaire,
laissant à la hauteur qu'il faudra deux ou trois doigts d'espace, pour passer le
mousquet en guise de canonière.' 'Mémoire pour Monsieur le Grand Maistre
de l'Artillerie' [La Meilleraye] by Richelieu, 19 June 1639, ibid. vi. ccxv.

Louis referred to Sublet in his letters to Richelieu, but in contrast to his comments about Chavigny, he expressed no affection for him.[1] The king and the secretary co-operated closely on military questions; Louis wrote to Richelieu: 'I will wait for Monsieur de Noyers in order to find out what troops are most ready to march'; and 'Monsieur de Noyers will send me the names of the absentee officers of the garrison at Doulans . . . so that I may have those who are here arrested.'[2] Sublet furnished information to the king daily, and frequently the secretary filled the traditional role of his *charge* in the *Cabinet du roi*. Louis wrote to Richelieu: 'You will be informed by Monsieur de Noyers of the resolutions that I have made today. . . .'[3]

When the king and the secretary were not together, Louis often ordered his personal secretary, Monsieur Lucas, to write to Sublet, but again these letters concern only military affairs and do not help to discover the influence of the secretary on the king.[4] Perhaps the fact that Sublet was disgraced barely two months after the death of Richelieu best describes the secretary's relationship with the king.[5] He was solely dependent on the cardinal for his favour and power, and though he performed his duties well, this factor was certainly not always uppermost in determining which ministers were to serve the Crown.[6]

---

[1] Comte de Beauchamp, *Louis XIII d'après sa correspondance avec le Cardinal de Richelieu* (Paris, 1902), *passim*.

[2] 23 Mar. 1636, AAE, France, 244, fol. 187; 4 Sept. 1634, fol. 245.

[3] 9 Mar. 1642, ibid., fol. 352.

[4] A good example is Lucas to Sublet, 24 Apr. 1637, where the king, through Lucas, ordered Sublet to send a transfer dispatch to an officer whose bad conduct had reached the ears of the king. AG, A¹, 36, fol. 36.

[5] The circumstances of his disgrace are mysterious. Frequently one finds references to Sublet's voluntary retirement from his offices and the court (Fauvelet-du-Toc, *Histoire des secrétaires d'Estat* (Paris, 1668, pp. 291 ff.), but his letters afterward indicate that he was politely disgraced. See Sublet to Séguier, 27 Mar. 1643, and 15 Apr. 1643, BN, nouvelles acquisitions, MS. 6210, fols. 67 and 69.

[6] The *Mémoires de la Houssaye* are of very questionable value, but the following anecdote captures something of the situation of the ministers as well as the humour of Louis XIII. 'Quand Louis XIII se plaignoit du Cardinal de Richelieu à Monsieur de Noyers (ce qui arrivoit souvent) ce secretaire qui estoit la creature du Cardinal ne desseroit pas les dents. Le Roy avoit beau le presser, il ne luy répondroit jamais sur cet article que pour hausser les espaules, n'osant pas excuser le Cardinal de peur d'offenser le Roy; ny

Like Louis, Richelieu did not express personal affection for Sublet; however, his creature's austerity and efficiency inspired confidence and trust. Sublet, like Chavigny, was entrusted with personal as well as political duties by the cardinal. In 1642, just before the death of Richelieu, he purchased a library for the cardinal and also prepared the latter's last will and testament.[1] In those difficult months Sublet's letters to Richelieu are a mixture of affection and business, and show once again that the cardinal was not a Machiavellian who kept his political and personal actions shrouded in mystery.[2]

Like the king, Richelieu gave the secretary of state for war orders to prepare royal letters. As with Chavigny, these were often in the form of *mémoires*, a series of short statements, each with a request that something be done in the king's name. Richelieu did not delegate the lesser details of army administration to subordinate ministers, but at the same time his attention to them was sporadic and influenced by his health. The *mémoires* addressed to Servien often indicate that Richelieu alone felt responsible for the failure or success of the military effort.[3] Judging from the tone and the more frequent use of the first person, the cardinal entrusted Sublet with more of the details. He wrote to Sublet:

I have so much faith in what comes from Monsieur de Noyers that it is not necessary for him to send me musters and troop reviews which he well knows that I never see. It is sufficient that he take the trouble to write me what is happening.[4]

approuver les raisons du Roy de peur d'offenser le Cardinal. . . . Sur quoy le Roy disoit plaisament, qu'il avoit un Secrétaire d'Estat qui avoit la langue aux espaules.' Quoted from BN, Collection Cangé, MS. 68, fol. 134.

[1] The purchase of the library of the Sieur de Cordes is mentioned in several letters. Sublet was given careful instructions. Avenel, ed. cit. VII. xxxii, xxxviii, xlix, li, lvi, and lxi. These letters indicate not only Richelieu's confidence in Sublet but also his interest in libraries and his business acumen. For the preparation of his will, see the Duc de La Force, *Histoire du Cardinal de Richelieu* (Paris, 1933), vi, pp. 119 f.

[2] For example, Richelieu confided to Sublet his relations with the king, 10 May 1642, Avenel, ed. cit. VI. cccclxiii. After having received news of the cardinal's poor health, Sublet replied: 'Nous pouvons bien chercher la paix et le repos dans les créatures, mais il est certain que nous ne l'y trouverons jamais. . . . Où irons-nous donc, sinon à celuy à qui saint Augustin disoit: *Tu solus requies*?' 14 May 1642, p. 912 of the same volume.

[3] A good example is Richelieu to Servien, 16 Oct. 1635, ibid. v. cxliv.

[4] 30 July 1642, ibid. VII. xxxv.

The cardinal also frequently requested information from him.[1] Plans for future armies, budgetary details, and reports of conditions in the field were frequently requested, and serve to prove that the cardinal was truly dependent upon the secretary. Richelieu asked Servien how many cavalry-men and foot soldiers could be raised with the credits allotted by Superintendent Bullion.[2] He wrote to Servien: 'Monsieur Servien will diligently send me a muster list by which I may be relieved of my doubts; and if he is not really certain of his calculations, and if new orders should be necessary, he will come here to resolve what must be done. . . .'[3] On other occasions, when speedy action was required, the secretary summarized the problem and asked questions in a *mémoire* addressed to the cardinal.[4]

Sublet also counselled Richelieu, often on administrative details.

The king has ordered that Monsieur [Gaston d'Orléans] is to have a review of the army that he is commanding, according to the notice that I had given him . . . but I think that, if the king agrees, the review could be put off until the forts are more advanced, because we consider that it would not be appropriate to give pay to the soldiers while they are obliged to work on the forts.[5]

Because of the lack of records of the *Conseil d'en haut*, one can glimpse the more important aspects of the secretary's position only when the ministers were widely scattered. For example, Richelieu wrote to Claude le Bouthillier: 'I think it appropriate that you and Monsieur de Noyers work on

[1] Richelieu wrote to Sublet (who was also Baron de Dangu) about the latter's failure to inform him of the king's orders to Guiche: 'Ce billet est pour dire à Monsieur de Noyers que je suis en peyne de ne sçavoir point quel ordre le roy a donné à Paris, pour pourvoir au malheur arrivé à Monsieur le mareschal de Guiche. Sa Majesté me mande que Monsieur de Noyers me fera sçavoir tout ce qu'elle a fait; et cependant ny Monsieur de Noyers, ny Monsieur de Dangu ne m'en mandent rien, ce qui ne met pas en petite peyne une personne qui a passion pour l'Estat comme moy.' 10 June 1642, ibid. VI. cccclxxv.

[2] 'Monsieur Servien me mandera combien on peut lever de compagnies de cavalerie et de gens de pied, selon la supputation du fonds que Monsieur de Bullion a faict, afin qu'on n'excède pas le fonds qu'il y a. . . .' 16 Nov. 1635, ibid. V, p. 953.

[3] 23 Mar. 1635, ibid. IV. ccclxi.

[4] Sublet to Richelieu and Richelieu to Sublet, 10? Aug. 1636, ibid. V. cclxxxv.   [5] 12 Oct. 1636, AAE, France, 820, fol. 36.

the reduction of those expenses which you judge less important. . . .'[1] Sublet not only struggled with the superintendents
about army finances, but also participated in making up the
budget.

The cardinal's concern for Sublet is reflected in the
numerous gifts of patronage which Richelieu arranged for
his creature. After helping him become secretary of state,
Richelieu proceeded to arrange the purchase of Servien's
office from the royal treasury, an expense which usually
fell on the new secretary.[2]

In September 1638, through the good offices of Richelieu,
Sublet became superintendent of buildings, a position of
considerable importance even under Louis XIII. Richelieu
wrote to Louis: 'I dare assure [Your Majesty] that there is
no one more proper in France for that *charge* than Monsieur
de Noyers. I do not ask it for him, but Your Majesty's affairs
request it. . . .'[3] It would seem that Sublet took his new
office seriously. The château of Fontainebleau, where he

[1] 30 Aug. 1642, Avenel, op. cit. vii. lxiv.
[2] Bullion wrote to Chavigny, 15 Feb. 1636: 'J'ay receu la lettre qu'il vous
a pleu m'escrire sur le subject de Monsieur Servien, sur ce que vous me dittes
hier de la part de Son Eminence. J'ay fait expedier le contenu des 300,000
livres et n'ay manqué de donner de tres bonnes assignations pour les 200,000
livres et quand aux cent restantes, l'assignation en est bonne. . . .' AAE,
France, 820, fol. 119. Richelieu wrote to Servien, 13 Feb. 1636, after asking
him to go to Angers: 'Cependant on donnera dès demain à votre frère l'Abbé
toutes les assurances de la recompense de votre charge et gratification qu'il
plaira au Roy vous faire, ce qui sera suivy d'un effectif payement dont
Messieurs les Surintendants me donnerent hier parole. . . .' BN, Collection
Cangé, MS. 68, fol. 111ᵛ (copy).
[3] 29 Aug. 1638, Avenel, ed. cit. vi. lxxv. On the same day Richelieu wrote
to Chavigny, who was with the king: 'J'escris au roy pour la charge de Surintendant des bastimens pour Monsieur de Noyers. Je ne vous recommende
point de faire ce qu'il faut en cette affaire, parce que je suis asseuré que vous
n'y oubliérés rien. Je vous advoue que je désire cette affaire avec passion,
pour voir toutes les maisons du roy deslabrées et ruinées en bon estat comme
elles seront'; letter lxxvi in the same volume. See also the copy of the 'Provisions de la charge de surintendant et ordonnateur général des bâtiments et
France tapisseries et manufactures pour François Sublet, seigneur de Noyers',
14 Sept. 1638, BN, Collection Cangé, MS. 68, fol. 140 (copy). Richelieu's role
in the affair is obvious, when we see him thanking the king for the *charge*
given to his creature, 2 Sept. 1638, Avenel, ed. cit. vi. lxxxii. Regarding his
new office, Sublet expressed his anxiety to have the *provisions* as soon as
possible: '. . . et je vous prie qu'elle [the provision] soit conforme à celle du
deffunct parce que je suis adverti qu'il y a des intendants des bastiments qui
veillent à diminuer le pouvoir de la surintendance. . . .' 12 Sept. 1638, AAE,
France, 831, fol. 229.

was also *concierge*, was one of the first buildings to be repaired. In a letter from Richelieu to Louis there was mention that the lead roof of the ballroom was leaking everywhere. Sublet wrote to Chavigny: 'We are trying to restore this beautiful *demeure* which I found in great ruin, and I hope that this summer it will be made otherwise. If there is something to be done to a building you have only to give orders and you will receive service. . . .'[1]

Sublet might well have been referring to repairs for private property in his proposition to Chavigny. Only a thorough study of the expenditure for building repairs under Louis XIII would put the maintenance of private property by the Crown in proper perspective. Sublet once wrote to either Richelieu or Chavigny: 'I had already given orders for the repair of the breaches [in the walls] of your park, but since the laziness of my workers has caused you the trouble of writing to me about it. . . .'[2]

In addition to the administration of royal buildings, Sublet was occupied with the arts, and it was in that capacity that he received 'the Sieur Poussin, the excellent painter [newly] arrived from Rome . . .'.[3] He also watched over the Louvre; Richelieu commended him for driving out the hangers-on who lived there.[4] In the *Gazette de France* it was announced that 'the king went to visit his printing offices at the Louvre, and his new coinage mill. . . . His Majesty expressed his satisfaction to Monsieur de Noyers . . . for the care that he had taken of the two establishments.'[5]

The relatives of Sublet, like those of the other creatures,

[1] 21 Oct. 1638, Avenel, ed. cit. vi. cxxix; Sublet to Chavigny, 2? Jan. 1639, AAE, France, 833, fol. 9.

[2] Probably to Richelieu, because there are no classification numbers on the letter indicating that it was once part of the Chavigny correspondence. 24 May 1641, AAE, France, 838, fol. 196. It is also interesting to notice that the walls and moats around the new town of Richelieu were at least partly constructed by the Crown; see the budget of the Ponts et Chaussées, AAE, France, 801, fols. 288 ff. He was also supervising the mural paintings of the church at Richelieu for the cardinal, Avenel, ed. cit. vii, p. 149.

[3] *Gazette de France* for 22 Dec. 1640.

[4] Richelieu to Sublet and Chavigny, 22 July 1642, Avenel, ed. cit. vii. xxvii.

[5] 11? Jan. 1642; see also the interesting 'Project d'arrest touchant l'Establissement de l'Imprimerie Royalle au Louvre', 1640, AG, A¹, 58, fol. 315.

enjoyed royal patronage. His only son, Guillaume, later Seigneur de Noyers, held a minor position in the war department of his father. Sublet wrote to his first clerk: 'My son will have a commission of light horse sent shortly. . . .'[1] In 1640 Guillaume informed his father that the *bourgeoisie* of Arras was in great need of grain.[2]

The secretary of state for war had fewer friends than Chavigny,[3] and did not carry on private coded correspondence with provincial administrators. With the army officers Sublet remained aloof, but at the same time he extended favours to some and probably hindered the promotion of others. With Chastillon he occasionally interrupted his strict business-like manner to discuss the Maréchal's problems with the other ministers. He also came to his aid, at least in appearance, over a pension difficulty which had put Chastillon and Bullion at odds.[4] When La Meilleraye personally led a third attack, however, after the *Conseil de guerre* had decided against it, Sublet harshly scolded him.[5]

In the case of Guébriant,[6] who became general-in-chief of the armies with the help of Sublet, it is fairly obvious that the creatures of Richelieu also had their creatures.[7] The secretary wrote to his favourite: 'Finally we are generals-in-chief of the army. I say "we", because it seems to me that I have contributed to all the honour and fortune which has fallen on you.'[8] Sublet continued by giving advice to

---

[1] 10 Sept. 1636, AG, A¹, 29, fol. 190.

[2] Sublet to St. Preuil, AAE, France, 1677, fol. 312. In a letter from Sublet to Chastillon and Chaulnes, 4 June 1640, he mentioned that Richelieu had ordered his son to watch over the munitioners, BN, MS. 3763, fol. 55. Sublet wrote to Chavigny, 12 Dec. 1639: 'Envoiant mon fils en Champagne pour donner ordre aux fortifficacions . . . je suplie Monsieur de Chavigny de vouloir prendre la peine de signer les expeditions qui luy sont necessaires.' AAE, France, 834, fol. 170.

[3] For Sublet's relations with Chavigny, see above, p. 88.

[4] Sublet to Chastillon, 16 May 1639, BN, MS. 3762, fol. 18.

[5] Sublet to La Meilleraye, 19 June 1636, *Mémoires et documents inédits pour servir à l'histoire de la Franche Comté* (Besançon, 1912), i. cix.

[6] Jean-Baptiste de Budes, Comte de Guébriant.

[7] See Louis André, 'Le Maréchal de La Motte Houdancourt,' *Revue d'Histoire Moderne*, 1937, xii, *passim*, for an illustration of the role which a secretary of state might play in the rise of a young officer to power.

[8] 13 Oct. 1641, BN, Collection Cinq Cents Colbert, MS. 108, fol. 91.

Guébriant on how to control armies. In doing so he discussed absolutism in a practical way:

The king would very much like, in appointing you as general, that we no longer speak of *directeurs* or of any other extraordinary power in the entire army; and that the king, having paid for an army, be the absolute master of it. There are only two ways to achieve this: one by force, which is very difficult to come by at present, and the other by money; it is by that [means] that we intend to succeed. . . . And as to the suppression of this name *directeur*—if, however, you should encounter unforseen and insurmountable difficulties, the king does not mean that in our desire to re-establish order in the army we ruin it. . . . We must not make our weakness known and push the stubbornness and obstinacy of these people to the extreme, but [we] must delay and adapt ourselves to the moment and to their mood, seeking, however, other ways to achieve better order and to establish solidly the power of the king among your troops. We must even be more resolved that everyone see the common good of the *bon party* and come over to it individually, and that there is no other way to re-establish it so that we may reap from it the services for which we are hoping, for the good of Christianity, than by a monarchical order which binds everything into one. But as to telling you when and how that can be done, you must certainly be pleased that we leave it to your prudence; because, being on the spot, you may choose the moments and promote the changes of opinion. . . . [1]

The secretary of state for war under Louis XIII was already struggling against the multitude of traditions and individual rights which stood between the Crown and complete control of the army. Louis André, who conjectured that Sublet was jealous of Michel Le Tellier, future secretary of state for war, did not look beyond his hero to notice that Le Tellier, as intendant with the armies in Italy, was doing only what the other intendants were doing, and not more.[2] Gremonville, intendant with the armies in Champagne, was another officer doing much the same as Le Tellier. He wrote Sublet long *mémoires* describing the organizational and financial problems of the army and asking for

---

[1] 13 Oct. 1641, BN, Collection Cinq Cents Colbert, MS. 108, fol. 91.
[2] Louis André, *Michel Le Tellier et l'organisation de l'armée monarchique* (Paris, 1906), p. 85. Much of what André described as army reorganization under Le Tellier rests only upon a close analysis of the *règlements*.

instructions.[1] Sublet wrote his comments on each question in the margin, then probably turned it over to his first clerk to prepare for dispatch.[2] There is no indication that Sublet consulted the king or the other ministers; his comments seem to be personal decisions.

Through the *mémoires* of the intendants, as well as by means of the reviews and musters ordered by the officers and supervised by the intendants, the secretary was already becoming much better informed than in the previous reign of conditions in the armies. The officers did not always seek personal gain at the expense of the army; and, while intendants were certainly not always welcome in every army encampment, at least one commander requested one.[3]

Sublet worked continuously to establish strong armies and to assure their complete obedience to the king. In his relations with all save his peers, he did not hesitate to criticize and demand action. When he wrote to Le Tellier: 'The king has found it very bad that you were unable to collar those officers who were imprudent and spiteful enough to write to their companies in France to withhold as much money as possible from their recruits . . .',[4] the essential elements for a new order were determined: the secretary spoke and wrote in the name of the king, and the goal, the unification of the entire military administration, was already established.

---

[1] Nicolas Bretel, Seigneur de Gremonville, probably became influential through the good offices of Chavigny. See Avenel, ed. cit. vi, p. 720.

[2] 15 Dec. 1640, 'Mémoire touchant les payements qui sont à faire en Champagne', AG, A¹, 61, fol. 424.

[3] André's generalization of the conduct of officers is accurate, but has exceptions; op. cit., pp. 115 ff.

[4] 22 Apr. 1641, BN, Collection Cangé, MS. 25 (copy).

VI

The Superintendents of Finance

IN 1639 Claude le Bouthillier wrote to Richelieu : 'Finances are the nerves of war.'[1] After the beginning of open war in 1635, the cardinal realized this more than ever before. His increasingly ambitious plans for the *gloire* of Louis XIII strained the treasury to the breaking-point, forcing him and his creatures to accept any means at hand to avoid financial catastrophe. The personality of the cardinal was itself an important element in the direction of financial administration. In contrast to other areas of government, particularly military and diplomatic, financial policy was only supervised by Richelieu, who left the details to the superintendents of finance.

Financial problems were traditionally aired *en conseil*, and the king presumably made the decisions with the help of a few wise old councillors experienced in the complexities of finance in the *ancien régime*. However, ever since the reign of Francis I broad powers to administer the king's finances had occasionally been given to a *surintendant des finances*. While having great powers, he did not himself spend or collect the king's money; consequently he was not 'responsible before any financial jurisdiction, rendering account only to the king, and recognizing no other rule than that of the *bon vouloir royal*, no other law save his own conscience'.[2] Historians have carefully described some of these great finance ministers, particularly Semblançay and Sully, but for the reign of Louis XIII little has been done.[3]

Though the superintendent was recognized, along with the chancellor, as the chief councillor to the king, the powers

---

[1] 2 Sept. 1639, AAE, France, 834, fol. 48.

[2] A. de Boilisle, 'Semblançay et la surintendance des finances', from the *Annuaire-Bulletin de la Société de l'Histoire de France* (Paris, 1882), p. 35.

[3] See H. Sée, A. Rébeillon, and E. Préclin, *Le XVIᵉ siècle* (Paris, 1955), *passim*; E. Préclin and V. Tapié, *Le XVIIᵉ siècle* (Paris, 1956), *passim*.

of the office of superintendent of finance, unlike those of the secretaries of state, were not defined by *règlements* under Louis XIII. Even so, it was a position of far greater prestige and influence than that of any of the secretaries of state in this period. The superintendent presided over the financial administration, which was frequently changed by council *règlements*; but the office itself was immune from such proceedings.[1]

Faced with the great powers of this office, Francis I disgraced the first holder of it, Semblançay, when he became too powerful and a threat to the prestige and authority of the Crown.[2] During the minority of Louis XIII the highhanded Sully, who had refused to conduct financial affairs *en conseil*, was disgraced in 1611 when the Regent, Marie de Médicis, wished to have greater personal control over finance.[3] To make sure that it did not again come under the control of one man, Marie left the office vacant and established an elaborate system in the councils to deliberate and establish financial policies.[4] Judging from the numerous changes and additions made in the procedure, and from the short time which passed before a superintendent was again appointed in 1619, this method was probably ineffective.[5]

Only a thorough study of financial procedure after 1619 would permit one to measure how much the office of superintendent was modified by the retention of council procedures established in the Regency. Judging from a *règlement* of the council made in 1624, however, the superintendent was obliged to present his decisions for review, not only before the king, but before the administrative councils as well. This and other measures provided a check on the office; even so, as the head of the councils which met for financial

---

[1] Even the *règlement* discussed in the following chapter, which was really against the extended powers of the superintendent, was only called a *règlement des finances*. See Appendix B.

[2] See H. Lemonnier, *Histoire de France*, ed. by E. Lavisse (Paris, 1903), v, part 1, pp. 228 ff.

[3] J. H. Mariéjol, *Histoire de France*, ed. by E. Lavisse (Paris, 1911), vi, part 2, pp. 146 f.

[4] See the *règlements* published by R. Mousnier, 'Les Règlements du Conseil du Roi sous Louis XIII', *Annuaire-Bulletin de la Société de l'Histoire de France*, 1946–7, pp. 38 f.

[5] For a list of the superintendents, see Boislisle, loc. cit., pp. 38 f.

measures, the superintendent often had his way. By a *règle-ment* of 1624 the superintendents (the office was frequently held jointly) were to hold at least two councils a week for financial affairs, to calculate current expenditure, and to sign ordonnances for payment up to 1,000 *livres*.[1] Every fort-night accounts must be verified and signed by the king; the superintendents must prepare an *état général des finances*, a sort of budget, and at the same time were expressly for-bidden to order a payment alone or make assignations or reassignations without verification *en conseil*. Apart from these details, council legislation provides much information about financial procedure, but little about the participation of the superintendent.

Throughout the *règlements*, treatises, and commentaries on the nature of government written in the seventeenth century, the superintendent appears as a great councillor, and it is as such that he will be described here. In this posi-tion he participated in the councils, where both judiciary and legislative decisions influenced every aspect of the political, social, and economic life of the realm. As chief councillor, it was his duty to sign the minutes of the deci-sions handed down by the various branches of the council. For the last decade of the reign of Louis XIII, the signatures of Séguier, Bouthillier, Bullion, and a council secretary have survived by the thousands on the minutes for the *arrêts* of the king's council.[2] Usually both superinten-dents signed, but sometimes only one did. On one occasion, after Bullion and Séguier had both signed a minute, Bout-hillier evidently refused to do so. After crossing out the sig-natures of the others, he proceeded to explain why the legislation in question was changed.[3]

The superintendents exercised powers almost as broad as the councils in whose name they announced decisions. They

[1] Mousnier, loc. cit., pp. 38 f.

[2] AN, séries E. These minutes are not as illuminating on the functions and duties of the superintendents as they might seem, because normally the decision only is given with no details of how it was made. For further inform-ation on the signing of *arrêts*, see Georges Pagès, 'Le Conseil du Roi sous Louis XIII', *Revue d'Histoire Moderne*, 1937, pp. 315 f.

[3] Aug. 1636, AAE, France, 821, fol. 243. The document survived as part of Richelieu's or Chavigny's correspondence, indicating that other ministers were also informed of the change.

received orders to make arrests in the king's name[1] and, with the chancellor, they kept a close watch over Paris for disturbances due to unpopular measures, for which they themselves might have been responsible in a council decision concerning taxes or prices.[2] The superintendents also listened to grievances and personally received petitions from subjects and institutions; for example, Bullion informed Richelieu that the *prévôt* of merchants and the *échevins* of the city of Paris had come as deputies from the general council of the city to inform him that they could not raise the 100,000 *livres* for military expenditure which they had promised the king.[3]

The superintendents could not send orders alone in the name of the council. After council minutes were properly signed, the chancellor or keeper of the seals reviewed the decision before sealing it.[4] This elaborate system of checks served to make legislation more explicit by having it reviewed by several persons at different stages of the council procedure and of course it helped to maintain powerful boundaries on the roles which great officers could play individually.

With the councils, and *vis-à-vis* the other ministers, the chief councillors acted as reviewers of proposals presented *en conseil*. If the superintendents or the chancellor disapproved of an important proposal, they presented it in the *Conseil d'en haut* to the king and Richelieu—each of whom sought the advice or consent of the other if they were separated. This also occurred between ministers; on one occasion Bullion asked for Chavigny's and ultimately Richelieu's support against a measure proposed by a secretary of state.[5]

[1] Bullion once had the wrong man jailed because of confusion over the spelling of an English name. See Bullion to Richelieu, 1 Feb. 1637, AAE, France, 826, fol. 103; also Bullion to Richelieu, 8 Sept. 1636, Richelieu, *Lettres, instructions diplomatiques et papiers d'Etat*, ed. by M. Avenel (Paris, 1853–77), v. cccxviii.

[2] During the tension between the council and the sovereign courts over the registration of council-sponsored new officers, revolt was imminent several times in 1636–9. See the *règlement* for police powers for the city of Paris written in Bullion's hand, 1635? AAE, France, 813, fol. 328.

[3] Bullion also reported fortification problems for Paris to Richelieu, 3 Sept. 1636, AAE, France, 821, fol. 270.

[4] Bullion to Chavigny? 28 Sept. 1635, AAE, France, 815, fol. 273.

[5] This was over the Vitry affair of 1635. Bullion wrote to Chavigny: 'Je seray le premier quand on m'en demandera mon advis à le condamner, mais

In the almost daily sessions of the councils, the chancellor and the superintendents were responsible for directing the deliberations and, in some ways, even for the decisions or mistakes of the councils.[1] Sessions were held for both formal deliberation and the execution of legislation already prepared by the king and his ministers. After assuring him that he had informed Séguier of the cardinal's requests, Chavigny wrote to Richelieu:

> Yesterday morning we met together at the Keeper of the Seals' house [Séguier did not become Chancellor until 1636], Monsieur de Bullion, my father [Claude le Bouthillier], and I. It was decided that we would prepare an *arrêt*, which was done immediately so that it could be sent to the provinces. . . . We would have made it a declaration but we would have lost a great deal of time in having it verified. . . .[2]

This occasion was no doubt exceptional, as the lesser councillors do not seem to have been present, but it illustrates the broad powers of the chief councillors.

The superintendents—in addition to preparing legislation ordered by the king and preparing the decisions of the council on judicial cases—jealously watched over the rights of the Crown. Bullion, an old and crafty councillor, stopped proposals when they granted royal privileges unnecessarily. He angrily complained to Richelieu about a governor who had 'given away more than half the just pretensions of the king' in his region.[3] Bullion also reviewed a draft for a commission to establish an intendant in the Dauphiné. He sent it back to its author with specific comments on its illegality and expressed fear that the new officers would cause a loss in tax revenues.[4]

si le Parlement sans le commandement du Roy peut informer contre un Gouverneur . . . cela seroit de perilleuse consequence. . . .' 9 Jan. 1635, AAE, France, 813, fol. 11. Servien was the secretary preparing the commission of inquest.

[1] Richelieu angrily wrote to Bouthillier: 'Je vous avoue que je ne sçay comme vous ne pensés un peu plus que vous ne faictes aux conséquences des résolutions que vous prenés dans vostre conseil des finances.' 28 Aug. 1639, Avenel, ed. cit. vi. cclxix. This clearly indicates that the cardinal held the superintendents responsible for council decisions, and his complaint is a measure of the relative freedom he left them.

[2] 26 July 1634, AAE, France, 810, fol. 363.

[3] Bullion to Richelieu, 25 Oct. 1634, Avenel, ed. cit. iv, pp. 637 f.

[4] Bullion to Sublet, 19 Nov. 1638? AG, A¹, 49, fol. 256. Bullion added

Apart from these general activities, the superintendents performed the bulk of the higher financial administration. This began with the preparation of the *état général des finances*, a budget showing estimated revenues and allocations for expenditure. Such budgets had never been prepared with regularity before 1632, but from the beginning of their administration Bullion and Bouthillier decided that they should be.[1] Allocations for various branches of the government were sometimes tried within the budget in the last decade of the reign, but particularly in 1635, when Bullion proposed raising 36,000,000 *livres* for military expenses. Richelieu wrote to him: 'We have miraculously worked not to exceed by a single *double rouge* the fund of thirty-six millions which you have destined for war expenditure. . . .'[2] Certainly the intendants of finance, the general comptroller, the secretary of state for war, and, above all, Richelieu, had worked to establish the figure along with the superintendents. Indeed, Bullion wrote to Richelieu barely a fortnight after the cardinal had proudly announced that expenditure was within Bullion's budget: 'Your Eminence is making a very good decision not to exceed the budget for soldiers established according to the project he prepared. . . .'[3] The cardinal had thus prepared part if not all of the war budget, either by giving the number of soldiers needed and simply letting Bullion calculate the cost, or by giving the actual figures for the budget.[4]

that if Richelieu really wanted to establish the intendant, that he would do nothing but accept, but concluded by saying that he was sure His Eminence would consent with 'uneasiness'.

[1] Bullion really emphasized it. See the *mémoire* made by Bouthillier when they took office, published in Appendix B, and below, p. 167.

[2] 20 Apr. 1635, Avenel, ed. cit. IV. ccclxxix. The *double rouge* was a small copper coin worth 2 *deniers* and was synonymous with 'little more than nothing'.

[3] Bullion continued: 'en faire ceste chose qui tournera au grand honneur et proffit de Vostre Eminence parce que sans desordres avec l'ayde de Dieu on pourra continuer, et que quand on vouldroit en user autrement il seroit impossible et cela mettroit tout en confusion. J'assure Vostre Eminence qu'en mon particulier c'est me donner la vie que de voir le moyen de pouvoir faire subsister Vostre Eminence dans sa grandeur et réputation', 4 May 1635, AAE, France, 814, fol. 17.

[4] Nevertheless, Bullion was given the credit. Augier wrote to the English court: 'Ledit Sieur Cardinal a escrit icy à Messieurs le Garde des Seaux et Bullion de venir faire un tour audit Chasteauthierri. Ils s'y acheminerent hyer ayans laissé en cette ville le gros du conseil où ils ont promis d'estre de retour

Budgets on the state level were subject to radical changes by the turn of events even in the seventeenth century, but the essential point described here is that royal administrators were already using them as a tool, crude though it was, to fix limits of expenditure. Expenses not influenced by war changed very slowly in the reign of Louis XIII, for he was not a great builder or an extravagant spender on court functions. The costs of the *maison du roi* and other households climbed slowly from year to year, but these corresponded to the 'fixed costs' of a modern corporation.[1] Building costs, ambassadorial expenses, and pensions also varied little from year to year, as is shown in the numerous budgets preserved in the Archives des Affaires Etrangères.[2]

After the great effort to prepare the realm for war in 1635-6, elaborate budgets virtually disappeared because of the chaos of arrears, separate accounts, borrowing, and so forth. After 1636 there is no evidence indicating that even the army was allotted a fixed sum by the Crown; only the hard realities of expenditure and revenue were considered, and there was no attempt to allocate the funds. The treasury (*épargne*) frequently prepared short balance-sheets showing the financial position of the realm;[3] only from these did the superintendents calculate expenditure and receipts for the fiscal year.[4]

The superintendents worked with the treasury officers throughout the year and supervised the accounts. Once the treasurer in charge had accounted for all payments and disbursements, it was their duty to sign the great treasury rolls

en peu de jours. Ledit Sieur de Bullion resjouira(?) Sadite Majesté par la presentation de l'estat des finances qu'il a dressé pour le maintien de la guerre.' 15/25 May 1635, PRO, State Papers, 78, vol. 97, fol. 247.

[1] These included guards, charity, food, maintenance of royal residences, salaries for doctors, musicians, and historians, and so forth. See E. Griselle, ed., *Supplément à la maison du Roi* (Paris, 1912).

[2] France, *passim*.

[3] See the photo-copy of the *extraict de l'espargne*, 1640, pub. by Avenel, ed. cit. vi, p. 745.

[4] See below, p. 171. The fiscal year was the calendar year, but July was very important for new tax levies, especially for the *taille*, determined *en conseil* and assigned to the *généralitiés*. Claude de Beaune, *Traicté de la chambre des comptes* (Paris, 1647), p. 220. For an excellent introduction to taxation and its collection in the *ancien régime*, see G. T. Matthews, *The Royal General Farms in Eighteenth Century France* (New York, 1958), *passim*.

upon which the various royal accounts were inscribed.[1] When disagreement arose among the treasurers over their duties, the superintendents stepped in to settle them.[2]

Because of the complex system of revenues and expenditure, the superintendents enjoyed powers which in the last decade of the reign were subject to review by neither the council nor the Crown. Under Louis XIII the revenues were either dispersed as cash, or expenses were assigned to be paid from certain revenues collected by royal officials and tax farmers when the latter were received by the Crown. These varied with the size and importance of the disbursement to be made, as well as with the conditions of the royal treasury at the moment. Munitioners and merchants of all kinds were accustomed to advance money to officers seeking army supplies, but they were careful to protect themselves by not granting full credit, in case economic conditions, revolt, or a war endangered the revenue assigned to their clients. Neither Louis nor Richelieu interfered with the making of the ultimate decision determining from what revenue a given item of expenditure was to be paid. The greatest single power of the superintendents was the right to fix assignations and to decide if a payment was to be made in assignations or in cash.

On paper, assignations were equal in value to a cash payment, but to collect them at face value was another matter. The superintendents, with the help of the intendants of finance, assigned revenues quite arbitrarily and generally to the king's advantage; but when two projects of seemingly

---

[1] Bullion wrote to Richelieu: 'Hier matin nous avons compté avec l'espargne. . . .' 16 Jan. 1635, AAE, France, 813, fol. 31; Bouthillier to Richelieu: 'J'ay arresté cette année bonne quantité de roolles jusques 7 ou 8 qui estoient en arriere, et les deux collegues ont mesme veriffié leurs estats au vrai chacun, de sorte qu'à leur egard il n'y a plus rien du tout à faire du passé. . . . Il y avoit quantité d'affaires qu'il faloit comprendre, dans son cinquiesme Role que j'arresterai jeudi, et ensuitte je luy ferai presenter son Estat au vrai devant la fin de cette année. Apres cela toute l'espargne sera nette, ce qui n'a pas esté il y a longtemps. . . .' 19 Nov. 1641, AAE, France, 839, fol. 356ᵛ.

[2] Bullion to Richelieu: 'Hier on me donna advis qu'il y avoit de la difficulté entre les thresoriers. J'ay terminé sur le champ leurs differends et ose asseurer Vostre Eminence que les commis de l'un et l'autre partent presentement et que l'argent sera dans Nancy. . . .' 24 July 1636, AAE, France, 821, fol. 104.

equal importance were to have revenues assigned to them and there was a lack of cash, personal influence in the ministry often determined which person had a better chance to collect his money. As the war continued and the financial crisis worsened, assignations were given on revenues not due to be paid until the following year. The worst aspect of the system was its tendency to aggravate the financial crisis by spending in advance revenues needed in difficult times ahead.

When France was at war, the power to command money by assignation—more than elaborate budget plans or the courage of the generals—often determined the success or failure of a military campaign.[1] The system itself was not directly responsible for campaign failures, because it only reflected the basic problem, lack of funds; but the question of which armies were to be eliminated or reduced often depended upon the superintendents and their power to assign revenues.

There is little evidence that Richelieu intervened in this domain, nor, for that matter, does it seem that he was familiar with the details of accounts and conditions of the different tax jurisdictions which made certain revenues coveted for assignations and others undesirable. Richelieu occasionally requested the superintendents to give a good assignation, but such a general request, without knowledge of which revenues were better than others at the moment, was ineffective with Bullion. The superintendents usually reported their decisions in vague terms, without specifying the financial details needed to evaluate them. Richelieu probably preferred to remain aloof from the details of revenues due to be paid, as well as ignorant of what the superintendents had already spent by assignation in previous months.[2]

---

[1] A striking example was Rohan's campaign in the Grisons in 1636–7. See Mariéjol, op. cit., pp. 343 f., and the copies of the correspondence written during the campaign in BN, MS. 5190, *passim*; and below, p. 149.

[2] Richelieu sent orders that certain expenses were to be met by assignation, and then he left the creatures to work out the details. Bullion wrote to Richelieu: 'Demain Dieu aydans nous travaillerons avec Monsieur de Noyers sur les assignations dont il a pleu à Vostre Eminence me parler. . . .' 12 June 1636, AAE, France, 821, fol. 29.

In other areas, also, Richelieu left the details to the super-intendents and the council. The lack of comments in the correspondence on such questions as the amount of tax to be collected by the *taille*, for example, would seem to indicate that such matters were deliberated *en conseil* and submitted to Louis and Richelieu in the *Conseil d'en haut* for review. The same was true for not only the *taille* but for the *aides* and the extraordinary levies such as the *subvention générale*, which made it possible to continue the war.[1] The *répartition*, or division of taxes to be raised in each *généralité*, was also done in council, where the superintendents and the intendants of finance again dominated the scene, because they were better informed on local economic conditions, including the hostility toward higher taxes in various areas of the realm.

The councils also sent out royal orders announcing new tax measures, but more important, they—or the chief coun-cillors in private—negotiated contracts to collect taxes with the *traitants*.[2] Mariéjol astutely observed Bullion's alliance with the *traitants*,[3] but he did not describe the difficult task of negotiating such contracts or why it was inevitable that the superintendents co-operated with some of the most powerful financiers of the realm. The Crown often lacked a strong position in bargaining, and was forced to accept contracts with exorbitant losses in revenue. Indeed, the administrative procedure in making tax contracts during the ministry of Richelieu depended upon the relationships between the superintendents and the *traitants*; but in spite of such alliances, the former generally struggled valiantly for the benefit of the king. Bullion, for example, after nego-tiating with a *traitant*, proposed his plan to Richelieu:

We have a proposition for two millions in *douzains*.[4] I am sending

---

[1] See the *Mémoire sur l'état des finances depuis 1616 jusqu'en 1644*, published in *Archives curieuses de l'histoire de France*, series 2, vol. vi. 'Et c'est à cause de l'augmentation de la taille et des fermes, et particulièrement des deniers des levées extraordinaires en sy grand nombre que, depuis l'année mil six cent vingt seulement l'on veriffia qu'il s'est porté à l'espargne plus de sept cent millions de livres, non compris plusieurs frais pour les taxations et aultres despenses employées dans les comptes de ceulx qui ont mangé lesdicts deniers . . .', p. 60. The great sums consumed by royal officers and tax farmers in collecting revenues were a problem never attacked under Louis XIII.

[2] See below, p. 155.   [3] Mariéjol, op. cit., p. 427.

[4] The *douzain* was a silver coin having the value of 12 *deniers parisis*, hence

the whole plan. . . . The *traitant* will gain four hundred thousand odd *livres*. The remainder goes for charges without which the thing cannot succeed. The net return is two millions payable in three years. . . . The best would be to do nothing if we had other ways to acquire money; but because of the necessity, I humbly implore Your Eminence to help us, because truthfully we are behind more than five or six millions.[1]

Richelieu was often left with no choice but to accept any possible means that would bolster the royal treasury. This time Bullion sought Richelieu's approval; at other times he merely informed the Cardinal of what had already been arranged. Having negotiated the contract to raise taxes on the *cinq grosses fermes*, Bullion reported, probably after its approval by the council:

The farm of the *cinq grosses fermes* has been continued with Monsieur Rambouillet and those of his company, in augmenting [*illegible*] by 760,000 *livres tournois*. We estimated, with the good pleasure of Your Eminence, to employ it this way, as we have saved a million and more in compensations [*dédommagement*]. . . . I almost forgot to tell you that I do not know how to come to final terms with the procurator general about the treasury deposits [*consignations*]. It comes to three million; I think that a letter from Your Eminence would be infinitely useful.[2]

The complexity of revenues might lead one to believe that some were not endangered by the arrears in others, but this would be mistaken. Even the *taille*, the most reliable income of the Crown, became endangered by agreements with the *traitants*, because, like the other taxes, it was more easily collected in some provinces than in others.[3] The super-

the name. It was coined off and on during the reign of Louis XIII, notably in Montpellier and Montauban in 1628–9 and in 1640. See BN, MS. 18504, fol. 54, for the authorization in 1640.

[1] 18 June 1639, AAE, France, 833, fol. 191. It was probably not an oversight by Bullion in failing to mention the total cost of the project in royal revenues.   [2] 11 May 1635? AAE, France, 814, fol. 34.

[3] Bullion to Richelieu, 7 Apr. 1638?: 'Monsieur de Noyers a veu l'estat des depenses jusques à present mais le pis de tout est que nos traitants ne veulent payer sur l'aprehension et mesme assuranße qu'on leur donne des provinces qu'il ne se payera rien de la taille qui est l'assignation de leur renboursement. Je n'oublieray ny l'affection ny la fidelité que je doibs à Vostre Eminence mais si le secours des tailles ne vient ayant usé de toute la prevoyance possible je craint que nous ne tombions tout à faict dans l'impuissance. . . .' AAE, France, 830, fol. 97.

intendents attempted to control these problems, but often their efforts were futile.

Taxes on foreign commerce were related to internal impositions; and perhaps even before the taxpayers complained the *traitants* did so, because they feared a diminution of the revenues that they were to collect. Bullion wrote to Richelieu, probably after having received an order to impose an additional tax on commerce:

Before receiving the letter from Your Eminence about the Marseille affair for the three per cent. imposition on Levantine commerce, I worked with the farmer of the *cinq grosses fermes*, who held that the justice of Your Eminence [who was superintendent of commerce] would not sustain a three per cent. imposition on Levantine commerce, and even on that [commerce] which will be unloaded in Atlantic ports because the contract for the *cinq grosses fermes* obliged the king to impose only five per cent.; to levy three more, that would raise it to eight per cent., [and] that the king was the master and could order what he pleased, but the farmer could reasonably request to be discharged from his tax farm. . . .[1]

Even so, on the same day Bullion again wrote to Richelieu: 'With a great deal of trouble I arranged the three per cent. affair, and now the farmer has consented.'[2]

When taxes were not paid, and consequently when the *traitants* and farmers refused to pay, the Crown was constrained to borrow money. Often it was forced to borrow from the *traitants* themselves. The superintendents negotiated loans and bargained to gain the lowest interest rates. Bullion wrote to Richelieu:

I negotiated with Messieurs de Rambouillet and Talmon [Talmond] for 150,000 *livres*, with 100,000 payable May 31, and 50,000 on June 15. It was impossible to make them advance the term even though I promised them 30,000 *livres* interest. There, Monseigneur, is what I could do with the said Rambouillet and Talmon, who excuse themselves for not having advanced the time because of the 100,000 *livres* which they are furnishing next April 20, for the passage of troops from Holland. . . .[3]

During the war the royal revenues, inadequate in peace-time,

[1] 11 Aug. 1638, AAE, France, 831, fol. 25.
[2] 11 Aug. 1638, ibid., fol. 24.
[3] 31 Mar. 1636, AAE, France, 820, fol. 184ᵛ. Bullion continued, 'S'il plaist à Vostre Eminence agreer ce qui a esté fait. . . .'

became grossly insufficient. Borrowing was only one of the expedients to which the ministers turned; the other will be discussed later in this chapter.

Working with the chancellor, the superintendents provided a work-a-day liaison with the sovereign courts and other institutions outside the *Conseil du roi*. Apart from occasional and very dramatic interventions in the Parlement, the king and his principal minister left to the chief councillors the arduous task of negotiating with the members of the Parlement for the registration of edicts and other legislation. Bullion, perhaps even more than Séguier, kept Louis and Richelieu informed of the moods in the Parlement, and often carefully advised them when there were difficulties. If legislation was registered with little difficulty, Bullion quickly informed the cardinal and attributed the success to Richelieu's prudence.[1] The cardinal, who remained responsible to the king, led the initiative, while the ministers attempted to execute his orders. Both superintendents jubilantly wrote to Richelieu: 'We are dispatching this courier to inform Your Eminence that (according to the resolutions made yesterday, fulfilling your orders given to Monsieur the Chancellor) everything went as planned.'[2] Bullion and Bouthillier then continued by describing the mood and political temperature of the Parlement.

Bullion willingly approved when Richelieu took stern measures with the Parlement. When the latter came to register legislation earnestly desired by the councillors, the old quarrel between the council and the Parlement was never remote. The superintendents were particularly interested in the fate of some edicts, especially those creating new offices to pay for the war. Bullion showed little patience with the court, for when the cardinal did not move quickly to force the Parlement, he wrote: 'I humbly beseech His Eminence to remember the Parlement of Paris, because the expenditure for war is in part based upon edicts on which [it] must please the king.'[3] Only the presence of the king in the

---

[1] 30 June 1635, AAE, France, 814, fol. 215.

[2] Bullion and Claude le Bouthillier to Richelieu, 18 Jan. 1636, AAE, France, 820, fol. 42.

[3] Bullion to Richelieu, 6 Apr. 1637, AAE, France, 826, fol. 257.

Parlement to impose his will by *lit de justice* could make the court give way. On one occasion the Parlement procrastinated desperately for six months in the hope that Louis would soon leave the Île de France. Bullion sternly wrote to Richelieu that the Parlement was merely attempting to 'draw out the business', and recommended stern measures.[1]

After a victory in the Parlement of Rouen, Bullion jubilantly wrote: 'God be praised that the affairs of Normandy worked out well. It is now necessary to speak with Messieurs of the Parlement [of Paris] and bring them to reason so that the king may receive the help he desires from edicts published in his presence.'[2] The superintendents supervised the struggle for registration in other courts as well. Bullion wrote to Nicolay, first president in the *Cour des comptes de l'Hôtel de Ville*:

Monsieur, six weeks ago I negotiated with you on the business of the *Chambre* and arranged the conditions. I have always expected that they would be accepted. I am astonished at the long time which has passed without having those conditions, [already] ratified by the *Chambre*, executed. I beseech you to finish up the affair by the end of this week at the latest. Otherwise I will have reason to complain, and I will be obliged, for the king's service, to use means judged necessary.[3]

The superintendents also watched over monetary policy and also the mint. Bullion worked to establish currency stability, even though several devaluations took place during the period. 'We are working hard and firmly on the matter of the currency. If commerce can be re-established quietly and without fanfare, God will give us the grace, if it please Him, to make abundance return'.[4] Bouthillier wrote to Brézé: 'Monsieur de Bullion and I will be in Paris in three weeks, at the latest, to mint money to furnish for the expenses of the troops.'[5] The role of superintendents in the direction of the mint is obscure. This is the frontier of ministerial responsibility, indicating that a detailed study of their

[1] 18 July 1637, AAE, France, 827, fol. 239.
[2] Bullion to Richelieu, 29 Mar. 1637, ibid., 826, fol. 243.
[3] Aug. 1640, A. M. Boislisle, *Histoire de la maison de Nicolay* (Nogent-le-Rotrou, 1873), p. 405.
[4] Bullion to Richelieu, 24 July 1636, AAE, France, 821, fol. 104.
[5] 21 Sept. 1633, British Museum, Egerton Collection, MS. 1687, fol. 45.

relations with the lower administration would be valuable. Who was actually responsible for first coining the *louis* and the beautiful ten-*louis* pieces designed by Warin in 1640?[1] No text exchanged between the ministers has offered an answer to this question. Only a careful study of the *Hôtel des monnaies* would enable one to discover who made such decisions. But the inflationary policy of changing metal ratios was certainly made by Richelieu and his creatures, who pushed the Parlement to register the necessary edicts.[2]

The superintendents wrote to officers in provincial institutions as well, often on the basis of friendship mixed with business. The same was true with governors, generals, ambassadors; in short, there was no limited sphere of action. Finance was not the only matter which concerned them.

Louis's brief letters to the superintendents usually contain orders or requests for money. Louis never asked if there was money available; he simply requested it.[3] Often the king gave orders to the superintendents through Richelieu. He would write: 'Speak to Monsieur de Bullion to send funds with me [on a voyage] for the muster of the new companies of guards. . . .' Later, in the same letter, 'Madame de Lorraine is complaining a good deal about the bad treatment that she is receiving from Monsieur de Bullion concerning her pension. I wrote to him about it; you will say a word to him about it.'[4] This indicates Louis's attitude regarding financial problems and also shows how he made Richelieu supervise the actions of the other ministers.

[1] Mariéjol, op. cit., illustration 17, p. 330. See also the monumental *L'Economie mondiale et les frappes monétaires en France*, 1493–1680 (Paris, 1956), by F. C. Spooner, after which it should be possible to go further politically by studying the personnel of the *hôtels* and their relations with the *conseil*.

[2] Bullion to Richelieu, 1 Mar. 1635. 'Suivant vos commandements l'Edict de la reduction des monnoyes a esté mis entre les mains de Monsieur le Procureur General du Parlement dès lundy dernier, Monsieur Cornuel [a council secretary and later intendant of finance] luy a parlé et mesmes luy a faict cognoistre que l'estoit chose pressée.' AAE, France, 813, fol. 99. See Bullion's pleasure after Richelieu decided to bring the court to terms, 22 Mar. 1635, ibid., fol. 182.

[3] Louis to Bullion and Bouthillier, 1 Jan. 1636, AAE, France, 244, fol. 171, is a good example of many letters with the same tone and formality. Once, after Richelieu had proposed to Louis the raising of cavalry in a foreign country, the king accepted the idea and as an afterthought added: 'Et pour Monsieur de Bullion elle ne coute pas tant.' 12 Sept. 1634, ibid., fol. 66.

[4] Louis to Richelieu, 20 Aug. 1635, AAE, France, 244, fol. 131.

Louis carefully watched over his court budget, but there is no evidence that he assisted his ministers in meeting the financial crisis caused by the war.[1] In the great mass of letters which Richelieu wrote to the king, the real financial peril so carefully described to the cardinal by the superintendents was seldom mentioned or emphasized.[2] Louis may have been informed, however, for perhaps Richelieu and the superintendents did so in the *Conseil d'en haut*. The superintendents might also have directly informed the king of the precarious state of the treasury, but their correspondence with him has not survived.[3]

Even though Richelieu was principal minister, and Bullion his creature, he often turned to Louis for support against the wily old minister. The cardinal wrote to the king:

Monsieur de Bullion will go to see His Majesty tomorrow. It is absolutely necessary that it please him [Louis] to tell him that it is absolutely impossible that the troops which he [Louis] has in Holland can survive without an eighth muster. . . . Only Your Majesty can force this affair on Bullion, which is so important and necessary. . . .[4]

Richelieu needed the king's support in extracting money from the superintendents. He prepared the king for the superintendent's excuses, adding: 'If Monsieur de Bullion brings up the consequences [of an additional payment] on His Majesty's other troops, it would be easy for him to reply that they [the troops] are so separated from each other that their example cannot be of consequence to the others.'[5] As

---

[1] About his court budget, Louis wrote to Richelieu, 9 May 1636: 'J'ay donné ordre pour l'aumoine extraordinaire laquelle j'avance sur menus plesirs, mais il faut que Monsieur de Bullion me rembourse. . . .' AAE, France, 244, fol. 207.

[2] There are numerous references to momentary financial peril at a siege, of which Richelieu's letter to Louis of Nov. 1636, Avenel, ed. cit. v. ccclⅳ, is an example. But without describing the entire problem to Louis, Richelieu assumed the burden of financial responsibility often thrown upon him by the superintendents.

[3] Bullion's letter to Louis of 9 May 1636 supports the idea that the superintendents did inform the king, but only in a general way. This letter includes Bullion's explanation of the Rohan affair in the Grisons, where he attempted to place the burden of responsibility before the king on the cardinal, AAE, France, 820, fol. 258; also see below, p. 149.

[4] 2 Dec. 1635, Avenel, ed. cit. v. clxxv.

[5] Ibid. v. clxxv. On another occasion Richelieu wrote to Louis: 'Sire, la

a matter of fact, only the cardinal's favour with the king enabled him to impose on the superintendents what was essentially a ruinous financial policy for France. When it seemed that the superintendents were compromising the war effort, he had to seek help from the Crown.[1]

The cardinal's difficulties with finances, and consequently with the superintendents, partly resulted from his own opinions on finance. There is this frequently quoted comment written to Bullion:

> I confess fully my ignorance on financial matters, and realize that your [knowledge] is so vast, that the only advice which I can give you is to use those [people] whom you find most useful to the king's service, and [I] assure you that I will second you in every way I can. . . .[2]

In order to meet the Hapsburg threat and fulfil the *gloire* of Louis XIII, Richelieu plainly subordinated internal affairs to diplomacy and war. In doing so, he placed second in importance the evils resulting from financial affairs, tax administration, the sale of offices, excessive borrowing, and a host of lesser matters. The cardinal wrote to Sublet, who was busy supervising the construction of northern fortifications:

> If you lack cash, it is necessary rather to take it on interest, and I am offering sooner to do so myself by bond, having decided to do what I did at La Rochelle for immediate matters; that is, to find as much money as possible to advance the *service du roi*.[3]

Richelieu was prepared to place ends above means in financial matters, but he was confronted with faithful superintendents more conservative than he who, in spite of their efforts, could not amass sufficient funds to carry on the war properly.

After Richelieu and Servien began to go beyond the

lettre qu'il a pleu à Vostre Majesté m'escrire pour faire de nouvelles levées et la nécessité que l'on en a, ont réduict Monsieur de Bullion à y consentir. . . .' 8 July 1635, letter xlix of the same volume.

[1] Louis wrote to Richelieu, 14 Mar. 1636: 'J'ay escrit une lettre bien seche à Messieurs de Bulion et Boutilier sur le paiement des troupes de Hollande; je croy qu'ils en prendront l'alarme bien chaude.' AAE, France, 244, fol. 185.

[2] 23 Apr. 1635, Avenel, ed. cit. IV. cccxci.

[3] 23 Apr. 1635, ibid. IV. ccclxxxix.

36,000,000 *livres* budget established for war, instead of looking for a means to increase tax revenues generally, the cardinal and the superintendents turned to the sale of offices, *subventions générales*, reduction of *rentes*, reducing pensions, and borrowing money personally to pay for troops. As the war continued, each of these practices was extended to the maximum.

There is no evidence that either Richelieu or the ministers introduced really new tax schemes; they were content to push the old ones to extreme limits and to revive old rights that had been dropped in periods of weak central government. On one occasion—after edicts had been signed, sealed, and registered for levies on the clergy—the ecclesiastics sent an agent to negotiate the matter with Richelieu, who turned to Bullion for the necessary details. He wrote: 'I ask you to inform me sincerely up to what figure the said edicts may be [valued], and what you must really have, so that we may prevail upon them to find money in another way which they deem less prejudicial.'[1] Again Richelieu, as the principal minister, did the actual negotiating, but he depended upon the superintendents for the details of both the legislation and what the government expected to collect.[2]

When uprisings occurred, because of the rapacity of the *traitants*, Richelieu angrily wrote to the councillors:

If Messieurs of the Council continue to let the farmers and *traitants* unrestrainedly treat the king's subjects according to their own uncontrolled appetite, there will be some disorders in France similar to those in Spain. The Sables affair is an example. I could point out several others which they know as well as I. . . . In desiring too much we will reduce affairs to nothing, and have nothing at all, and in banishing commerce we will deprive France of that on which she has mainly survived. I place on Messieurs of the Council the responsibility for disorders which can happen by the malice of the *traitants* and others similar to them,

[1] Richelieu to Bullion, 2 Sept. 1639, ibid. vi. cclxxvi.

[2] Here again the principal purpose was to raise money, and Richelieu was not concerned with the exact enforcement of the edicts, a discrepancy that makes the study of finances in the *ancien régime* very difficult. This developed where direct taxation was incompatible with tradition. The idea was not lacking, e.g. the *taille*, which was old; but the 'absolute' government of Louis XIII was incapable of imposing any fundamental change on the three estates, especially in time of war.

and implore you to punish some of them so that the others will be constrained by their example.[1]

Bouthillier coldly and logically replied by explaining that in the Sables affair, if the Crown ceded the tax to those in rebellion there, the *subvention générale* and other taxes fixed by the Crown would be endangered in Guyenne, Languedoc, Dauphiné, Burgundy, Brittany, Béarn, Poitou, and other regions.[2]

Thanks to the work of Mousnier, the magnitude and importance of the sale of offices in the reign of Louis XIII is well known.[3] All that one may add is an outline of the role of the superintendents in the planning and execution of the numerous edicts for office creations. They often planned which offices were to be created, and then presented projects for Richelieu's review. Bullion wrote to Richelieu:

I have been working . . . for next year, and it is necessary that Your Eminence order what he wishes to be done on the extraordinary means [for raising revenue] for next year, which is [estimated at] fifty two millions. I have about thirty millions for and from the Parlements, provided that the merchandise [offices] will sell. We still need . . . twenty-two millions. When I have the honour to be with His Eminence I will show him by which way we can come out of it, according to my feeble counsels. . . .[4]

The superintendents, perhaps even more than Richelieu, urged the sovereign courts to register the edicts for new officers.[5] Bullion informed Richelieu:

We need four or five *lettres de cachet* to use against the President Maupeou and some councillors in the *Cour des Aides* if they continue in their rebellion. If we do not have the said letters the [new] presidents will not be established and we will not have the money that we planned for the million ordered to be sent to the army.[6]

---

[1] Richelieu to Séguier and Bouthillier, 10 Oct. 1641, Avenel, ed. cit. VI. ccccxlii.

[2] Bouthillier to Richelieu, 17 Oct. 1641, ibid. vi, p. 882: '. . . n'y ayant rien qui désespère d'avantage que l'inégalité des charges. . . .'

[3] Roland Mousnier, *La Vénalité des offices sous Henri IV et Louis XIII* (Rouen, 1945).

[4] 11 Oct. 1639, AAE, France, 834, fol. 93.

[5] See Bullion to Richelieu, 1 Mar. 1637, AAE, France, 826, fol. 194. Bullion may even have thought of establishing a Parlement at Nîmes to 'bring to reason' that of Toulouse, Bullion to Richelieu, 6 Apr. 1637, AAE, France, 826, fol. 257.   [6] Undated (Oct. 1636?), AAE, France, 822, fol. 75.

Bullion and Bouthillier informed the cardinal about the progress in the sale of offices. They not only planned the sale and watched over registrations in the courts, but they actually negotiated with prospective office buyers. Bouthillier remarked: 'I am assured of the sale of four of the new offices of *maître des requêtes* at 54,000 *écus* each. There are two of them left and I will have great difficulty in disposing of them as they are for the July quarter.'[1] Even when such officers died, and there was a question about conferring their *charges*, the superintendents advised Richelieu of the exact details in the *provisions*.[2]

While working to raise revenues, the superintendents also struggled to reduce expenditure. These reductions often took the form of war measures, and were temporary; but they led to certain reforms. Some of the numerous *rentes* were reformed according to Richelieu's counsel by giving fixed sums instead of assigning income from royal revenues,[3] permitting the Crown to control more effectively the income of the *rentiers* in war-time.

In the last years of Louis's reign, there was even a great effort to reduce temporarily the pensions given by the Crown. In 1641 over two million *livres* were cut from the incomes of courtiers, royal officers, and even the princes of the blood. Bouthillier negotiated with important pensioners to gain their approval and to use them as examples for the others. Meanwhile, all the treasurers, secretaries of state, superintendents of finance, and other officers were to have their pensions reduced by one-fourth.[4]

When all other means failed, Richelieu and the creatures personally borrowed money to pay for troops and fortifications. The cardinal had supreme powers in finance, but

[1] 1 Feb. 1642, AAE, France, 842, fol. 29.
[2] Bullion to Richelieu, 26 Sept. 1636, AAE, France, 821, fol. 326.
[3] Bullion to Richelieu: 'Nous travaillons au faict des rentes pour faire voir la verité des payements et que jamais Roy de France n'a fait à l'esgard des rentes ce que Sa Majesté a resolu en telle occasion par le bon advis de Vostre Eminence. Il fauldra Dieu aydant renvoyer dans chaque province les rentes constituées au lieu des droits et oultre cela adviser pour les autres rentes que le prevost des marchands du contentement des rentiers, fasse commetre des receveurs affin qu'ils voyent s'il tient au Roy ou à son conseil que les rentes ne se payent. . . .' 30 Mar. 1638? AAE, France, 830, fol. 86.
[4] Claude le Bouthillier to Richelieu, 9 Dec. 1641, AAE, France, 839, fols. 385 f.

even so he was powerless before budgets, customs, and the threat of revolt.[1] So he borrowed great sums, and maintained entire regiments himself. He asked the king through Claude le Bouthillier for a letter which would appear as a royal request to borrow money to raise six regiments and six companies of cavalry, in the event that Bullion made difficulties.[2] Richelieu dictated the letter word for word to his old friend, indicating that he counted on Bouthillier in the most intimate financial affairs.[3] The cardinal had made the request on 30 June 1635; on 18 July Servien woefully wrote to him that the 200,000 *écus* which he had furnished were already spent.[4]

The struggle continued. Richelieu wrote: 'The garrison of St. Quentin is breaking up because of lack of payment; and, although the superintendents could not, Monsieur de Noyers and I have found some money.'[5] Indeed, the secretaries often took the initiative when royal funds were lacking. Chavigny reported: 'I found on my credit 360,000 *livres* in this town.'[6] Such methods were at best only temporarily helpful, but remain a good example of the energy and resourcefulness of ministers in the *ancien régime* and the peculiar form which this *élan* took.

The position of the superintendents *vis-à-vis* the other ministers, and particularly the secretaries of state, placed the former in a dominant role. Together with Richelieu, they shared the struggle to meet army payments and other expenses, the scene of action being again the *Conseil du roi*. The superintendents limited the ambitious spending projects of the secretaries; but when the latter thought that their cause was good, they appealed directly to Richelieu for help

---

[1] Regarding supreme powers, Bullion wrote to Richelieu: 'J'estime que Vostre Eminence jugera à propos pour la recepte de nous donner de l'authorité depandante de vous [Richelieu and the king] seuls, [les] commandements pour la despense.' 6 Sept. 1638, AAE, France, 831, fol. 199.

[2] Richelieu to Claude le Bouthillier, 30 June 1635, Avenel, ed. cit. v. xli.

[3] But was the letter really meant for Bullion? It might well have been used to induce *honestes gens* to lend Richelieu money. Richelieu to Louis, 8 July 1635, ibid. v. xlix.

[4] 18 July 1635, AAE, France, 815, fol. 7.

[5] To Chavigny, 24 Aug. 1636, Avenel, ed. cit., v, p. 988.

[6] 8 July 1642, AAE, France, 843, fol. 58. He was in Lyon. See BN, Clairambault, MS. 385, fol. 36.

against Bullion and Bouthillier.[1] In numerous references the secretary, on his word, could not make the superintendents order a payment from the treasury.[2] In spite of the co-operation and mutual trust among the creatures of Richelieu, only royal letters, properly signed and sealed, were effective.[3]

The secretary of state for war and the superintendents worked together, but kept separate accounts of army expenditure as a form of control between the two ministers. Bullion kept muster lists showing the number of troops and their type, and other ministers also used them. When the superintendents wanted a new *contrôle* giving sizes and conditions of the armies, the principal minister turned to the secretary of state for war for the details.[4] In return, the superintendents sent the secretary a statement showing all unpaid credits for the armies.[5]

---

[1] Servien (his secretary's hand) wrote to Richelieu, 30 ? July 1635 : 'Ayant expedié l'ordonnance pour la levée des compagnies d'augmentation au Régiment des Gardes, Monsieur de Bulion a faict difficulté d'en faire le fonds, sur ce qu'il dict que Monseigneur luy a faict l'honneur de luy dire qu'elle seroit payée. . . .' AAE, France, 815, fol. 48.

[2] Sometimes controversies arose between the officers, and as a result the secretaries took measures into their own hands and ordered payments without passing through the superintendents. Servien wrote to Richelieu : 'Il s'est presenté une difficulté au payement des troupes de Monsieur de Vignolles dont la cavalerie s'est trouvée fort complete et le fonds deffectueux [and so that they will] . . . ne tomber pas dans les longueurs qui eussent peu faire dissiper les troupes j'ay commandé l'affaire sur le champ avec le tresorier lequel sur ma parolle a renvoyé un nouveau fonds pour payer lesdites troupes . . . comme il a fallu pour la descharge du tresorier une ordonnance du Roy pour passer pardessus la regle de Messieurs les Surintendants il fault pour la mienne qu'il plaise à Son Eminence m'en envoyer un commandement de sa part. . . .' 19 Nov. 1635, AAE, France, 816, fol. 132.

[3] Particularly payments to be made in foreign countries. See Richelieu to Chavigny, 18 Aug. 1638, Avenel, ed. cit. VI. lix.

[4] Richelieu to Servien : 'Monsieur Servien m'envoyera, s'il luy plaist, l'estat par le menu des trente cinq ou trente six mille hommes et six cens chevaux qui sont en garnison, parce que sans cela il m'est impossible de faire le controolle que désire Monsieur de Bullion. Et avec ledit estat je justifieray clairement qu'avec toutes nos nouvelles levées les despenses de la guerre n'excèdent point les cent trente deux mil hommes que Messieurs les surintendans ont faict estat de payer l'année 1635.' 21 July 1635, ibid. v. lix.

[5] Bullion also specified that Sublet de Noyers was to show the statement to Richelieu. 'J'ay envoié et envoie encores à Monsieur de Noyers l'estat de tout ce qui est deub tant pour l'armée, garnisons, qu'autres despenses tant par l'espargne que sur les subsistances et prie Monsieur de Noyers de le faire voir à Vostre Eminence.' Bullion to Richelieu, 6 Oct. 1639, AAE, France, 834, fol. 87.

The superintendents acted with the chancellor in council decisions, helped formulate policies of the Crown regarding the sovereign courts, and negotiated together on various matters including wheat purchases.[1] Together, their range of action was practically unlimited, and after those of the king and Richelieu, their powers were the greatest in the realm.

In the following chapters various aspects of the position of the superintendents of finance will be discussed in more detail. To great officers in the realm, a certain independence—not only from Richelieu but from the royal authority itself—was possible, owing to the nature of their duties in finance.

[1] Bullion to Séguier, 28 Oct. 1636, BN, nouvelles acquisitions, MS. 6210, fol. 72.

VII

Claude de Bullion, Superintendent of Finance

I N 1857 Caillet remarked: 'The administration of Bullion
and Bouthillier was not marked by any financial measure
worthy of mention. They had recourse to the usual expedients when ordinary revenues were insufficient, that is,
creating *rentes*, selling offices, and so forth.'[1] No generalization could be more accurate from the point of view of
institutional development or reform. Nothing new was
added, and old administrative evils were pushed to extremes.
This, however, was only part of the story.

When Bullion proclaimed it impossible to find, annually,
more than 40 million *livres* in cash for the royal treasury, it
was not so much an apology as a statement of achievement
under trying conditions.[2] The contrast between Caillet's
analysis and Bullion's statement sets the tone for this
chapter. For Louis and his ministers, and for Richelieu in
particular, financial policy was not a question of means but
of ends. The superintendents were fully aware of the disastrous results of their policies; but in the face of an ever
increasing demand for money, no broad and general reform
could have been formulated. The question arises: if a real
reform of taxes and tax administration had been proposed,
would the Crown have had the power to enact it and fight
the Hapsburgs at the same time? Later, the fate of one
attempt at reform will be noted in the relations and activities
of Bullion in the ministry of Richelieu. The ultimate control
of finance in the realm was at stake.

When the superintendency was held jointly, as it was

---

[1] J. Caillet, *De l'administration en France sous le ministère du Cardinal de
Richelieu* (Paris, 1857), p. 271.

[2] Bullion to Richelieu, 7 Nov. 1635, AAE, France, 811, fol. 120. The
following spring he wrote: 'Il nous fault trouver jusques à cinq millions et
peut dire que je suis fier de moymesme quand je voy ces despenses en argent
content [comptant] au temps où nous sommes. . . .' 28 Mar. 1636, AAE,
France, 820, fol. 178.

several times under Louis XIII, there was no division of
duties or authority between the two officers. They worked
on the same problems, signed the same documents, often
wrote letters in common, and advised the king *en conseil*
together.[1] This did not mean, however, that one of the
superintendents was not more influential than the other.
For reasons of age, intelligence, experience, political friendships, and prestige, Claude de Bullion was more influential
from the very beginning, when he and Bouthillier took office
in 1632, and he continued to be foremost until 1640.

In 1632 Louis XIII could probably not remember when
Bullion had first joined that inner circle of courtiers always
surrounding the king or regent in the *ancien régime*. The
wily old councillor had spent more years in the service of
the Crown than any of the other ministers, and he was not
one to let them forget it.[2] He enjoyed great prestige, had
a good sense of humour, but was occasionally given to fits
of anger and despair. Constantly at work in the councils,
except during occasional attacks of gout, Bullion by 1635
appeared as a grizzled and portly old man in his sixties.[3] He
had great patience with governmental problems and a mind
for details, and was eager to perform his duties without
ever thinking of bold reforms.[4] In spite of the financial
tempests which burst about him, Bullion remained at his

[1] It has not been possible to determine if the superintendents were obliged
to consult each other when one of them did not attend the king's council.
Because of Bullion's greater influence, Bouthillier more frequently commented that he would have to consult his colleague before making a decision.
However, there is evidence that Bullion consulted Bouthillier.

[2] This was true even with Chancellor Séguier, who was some twenty years
younger than Bullion. The relationship between the two men is impossible
to describe in detail, because the letters received by Bullion have largely
disappeared, and he does not figure among the correspondents of Séguier in
that part of the chancellor's letters in the BN.

[3] See the small engraving by B. Moncornet, and also the 'Ceremony of
the Ordre du Saint Esprit in 1633', painted by Philippe de Champaigne in the
Musée des Augustins, Toulouse.

[4] There was one great exception. After reflecting on the financial chaos
brought on by the years of war, Bullion prepared a *mémoire* in which he carefully described how the Crown's finances should be administered as *before* the
war. This meant cutting the cash expenditures and returning to the old system
of assigning payments to revenues. He also expressed a desire for more
accurate revenue inventories, indicating that he himself was probably unsure
of just what resources the Crown had at its disposal. BN, Collection Cinq
Cents Colbert, 194, fol. 273 (copy).

CLAVDE DE BVILLION *Conseiller du Roy en ses Conseils,*
Commandeur et garde des seaux des ordres de sa Mayeste,
et surintendant des finances de France.
B. Moncornet excū

post, thinking that 'with God's help and a little time' every-thing would come out all right. One can never quite be sure that Bullion felt as desperate and worried as his letters to Richelieu seem to show him. The situation was certainly grave, but Bouthillier, whether for personal or administrative reasons, never reflected the same anguish and despair, yet he held the office under the same conditions.

There was never a question of open disobedience to Richelieu or of an open challenge to his superior authority based upon his relationship with Louis XIII, but Bullion often thwarted Richelieu's will, and Louis's too, because of confusion over financial details. He did not keep them properly informed of all his actions, and he often brushed aside the cardinal's orders after having solemnly promised to carry them out. This was not done openly. Behind the innumerable details of different armies, budgets, assignations, ordinary and extraordinary revenues, Bullion exercised broad powers, even though the king and the cardinal easily held the power to bring him to his knees or even to disgrace him. It is not easy to describe Bullion's touch-and-go insubordination.

As the war dragged on and his task of paying for it became more and more difficult, there was a marked evolution in Bullion's thinking. In 1635 there was already a tone of pessim-ism in his letters,[1] but in the end he not only questioned his own policies, but also feared a national collapse if peace were not made. He wrote to Richelieu in 1639: 'Expenditure in cash is up to at least 40 millions, the *traitants* are abandoning us, and the masses will not pay either the new or the old taxes. We are now at the bottom of the pot . . . and I fear that our foreign war is degenerating into a civil war.'[2]

---

[1] 23 Apr. 1635: 'Je suis tres ayse que Monseigneur n'aie eu desagréable ce que je luy ay escrit; j'ay très bonne résolution, Dieu merci, mais je vous advoue que le fardeau est si pesant que je crains de succomber tout à fait. Si Monseigneur se resoult d'executer ce qu'il luy a pleu résoudre pour les 40 millions du content [comptant], et le nombre des 132 mil hommes et 12 mil et tant de chevaux, soyez asseuré qu'avec l'ayde de Dieu tout ira bien, et que cela me donnera la vie. Si au contraire, les affaires tombent en désordre, ce que je ne veux croire, ayant trop de confiance en la prudence et prevoyance de Mon-seigneur, que je ne survivray guere un tel malheur.' AAE, France, 813, fol. 301.

[2] 25 Oct. 1639, Richelieu, *Lettres, instructions diplomatiques, et papiers d'État*, ed. by M. Avenel (Paris, 1853–77), vi, p. 608.

On more than one occasion Bullion indicated that he was not as resolute a warrior as Richelieu.

Bullion was always a respectful creature; but confronted with insuperable financial difficulties, he hinted to Richelieu that he longed for peace:

I pray God that Your Eminence has good news from Turin, because the truce or peace depends on those two fortifications. If God will give . . . Your Eminence the grace to establish a good and assured rest for France and for Christianity. . . . Your Eminence by giving order to public affairs [will cause] the name of Your Eminence to be respected and revered for ever, and your *règlements* and reforms [would be] followed and maintained to the last point. May God give us the grace to see this golden century.[1]

Here Bullion summarized the old problem which had haunted Richelieu, the diplomatist, warrior, and internal reformer, ever since he had become influential in the council of Louis XIII. To choose between these different roads to *gloire* was probably a difficult decision for the cardinal. But as Bullion correctly noted, the decision was not all Richelieu's; it depended upon French arms, diplomacy, and the capacity of the Hapsburgs to make war. To understand Bullion in particular, it is important to notice the pressure on Richelieu within the ministry itself to make peace. This was done gently but firmly by emphasizing an alternative to military and diplomatic *gloire*.

Richelieu retained much of his affection and confidence in Bullion right up to the latter's death, but his dissatisfaction with him increased slowly over the years and especially when the lack of money forced the superintendents to raise taxes which might bring on revolt. The cardinal refused to accept responsibility for such measures before the king.[2] He wrote ironically: 'I have often heard it said to Monsieur de Bullion that only the word of the superintendents enables them to find money. If that is so, and I hold it to be true, Messieurs of the Council must recognize that nothing is more necessary than that the king hold the hearts of his subjects.'[3] This was a frequent theme in Richelieu's letters

---

[1] 11 Aug. 1640, AAE, France, 836, fol. 25.
[2] Richelieu to Louis, 29 Mar. 1637, Avenel, ed. cit. v. cdxxix.
[3] Richelieu to Bullion and Bouthillier, 21 Aug. 1638, ibid. vi. lxiii.

to the superintendents, but he himself rarely grappled with the problem of raising revenues.

Bullion agreed with Richelieu when the latter complained about the tax measures made by the superintendents, but he saw no alternative while faced with the exigencies of war. Bullion wrote to the cardinal:

Our calamity is that we no longer have a choice between good means [to raise money] because of past expenditure—the present expenditure cannot be met without extraordinary means. It is necessary to find forty millions every year because of advances made in cash... while [we] have just so much money and so many places where it is to be distributed. I am beside myself most of the time . . . but with the support of Your Eminence, I will do the impossible and take for my motto: *Te stante virebo.*[1]

Bullion made every effort to support the war, risking his own prestige by unpopular measures and in turn incurring Richelieu's wrath because of them.

Even if Bullion assumed the responsibility of finding the means to pay for the war, he did not stop with tactful references to peace and internal reform. Forcing him to order the treasury to make a payment was a difficult task; only Louis and Richelieu could bring him to authorize expenditure when he was reluctant, and in some cases the cardinal even sought the king's help against Bullion.[2] Aside from such dramatic crises, Bullion daily fought increased expenditure on every front. He informed Richelieu of council deliberations in such a way that the gloomy side was nearly always emphasized; when ambassadors or generals requested additional funds, Bullion was ready with a battery of figures indicating what had already been spent on each project. He would describe these disbursements in detail, emphasizing their magnitude, but without giving information on the success or value of the project in question. Often the executor of a particular project was an ambassador or general in the field who found it difficult to defend himself. In 1636, when Hémery requested more money for Italian affairs, Bullion did not openly oppose him, but his pressure to keep

[1] Bullion to Richelieu, 6 July 1640, ibid. vi, p. 707.
[2] See above, p. 135.

expenditure down was real when he emphasized how much had already been spent in Italy. He wrote to Richelieu:

> I do not want to go into despair when I think how difficult this year has been. . . . Your Eminence knows that more than 150,000 *écus* have already been spent in Italy. Monsieur d'Hémery wrote to me that he had taken money by credit letters for bread. I beseech Your Eminence to remember that at the beginning of the year Monsieur d'Hémery was paid 380 thousand odd *livres* for wheat. . . .[1]

Then Bullion described Hémery's new requests. Objection on principle was out of the question on most items, but the lack of funds obliged the superintendents to urge Richelieu to be thrifty.

With general military expenditure Bullion was even more bold. He wrote to Richelieu:

> If it were permitted for a servant to give his opinion to his master, I should say that half a muster payment to the officers and two payments to the soldiers would be enough, while using the remainder [in the budget] for wheat and other army expenses and necessities. Otherwise everything will remain [as planned], for when Your Eminence returns it will be necessary to decide to hold a council to consider what can be done for next year.[2]

The significance of this letter lies in providing an example of the rapid conclusions often reached by Bullion. He began by making a suggestion, and in the next breath stated that his suggestion was going to be carried out; but at least he was kind enough to inform Richelieu that there would be no other change in the plans. Richelieu was not consulted on the change; and in any case it would have been difficult for him to act quickly to restore the cut funds, because he was at that moment in the provinces on a military campaign.

The cardinal frequently chided Bullion for not doing what he had requested in the name of the king. Sometimes Bouthillier was also criticized. For example, in April 1636 Richelieu wrote to both superintendents: 'There are some affairs where we lose one hundred per cent. by putting off or deferring. A long time ago I pressed Messieurs the Superintendents to be so good as to give an afternoon to clearing up

---

[1] 18 Oct. 1636, AAE, France, 822, fol. 73.   [2] Ibid., fol. 73.

all claims from all the foreigners who are each in the pay of the king. . . .'[1] He pressed them to pay needy troops immediately, which often forced Bullion to juggle funds destined for other purposes to accounts where they could be promptly disbursed. This only postponed inevitable shortages. Richelieu once ordered Bullion: 'It is absolutely necessary to replace promptly the funds which were destined for the fortifications and munitions of the Val Telline, which were used for the musters of troops which arrived there.'[2] In a letter to Richelieu the next day, Bullion flatly denied that the funds had been transferred.[3] There was considerable controversy over the matter, and Bullion was reprimanded.[4]

As the months and years dragged on, the Duc de Rohan, commander in the Val Telline, suffered a defeat when the people of the Grisons went over to the Hapsburgs in March 1637. Richelieu informed Louis XIII of the disaster, and after throwing off all personal responsibility, blamed it on the lack of money and on *Messieurs des finances*.[5] But he saved his wrath for Bullion:

Only God knows if the Swiss will revolt against us for lack of money; God knows if following that Italy will hold firm; God

---

[1] 5 Apr. 1636, Avenel, ed. cit. v. ccxviii.   [2] 15? May 1635, ibid. v. v.

[3] 'Je responds à Vostre Eminence qu'il n'a esté diverty aucune chose du fonds destiné pour les fortifications et munitions des Grisons. . . .' 16 May 1635 (the letter is misdated), AAE, France, 820, fol. 271.

[4] Rohan wrote to Louis, 27 Apr. 1636: 'C'est avec un extreme regret que je reitere à Vostre Majesté les instances que je luy ay desja faites diverses fois de la misère de son armée. Mais j'y suis forcé par la pure necessité affin que la ruyne qui en est inevitable ne me soit imputée . . . la monstre de janvier pour un mois seulement tant pour les françoys qu'éstrangers, est arrivée icy le vingtiesme d'avril . . . les deux deffauts de ce desordre proviennent l'un de ce que Messieurs les Surintendans n'envoient jamais l'argent de la monstre suivant l'extraict des commissaires et controlleurs, mais selon ce qu'ils se persuadent qu'on peut estre de monde, tellement qu'il y a tousjours manque de fonds pour plus de deux mille soldats en chaque monstre. . . . Sy vostre Majesté, Sire, veut prendre la peine d'ouir Monsieur Doujat qui esté intendant des finances l'année passée en ceste armée. . . . Je n'ay manqué d'envoyer divers mémoires de nos necessités à Messieurs les Surintendans mais ou le peu de creance qu'ils ont en moy, ou bien d'autres considerations ausquelles je ne penetre plus. . . .' AAE, Grisons, 9, fol. 52. Many others asked the same question as Rohan. Was it because the superintendents ignored the pleadings of officers or generals, or were there other factors which obliged them to neglect fundamental needs?

[5] 29 Mar. 1637, Avenel, ed. cit. v. cdxxix.

knows if we will find safety in peace; and Monsieur de Bullion knows better than anyone else if he will find the millions in Switzerland necessary to carry on the war. This blow has occurred because of lack of money; for one *écu* that it was necessary to give at the right moment, it will now take ten, and even more will not repair the loss that we have made. I have been preaching to *Messieurs des Finances* for a long time that there are certain privileged things where you must see ahead of events before a catastrophe makes us recognize the peril. . . . Monsieur de Bullion will remember that he gave nothing for fortifications for 1635 and 1636, and that funds given in 1635 are neither paid nor assured.[1]

Richelieu could not have summarized more clearly his lack of real control over finances if he had wished. In spite of strict orders from the cardinal dating back to May 1635, Bullion had gone his own way.

To circumvent opposition from the superintendents, and particularly from Bullion, Richelieu took steps to oblige his creatures to act within the traditional framework of the councils. He also appealed to officials in the army and provinces to inform him directly when they were in financial difficulty.[2]

The first real effort to curb Bullion's powers was the *règlement des finances* of July 1638.[3] The story of the enactment is particularly interesting, not only for Richelieu's relations with Bullion, but also for the manner in which it was prepared and the significance given to it by the superintendent.

Bullion did not readily accept the new *règlement*. It was clearly aimed at him, for he had to prepare it according to Richelieu's suggestions. No reference is made to Bouthillier in the correspondence preparing this *règlement*. Richelieu confided to Bouthillier at the moment: 'As for the mood of Monsieur de Bullion, we must let it pass without worrying about it when it is bad. He told me that he would approve the *règlement*; if he has other ideas, he is wrong.'[4] Richelieu's

[1] 28 Mar. 1637, Avenel, ed. cit. v. cdxxviii.

[2] Chastillon, for example, was encouraged to seek Richelieu's help against Bullion, 6 May 1637, ibid. v, p. 1028.

[3] To our knowledge the *règlement* has never been published. See Appendix B. The document, undoubtedly a first copy which was later modified, is written entirely in Bullion's hand and is signed by him. AAE, France, 830, fol. 261.

[4] 20 July 1638, Avenel, ed. cit. vi. xliii.

confidence in Bouthillier, Bullion's own colleague, is evidence of Bouthillier's immunity and also an indication of the peculiar position of Bouthillier between Richelieu and Bullion.

Bullion wrote to Richelieu on 19 July 1638 that he had spoken to the king about the *règlement*, and that he was sending a draft of it to him, made in accordance with Richelieu's desires.[1] In preparing his draft, Bullion probably added an article to the effect that the *règlement* of 1629 must also be enforced. Furthermore, the document restated the older custom obliging the superintendents to administer in the council, and added other controls governing negotiations with *traitants*.

After reviewing the document, Richelieu prepared a letter to Bullion stating that he approved the modifications and additions made by the superintendent. The cardinal then presented the projected *règlement* to Louis, who was not pleased to see what he suspected was a reference to the *Code Michaud*, the *règlement* of 1629.[2] Later the same day, Richelieu rewrote his letter to Bullion and explained the king's objections by commenting: 'The deceased Monsieur de Marillac often said that he could not observe it [the *Code Michaud*] and did not know why Monsieur d'Effiat had had it made.'[3] Bullion must have added the article about the *Code Michaud*, even though it was not among the original suggestions made by Richelieu, for in rewriting his letter the cardinal asked Bullion to explain the whole matter and inform him of the exact contents of the *Code Michaud*.[4]

Bullion, who had faithfully promised to uphold the *règlement* and the clause in question, which he himself had added, admitted just two days later that he needed to look up the *Code* to find out what it stated. He replied to Richelieu in embarrassment: 'I received the *règlement* that Your

---

[1] AAE, France, 830, fol. 259. Bullion was probably referring to the draft written and signed by him, published below in Appendix B.

[2] Richelieu to Bullion, 20 July 1638, Avenel, ed. cit. VI. xliv.

[3] Ibid. VI. xliv.

[4] Ibid. VI. xliv. The *Code Michaud* was certainly the *règlement* intended by Bullion, for he referred to it as the *règlement* of Jan. 1629, precisely the time when the *Code* was promulgated. Louis himself only suspected that Bullion's *règlement* of 1629 was the *Code Michaud*, but he was right.

Eminence has sent me, and I will not fail to obey. I will particularly look up the *Code Michaud*—there are many good things in it which cut short the disorders which come up only too often.'[1] This incident—the haphazard preparation of the *règlement*, and especially Bullion's careless attitude toward it—raises the whole problem of the place of such documents in the administrative thinking of the time.

During the negotiations over the *règlement*, Bullion became concerned over a family problem which, as a result of the custom of the times, eventually made him vulnerable to Richelieu. No officer with such power and prestige was permitted to arrange for the marriage of his children without the king's approval. This sometimes was no mere formality. Bullion wrote to Richelieu that he had spoken to Louis about the marriage of his son, but that the king's reply had been very vague.[2] Bullion then asked Richelieu to use his influence to gain royal approval. Three months later Richelieu wrote to Bullion that he would speak to the king about the marriage.[3] Still a month later, that is, four months after Bullion had first spoken to the king, the affair was not yet settled. Bullion pleaded: 'I beg Monseigneur to remember his servant's affair, and to excuse a father if he cares for his children. This whole matter is without prejudice to public interest. I confess that I will work more light-heartedly [once the matter is settled].'[4] But time passed.

Finally, in January 1639, a half year after the first request, Richelieu came to terms with Bullion. He wrote:

Before proposing the marriage of Bullion's son to the king, I request him to take action on the following:

Firstly, to despoil himself of the passions which he [Bullion] sometimes gives vent to against one person or another, and to examine and settle all sorts of affairs reasonably.

Secondly, to limit carefully his fortune to the wealth he now possesses so that in the future he will desire no increase, thus contenting himself by serving the king in the *charge* which he holds, with the income and emoluments of it, according to the

---

[1] Bullion to Richelieu, 21 July 1638, AAE, France, 830, fol. 266. On the *Code Michaud* see J. Mariéjol, op. cit., VI, part 2, p. 427.

[2] 19 July 1638, AAE, France, 830, fol. 259.

[3] 22 Oct. 1638, Avenel, ed. cit. VI. cxxx.

[4] 28 Dec. 1638, AAE, France, 831, fol. 396.

limits to which they have been restricted by the *règlement* made by His Majesty on July 16, 1638.[1]

In the third place, to re-establish the old order, according to which one must not make any disbursements of any sort, be it for the purpose of gifts, secret, foreign, or otherwise, or for the commissions or contracts made in the *conseil*, unless one keeps a minute of it, passed in the *conseil de trois* in three months, signed by Messieurs the Chancellor, the superintendents, and all the intendants [of finance]; three copies will be made of the minute,[2] the first for the treasurer [of the *épargne*], the second for Messieurs the Superintendents, and the third for Monsieur the Chancellor. The entire process [is to be] as was practised previously to the bad innovation of burning the minutes of cash disbursements, made in this procedure since the Sieur de Cornuel has been in office [January 1634].

In the fourth place, to apply himself as carefully to financial reform and the relief of the people, as he did to his personal affairs before he took over those of the public. He is requested to do this, not only because of the public interest, but also so that he may one day be as opulent in heaven as he is on earth; this is the best wish which a person who loves him as I do can make.[3]

Bullion quickly accepted this stern but affectionate offer to come to terms by swearing to uphold the *mémoire*, which he quickly signed and returned to Richelieu.[4] The cardinal then speedily arranged the marriage for Bullion.[5]

[1] This was the *règlement* just discussed. The draft prepared by Bullion has no provisions limiting his income, hence Richelieu and Louis must have added them to the final document. In any event, Richelieu was not sure that Bullion was enforcing these provisions, as is evidenced by his inclusion of the same issue here six months later.

[2] Here there is a note in the margin: 'Je seray bien aise d'en avoir une copie.'

[3] 10? Jan. 1639, Avenel, ed. cit. vi. clviii.

[4] Bullion answered: 'Je remercie monseigneur le cardinal des bons avis cy-dessus qu'il luy plaist me donner, que je recognois nécessaires et justes pour le bien de l'Estat et mon salut particulier. Et luy promets, sur mon honeur, d'observer de point en point ce qui est convenu au dict mémoire, sans y contrevenir, ny soufrir qu'il y soit contrevenu en quelque façon que ce puisse estre.' Ibid. vi, p. 272.

[5] Chavigny wrote to La Valette, 28 Feb. 1639: 'Le filz de Monsieur de Bullion fut marié hier avec la fille de Madame la Marquise de Toussi. Monseigneur le Cardinal a fait ce mariage et ne laisse pourtant pas d'estre dans les sentiments pour le bonhomme où vous l'avez veu autrefois. Monsieur de Bullion doit se tenir à cette heure bien assuré par les exemples de Messieurs de Puylaurent et de La Valette.' AAE, Sardaigne, 28, fol. 87.

The cardinal cleverly used personal elements in the life of the superintendent to impose his will on this officer and thereby on the administration of finances. Bullion continued to be responsible to Louis and Richelieu, but he also continued to be vague in describing his actions. He was left great freedom of action in executing the orders given by the Crown. In theory, administrative practices were formal and fixed in the *ancien régime*, but in reality they were loose and easily adaptable for personal ends by strong officers.

Bullion was bound by the customs of his office and by those of the councils through which he acted, but there was always room for personal initiative. Richelieu knew this and sometimes took advantage of it, as in a mysterious case when he ordered Bullion to borrow money secretly and cover up the affair somewhere in the complicated details of the budget.[1] If the superintendent was able to carry on such irregular practices for the Crown, there was nothing to stop him from doing the same for himself and his friends. Richelieu, too, who was obliged to act secretly on occasion, compromised his own freedom of action by confiding in Bullion, who also knew very well that the cardinal's wealth was increasing rapidly out of the confusion between the king's and Richelieu's personal wealth. No aspect of the financial administration, however, was beyond Bullion's authority. Along with Bouthillier, he directed taxation policies, revenue collection, borrowing, and expenditure of all kinds. This was done in the framework of the councils and subject to the approval of the king and the principal minister. But in the realm of finance, with its many details and complications, few councillors were capable of challenging their decisions, because of the superintendents' prestige and knowledge of details. Louis and Richelieu exercised careful control, but again, it was supervisory, for neither of them was familiar with the necessary procedure in following day-to-day affairs.

[1] Bullion wrote to Richelieu: 'Sur le commandement de Vostre Eminence j'ay emprunté de touts costés affin de faire les six cent mil livres dont j'ay donné les lettres de change à Monsieur d'Ossenville pour Lyon avec l'ordre des deux cent mil livres dont personne ne doibt en sçavoir et je prends le pretexte pour des despenses secrettes de bleds et autres munitions . . .' (no date, but shortly after the death of the Duc de Saxe-Weymar in 1639), AAE, France, 834, fol. 11.

Illustrations of the unique position of the superintendents are found in their daily problems. Bullion and Bouthillier were the chief negotiators with the *traitants*, those who contracted to pay a fixed sum for the privilege of collecting certain taxes. When the authority of the Crown was strained by rebellion or an unpopular war, the *traitants* did not pay outstanding debts to the Crown. Bullion coerced them, but sometimes he was unsuccessful. He wrote to Richelieu: 'I am trying to hurry up people here and there who owe the king thousands, but it is with little success because money is being held up by the richest people for the purchase of offices.'[1] Often the actions of not only the *traitants* but of the government itself were paralysed by other factors, and in this case one government effort was failing because of another government policy.

Bullion frequently found it impossible to borrow money for the Crown, because of a massive sale of offices which he and the council had arranged. He wrote to Richelieu:

All money is held up for office purchases. If it please God, and with the king's and your authority, we will surmount this. We have about twenty millions to collect in the next two months; whatever the sympathy and harshness that we may show, the debtors affirm their willingness, but be that as it may, they [the *traitants*] cannot collect money. . . . If the penury continues, and there is every appearance that it will because of the suspension of commerce and the transfer of money out of the kingdom (from which immense sums have been transported in the last three years), I think that it will be necessary to manufacture *douzains*[2] in order to furnish the provinces of Champagne, Picardy, Normandy, and others, to facilitate trade and payments of troops. . . . The farmers of the salt tax, who are the richest, say that the masses owe them three or four millions, because the lack of money keeps them from paying.[3]

But this was only part of the story. The war was going badly. In 1636, the disastrous year of Corbie, government finances worsened because royal debtors feared a military collapse. After describing his great difficulties in borrowing money, Bullion joyously hoped that the good news from

[1] 18 Jan. 1636, AAE, France, 820, fol. 39.
[2] See above, p. 129.
[3] 31 Dec. 1635, AAE, France, 816, fol. 199.

Corbie after a victory 'would give heart to our financiers. With God's help, here we are in the month of October, and the general revenues are lacking so it is necessary to take cash to pay the expenses of the [royal] households. . . .'[1] It is difficult to know if Bullion was describing the financial condition of the realm with any degree of accuracy. The problem is inevitably tied to economic and social conditions in the last decade of the reign.[2]

Financial difficulties were due to the lack of money rather than to Bullion's capriciousness, though Richelieu often blamed the superintendents. Examples of disintegrating armies, work stoppage on fortifications, and diplomatic setbacks abound; and on such occasions either Richelieu or one of the other ministers declared that the lack of money was responsible. More often it was Richelieu who complained and held the superintendents responsible for such disasters. He well realized the fundamental problem, the lack of money, but he also accused Bullion and Bouthillier of poor planning and even hinted that they were dipping too deeply into the public coffers.

After having received a long *mémoire* from Bullion listing what he proposed to pay for troops and other liabilities,[3] Richelieu burst out angrily:

It is impossible to keep garrisons if we do not pay them in cash. I well know that *Messieurs des Finances* will say that they have made plans, but such stories are useless if we do not have the money in advance. And now I have just learned that one of the forts in the realm being eyed by the enemy is in very bad condition because the garrison is completely disbanded owing to non-payment. It is really much easier for *Messieurs des Finances* to collect money than for us [to collect] men. Once money is collected it does not get lost, but soldiers once assembled disperse immediately if they are not paid.[4]

But the lack of organization and planning in advance was only half the complaint. Commenting on a decision to cut

[1] Bullion to Richelieu, 1 Oct. 1636, AAE, France, 822, fol. 2.
[2] The literature on this subject is profuse. See the summary of the conflicting interpretations of the result of economic conditions made by Mousnier, 'Recherches sur les Soulevements Populaires en France avant la Fronde', *Revue d'Histoire Moderne et Contemporaine*, 1958.
[3] *Mémoire* by Bullion to Richelieu, Nov. 1638? AAE, France, 831, fol. 327.
[4] 18 Nov. 1638, Avenel, ed. cit. VI. cxliii.

in half the salaries of the *prévôts des maréchaux*, about which Bullion had written in his *mémoire*, Richelieu answered:

Thefts are so frequent that there could not be any more, and all the trouble comes from the cut in the income of the *prévôts des maréchaux* and their archers. His Majesty considers that it would be better to take the entire incomes of *Messieurs des Finances*, or at least deprive them of illicit profits, which are worth much more than their salaries. I know well enough that the first reply that I will have on these matters will be an exclamation about the difficulty of finding money. I know also that the second will be a verbal promise to execute everything. But on the last one, we sometimes build many hopes without result. I request Monsieur de Bullion to give us results which will remove all room for doubt from our good hopes. I am sure that he will do it, if he considers that I wish him to take up the king's affairs with the same passion and ardour that he demonstrates in his own.[1]

Richelieu exercised his authority, but it was necessarily vague, because of his lack of information on all aspects of the financial administration.

Bullion's problems, however, were real. He battled continually with dozens of men seeking money from the royal treasury for numerous reasons, most of which were legitimate. He fulfilled the responsibility of meeting the requirements, and only when matters seemed to have reached the breaking-point would he call upon Richelieu for help. He wrote to the cardinal:

The principal difficulty before us is whether we should make prisoners of all the *traitants*. The entire Council of Finance and especially Monsieur the Treasurer are protesting about the complete ruin of finances with regard to the *traitants*. If we put pressure on them, then most of them would go bankrupt; it would seem appropriate that your Eminence have a council held in his presence where you will take the trouble to hear them all, and afterward Your Eminence would make any decision which he pleased with His Majesty, which we will have executed immediately. We need a declaration to increase the value of the money—requesting Your Eminence to write to Monsieur the Chancellor about it so that he may send it.[2]

[1] Ibid. VI. cxliii. Avenel rightly concluded that Richelieu was referring to Bullion's struggle over the marriage of his son in the last line.
[2] Bullion and Bouthillier to Richelieu, 22 Feb. 1636, AAE, France, 820,

These were measures of desperation, and when Bullion asked for a council over which Richelieu would preside, it took place. The cardinal usually suggested some expedient which temporarily relieved the financial crisis. From the modern viewpoint, the French and indeed others as well seemed to be fighting haphazardly in the Thirty Years War. It was not a national effort, and in turn there was no national movement to force Louis XIII and Richelieu to make peace.[1]

The human element in the struggle to meet rising expenditure was never submerged. Ministers understood what was expected of them, and when they helped each other they did not lose their sense of humour. Richelieu commented: 'To conclude, 14,300 [troops] reduced, for the consolation of Monsieur de Bullion.'[2] Later in the same year he optimistically reported to Chavigny that there was a possibility of collecting a debt of over 1,200,000 *livres*, but that he sought more information in order to make 'Monsieur de Bullion happy, who, as you know, is overjoyed when somebody pays his debts'.[3] In spite of angry moments and much disagreement, Richelieu showed a certain sympathy for Bullion.

fol. 131. Bullion wrote substantially the same thing in Oct. 1640, AAE, France, 836, fols. 134–5. Faced with no alternative before the *traitants*, Bullion appealed to Richelieu, who took direct action by proposing changes in taxes for the province of Languedoc. See Bullion to Richelieu, 2 Nov. 1640, AAE, France, 836, fol. 141, where he thanked the cardinal for his intervention. A thorough study of relationships between the *traitants* and the chief councillors would be valuable; if accounts and correspondence from the *traitants* to men like Bullion could be found. Bullion was certainly obliged to play along with the *traitants* just as Sublet de Noyers did with munitioners in periods of grave financial need which placed the government at their mercy. There is no evidence, however, to show that Richelieu reproached Bullion for his negotiations with the *traitants*; but he complained bitterly when other abuses occurred, such as when the council failed to limit the abuses of the tax collectors. See above, p. 137.

[1] Opposition to the war in France was dramatically evident in the numerous plots against Richelieu and his creatures, of which the Cinq-Mars affair was perhaps the most serious. It is difficult to separate personal motives from pressures within the realm for peace. Was there opposition in other quarters? Evidence of this would be difficult to find, for openly opposing royal policy on the war was often fatal.

[2] 16 Apr. 1635, Avenel, ed. cit. iv, p. 708.

[3] Here there is also more evidence of personal loans to the Crown: 'On me veut donner deux advis, l'un de poids et de consideration puisqu'il est assés fort pour faire le remboursement de douze cens mil livres que l'un de vos meilleurs amis a avancez pour le service du roy. . . .' 12 Oct. 1635, ibid. v. cxxxvii.

In tracing the relations of Bullion and Richelieu, a confused picture of conflict and co-operation presents itself.
Hauser and d'Avenel conclude that it resulted from Richelieu's real financial incapacity,[1] but there is another aspect
to Bullion's insubordination. The cardinal never gave time
to questions of finance, and though he was conscious of
such problems, he put them second in importance, especially
after the beginning of open war in 1635. Caught between
lack of funds and an insistent master, Bullion sought refuge
in administrative confusion and broken promises. Before
Richelieu and Louis XIII, Bullion dared not refuse, but the
lack of money could not be evaded. His efforts to portray
the financial peril may well have been exaggerated, but with
purpose, for Bullion attempted in every possible way to
control the spending of Louis XIII and his principal
minister. Richelieu saw military and diplomatic ends, and
Bullion's greatest service to him was to curb spending in
every possible case. No one realized the value of Bullion
better than Louis XIII who, after the superintendent's
death, feared that Bouthillier would not have the courage
and moral strength to oppose Richelieu on spending.

Bullion did much besides limiting spending. Though the
methods were old and odious, he increased the king's
revenues enormously. Reforms were out of the question.
In 1640 Bullion may have proposed a *taille* for the clergy,
a bold gesture and—if he had really intended to do it—an
action that would have made great changes in the social and
economic relationships of the three estates. The rumour
that a *taille* was to be imposed on the clergy brought a dele-
gation of Parisian priests to complain to Richelieu.[2]

After this reaction Richelieu wrote to Bullion that such
a proposal 'was capable of making the most devoted minds
of the moment revolt, and make it possible for the con-
trary ones to profit from it'.[3] The very idea of a *taille* on the
clergy was condemned, which caused Bullion to reply: 'We

[1] H. Hauser, *La Pensée et l'action économique du Cardinal de* Richelieu (Paris,
1944), p. 171; d'Avenel, *Richelieu et la monarchie absolue* (Paris, 1884), ii, p. 181.
[2] See the extract of the *requête* of 30 June 1640, pub. by Avenel, ed. cit.
vi, p. 707. For Bullion's negotiations with the clergy, see Jean Tournyol du
Clos, *Richelieu et le clergé de France* (Paris, 1912), *passim*.
[3] 3 July 1640, ibid. vi. cccliii.

are not talking about imposing the *taille* on the clergy, although by the ordonnances they are obliged to pay the *taille* on non-ecclesiastical property which they possess. We are asking them [to pay] a tax for the privilege of confirmation of this right.'[1] The cardinal frequently intervened in financial affairs before finding out the real intentions of the *conseil* or of the superintendents; but this time, had Bullion really thought of putting a *taille* on the clergy? Today the question is not as important as the immediate and negative reaction of the cardinal to anything that would modify or endanger the precarious balance between internal peace and insurrection. Reforms of any consequence were out of the question.

While Bullion gave every appearance of being a harried minister, there were times when he went off for week-ends to Wideville or when he relaxed by dining heartily with friends.[2] On one occasion, after describing his negotiations with the English ambassadors to Chavigny, he expressed his desire to see him by adding, 'with God's help we will eat rabbit from Wideville together'.[3] In his letters there is a robustness and self-assurance unequalled by any of the other ministers of Louis XIII save Richelieu himself. He held the implicit trust of the king and with it exerted a certain freedom from Richelieu's domination; when he wrote to one or the other, he knew how to flatter them both without running aground in conflicting compliments. In a style which later became obsolete, Bullion compared France to a ship and Richelieu to her pilot without flourish or preciosity. He continued his compliment by a serious observation in code: 'It is true, and I have always recognized it, that 52 [Anne of Austria] does not have good intentions towards 59 [Richelieu]', after which he turned to describe how he was having libellists, opponents of Richelieu, arrested, and that he had taken all necessary precautions to safeguard the peace in Paris.[4]

[1] 6 July 1640, AAE, France, 835, fol. 256.
[2] Bullion was included in the dinner where the Englishman, Leicester, surprised them in their 'debauche'. See above, p. 77.
[3] 12 Oct. 1636, AAE, France, 820, fol. 44.
[4] Bullion to Richelieu, 12 Oct. 1636, ibid., fol. 45. Richelieu was in northern France when Bullion made this report on the situation in Paris. His prestige

Bullion also played a role in foreign affairs. It was never very great, and though he never saw these problems as lucidly as Richelieu, he nevertheless felt at ease to give his opinions.[1] He normally negotiated with the English ambassadors in place of Chavigny, but often they did so together. When he did not receive diplomatic instructions from the *Conseil d'en haut*, Bullion was obliged to reply to the English proposals independently.[2] His influence as a diplomat was minor, but again it illustrates the activity of a single minister in many domains.[3]

Bullion's influence was preponderant over Richelieu's other creatures. Servien's conflict with Bullion was one of the principal causes of the former's dismissal.[4] Chavigny and Sublet de Noyers were very careful to retain Bullion's favour. There is no evidence of conflict with his partner,

and ability to act with speed enabled Richelieu to leave the otherwise unsure city when Louis XIII was himself away from Paris. He continued: 'Le Parlement est contre nous excepté le procureur-general qui y faict ce qu'il peut. La cour des Aydes comence à se faire paroistre. Il a falu en deppit qu'on en ayt eu laisser les deux offices de president à cent cinquante mil chacun. . . .' It was this humour and serenity before serious troubles which gave Richelieu confidence in Bullion.

[1] Bullion wrote to Richelieu: 'J'ay veu par les lettres de Monsieur de Bellièvre [ambassadeur extraordinaire in Italy] les dificultez de Monsieur de Savoye. L'importance du faict est que le Duc s'oblige à la ligue offensive et defensive avec le Roy. C'est un coup mortel contre l'Espagne d'entreprendre en Italie. Monsieur de Savoye estant de la partie, l'interest de Vostre Eminence n'est pas de conquerir maintenant la Savoye. [Cf. Richelieu, 'Ligue d'Italie', Avenel, ed. cit. iv. ccli.] L'evenement de la guerre est doubteux, la paix se faisant. Il est impossible de part et d'autre d'executer les conditions proposées et cependant dans l'ocasion presente l'advantage est du costé de Vostre Eminence puisque vous engagez le Duc et une partie des armées d'Italie de vostre costé. A mesure que les armes du Roy prospereront on taschera de rendre la condition de Sa Majesté plus avantageuse. . . . Je demande pardon à Vostre Eminence de la hardiesse que je prends de luy dire mon foible advis sur ce subjet estimant en verité que la guerre d'Italie facilitera grandement la paix et que s'il fault continuer la guerre il est besoin d'avoir des amis de touts costez qui travaillent à afoiblir l'Espagne. Dans sa dimunition le Roy y trouve sa grandeur toute entiere.' 30 Apr. 1635, AAE, France, 813, fol. 324.

[2] This was an exception. Chavigny wrote to Richelieu: 'Monsieur de Bullion a fait luy mesme la response pour Monsieur l'ambassadeur d'Angleterre.' 3 Sept. 1636, AAE, France, 821, fol. 268.

[3] Both Bullion and Bouthillier with Charnacé were given powers to negotiate and sign a treaty with Holland in 1634-5. Avenel, ed. cit. iv, p. 652 and *passim*.

[4] For the influence of Bullion on Servien's dismissal, see the accusations of inefficiency and corruption made by Servien against Bullion in an undated document corrected in his hand, AAE, France, 820, fol. 217.

Claude le Bouthillier, although every one in the government knew that Bullion actually held the purse strings. On the delicate matter of appointments, Bullion spoke out frankly. After announcing the death of the Duke of Saxe-Weimar, who had long been in the pay of France, Bullion stepped forward immediately with two candidates to head the leaderless army.[1] His analysis of the conditions and the strong points of the men he proposed indicates his astuteness and knowledge of men and armies.

Unlike the departments of the secretaries of state, little is known about the operation of the office of superintendents of finance or of the personnel attached to it. As chief councillors they worked constantly with the secretaries of the council, who prepared the *arrêts* and even the organization of council deliberations, but for financial affairs, the superintendents relied heavily upon the intendants of finance to help them. Intendant Tubeuf was Bullion's special aide in preparing tax projects or in arranging expenditure.

Bullion urged Richelieu to advise Louis XIII to name his candidates whenever death diminished the number of intendants of finance. Both Cornuel and Tubeuf were appointed after Bullion's urging.[2] When Tubeuf was appointed, Bullion wrote to Richelieu a letter full of 'humble gratitude' for Louis's choice.[3] Substantially, this had occurred four years earlier when Cornuel was named.[4]

With other officers Bullion was no less important. When Guron, governor of Marans,[5] died, the superintendent came forward and asked for the governorship and the 3,000 *livres*

[1] Bullion to Richelieu, 26 July 1639, AAE, France, 833, fol. 243.

[2] Richelieu assured Bullion that he would speak to the king about the intendant needed to help bear the weight of affairs after the superintendent had proposed Tubeuf. 22 Oct. 1638, Avenel, ed. cit. VI. cxxx.

[3] 12 Nov. 1638, AAE, France, 831, fol. 341.

[4] Bouthillier and Bullion both expressed their gratitude (in Bullion's hand) in a letter to Richelieu, 9 Jan. 1634: 'Nous ne scaurions assez remercier Vostre Eminence de la grace qu'il vous a pleu nous faire de l'intendance des finances pour Monsieur Cornuel . . . si nous en sçaurions un plus capable pour nous donner les moyens pour soustenir les despences ausquelles Sa Majesté par necessité et sans laisser ruiner l'estat est obligé, nous irions au bout du monde pour le chercher, mais en verité, nous tenons pour chose tres assurée qu'il est tres capable. . . .' AAE, France, 810, fol. 11.

[5] The deceased was Jean de Rechignevoisin, governor of the city and château of Marans (Charante-Maritime) after 1626.

pension for the eldest son of the deceased officer.[1] While it
was customary for governorships to pass from father to son,
there were exceptions. Bullion gave his opinion on any
matter that he chose, but like the king himself, Richelieu
was not obliged to make it his own. He often did, however,
to the pleasure of Bullion and his friends, who depended on
him to acquire offices and other royal favours for them.

When Bullion overstepped his authority, it was felt by
the entire court, for the least little comment of disfavour
from Richelieu was enough to make any minister worry and
present his humble apologies. Once, when Bullion had
momentarily fallen from the cardinal's good graces, Chavigny
came to his aid by putting in a good word for the old councillor. Bullion thanked him by writing: 'I thank you with all
my heart for the kindness that it pleased you to do for me
with His Eminence. I prefer his good graces to all the
wealth in the world. You know the decision that we have
made together to live and die in fidelity and obedience to
His Eminence.'[2] No better evidence of the attitude of the
creatures *vis-à-vis* Richelieu and of the commitment of the
group as a whole is necessary.

Bullion may well have preferred Richelieu's affection, but
this did not stop him from amassing a huge fortune. Through
Richelieu's favour he continued to add offices and wealth to
his family even in the most difficult years of the war.[3] He
also interceded for his friends; Louis wrote to Richelieu:
'I grant the priory that Monsieur de Bullion is asking for,

[1] 16 Jan. 1635, AAE, France, 813, fol. 31.
[2] Bullion to Chavigny (as indicated by the allusion to the financial problems
of Gaston d'Orléans, for whom Chavigny was Chancellor), 16 Sept. 1636,
AAE, France, 821, fol. 289.
[3] There is some evidence to indicate that Richelieu made Bullion gifts outright. Bullion wrote: 'Je n'ay point de paroles pour remercier Vostre Eminence de la faveur extreme qu'il vous pleust de tesmoigner à vostre tres humble
serviteur . . . je suplie tres humblement Vostre Eminence croire que la hardiesse que je prends quelquefois de luy parler avec liberté ne procede que de
la passion et affection que j'ay au service de Vostre Eminence. Je feray
l'impossible et sacrificeray et ma vie et tout ce que Dieu m'a donné pour
l'employer à ce que je vous doibs par tant d'obligations que j'ay receu de
Vostre Eminence.' 11 May 1635, AAE, France, 814, fol. 34. See also the
chapter on Bullion by Gédéon Tallement des Réaux in his *Historiettes*, the
Pléiade edition (Paris, 1959), vol. i. At the same time we have found no
references to direct gifts to Bullion in the correspondence of either the superintendent or Richelieu, but such courtesies were often omitted from letters.

providing that you think the man for whom he is requesting it is capable.'[1] Favours for friends, while not ready capital, represented important assets for a minister in the seventeenth century. Bullion was very successful, so much so that one of his contemporaries estimated his revenues to be 1,500,000 *livres* annually.[2] This may well be a gross exaggeration, but no records are extant by which to measure Bullion's wealth.[3] Other offices, including the much coveted position of keeper of the seals of the order of the Holy Spirit, also added to his income as councillor and superintendent.[4]

His entire family profited from Bullion's favour with Louis XIII and the cardinal. His son, Claude de Bonnelles, became a councillor in the Parlement of Paris, and Bullion probably bought one of the newly created offices of president *à mortier* for himself.[5] Another son, François de Montloüet, received a special age dispensation to replace his brother Pierre in the Parlement of Metz in December 1638,[6] when Pierre became abbot of St. Faron of Meaux.[7] Bullion's brother became an intendant of finance and justice in 1635, when he was in Venice negotiating with merchants for funds to pay armies in Italy.[8]

Bullion presided carefully over family affairs, just as he did over those of Louis XIII, until in December 1640 a sudden attack of apoplexy proved fatal. Various interpretations have been offered about the cause of his death, but

[1] 22 Apr. 1636, AAE, France, 244, fol. 199.

[2] See the anonymous 'Observations curieuses sur l'Estat et gouvernement de France avec les noms et dignitez et familles principalles', Bibliothèque de l'Arsenal, MS. 4058, fol. 265ᵛ. After listing the superintendents, intendants of finance, treasurers, and secretaries of the council, the author commented: 'Tous ces Messieurs sont des plus riches de France et leur revenue n'est pas croyable tant il est immense et prodigieux estant la plupart riches des biens de leur maistre Louis XIII et la souffrance du peuple.'

[3] The private papers, except for seignorial documents, were apparently destroyed during the Second World War, in spite of efforts of the de Galard family, the descendants of Bullion, to save them.

[4] See his *provisions* (copy), 27 Feb. 1636, AAE, France, 820, fol. 138.

[5] See the *avis d'Augier*, 10/20 Dec. 1635, PRO, State Papers, 78, vol. 99, fol. 250; and the copy of the *provisions* for the latter office, 27 Dec. 1635, AAE, France, 816, fol. 190.

[6] *Despence d'aage*, AG, A¹, 49, fol. 289.

[7] Louis Moreri, *Grand Dictionnaire historique* (Paris, 1699), 'Bullion'.

[8] Comte de Laval to the Duc de La Trémouille, 11 June 1635, AN, 1AP, MS. 381 (no folio).

contemporary letters and comments fail to indicate anything unnatural about it.[1] After announcing the death, Chavigny wrote to Mazarin: '[Bullion] had decided to help you, and he had accomplished marvels for you at the moment of the treaty [between France and Savoy?]. We should have prepared ourselves for this accident a long time ago.'[2]

But the most interesting reaction came from Louis himself. He wrote to Richelieu:

I already wrote to you this morning about the death of Monsieur de Bullion, about which the more I think, the more I miss him for his firmness. . . . I do not think we can find one similar to him. I believe it is necessary that you tell Monsieur le Bouthillier that he be a little more firm and strict than he is; otherwise he will grant everything that we ask and there will be no money for the second half of the year. . . .[3]

The king understood perfectly the great service which Bullion had rendered to the government. Through his prestige, stubbornness, and common sense, Bullion had tempered the grandiose plans of the cardinal and was, as a result, in no small measure responsible for their success.

[1] See Mariéjol, op. cit., p. 438, where he perhaps relied a little too heavily on *mémoires*.

[2] 23 Dec. 1640, AAE, Sardaigne, 31, fol. 692.

[3] 23 Dec. 1640, *Mélanges publiés par la Société des Bibliophiles François*, ed. by the Vicomtesse de Galard (Paris, 1903), p. 27.

VIII

Claude le Bouthillier, Superintendent of Finance

OVERSHADOWED by Bullion during his first eight years as superintendent, Claude le Bouthillier exercised a principal role in finance in the last two years of Richelieu's ministry. Even while Bullion lived, however, Bouthillier was never far from the centre of the stage on which all policies and problems were debated. His frequent comments about thrift and fidelity to the king and Richelieu reflected the ideas of the *petite noblesse* of which he was a member. He sincerely loved the monarchy; Louis XIII and all his activities were a real source of pleasure to him, and when the future Louis XIV was born he joyously wrote all the details in the foreign affairs dispatches.[1]

He was just average in intelligence; he understood the duties of his office, but his letters clearly indicate that he was made to execute the decisions of others more brilliant than he. His star had risen with that of the house of Richelieu, and his gratitude to the cardinal was not only expressed —as was Bullion's—but was reflected in his actions as well. Richelieu's orders were sacred to him. He also sought to keep the cardinal fully informed on financial problems and decisions in an outright, forward way. In many ways Bouthillier appears as a check to Bullion in the financial administration.

There was never open recognition of Richelieu's special confidence in Bouthillier, but it was implicit in many of their letters. Richelieu was frequently perplexed by the innumerable details necessary to direct financial affairs. He wrote to Bouthillier: 'There are many things to clear up

[1] It was the custom to do so, but while Richelieu and the other creatures used the same expressions of love and devotion for the Crown, they lacked the ring of naïve sincerity found in Bouthillier.

MONSEIGNEVR CLAVDE BOVTHILLIER

Seigneur de pons sur seine et des Caues, Conseiller du Roy
en ses Conseils, secretaire d'estat et de ses, Commendemens et surintendant des
finances de france

with Monsieur de Bullion, about which only you know the details.'[1] At such times the cardinal used Bouthillier to make sure that his orders were executed in spite of possible opposition from Bullion. Sometimes Richelieu's reliance upon Bouthillier was almost complete:

As to the financial proposal about which you wrote me, you well know that I will not get involved myself. If the affair in question is not good, it is up to you to change it. However, if we talk about it before the king, and I am well instructed beforehand, I will say what I esteem most appropriate for his [the king's] service.[2]

This letter is an extraordinary example of Richelieu's reliance on a creature, and it is certain proof that even during Bullion's domination, Bouthillier was active in the formation of financial policies.

When Bullion and Bouthillier took office in August 1632 the latter wrote a *mémoire* on the financial conditions which they found. This document, published in Appendix B, is of fundamental importance to an understanding of the highest level of financial administration under Louis XIII.[3] On taking office Bullion and Bouthillier decided that their first task was to learn the exact financial situation of the Crown. To do this they requested the intendants of finance and the comptrollers general of finance to examine all the contracts made with the *traitants* since 1626, the year in which their predecessor had taken office.[4] The next task was to ascertain if the *traitants* had met their obligations. To do this, they examined the accounts of the treasurers of the *parties casuelles*, who kept records for the extraordinary revenues. The intendants were also asked to examine the administration of the general receivers and tax farmers by tax districts for the years 1630, 1631, and the first part of 1632.

The treasurers of the *épargne*, who recorded customary revenues, were asked to verify their accounts as well, so

[1] 10 Jan. 1639, Richelieu, *Lettres, instructions diplomatiques et papiers d'Etat*, ed. by M. Avenel (Paris, 1853–77), VI. clvii.
[2] 29 Dec. 1634, ibid. IV. cccxxxix.
[3] 'Mémoire fait par moy [in Claude le Bouthillier's hand] le 15ieme du mois d'aoust 1632 touchant ce que nous avons faict Monsieur de Bullion et moy au commencement que nous sommes entrés en la charge de Surintendant des Finances', AAE, France, 806, fol. 178. [4] This was the Maréchal d'Effiat.

that this and other information could be combined to furnish details for a general budget statement of revenue and expenditure. Finally, Bouthillier listed measures immediately necessary to meet current expenses. One of these was to convoke the Estates of Normandy, presumably for the purpose of negotiating the sum to be paid in taxes by the province.[1]

Bullion and Bouthillier began by co-operating closely, and they continued to do so. While Bullion assumed the responsibility of the great problems, including the onerous task of making economies, Bouthillier was often busy with minor but necessary tasks, e.g. he verified accounts, estimated costs for certain projects, worked on thousands of *arrêts du conseil* as a chief councillor, and intrigued in every possible way to assure the power and prestige of Richelieu.

These activities covered the gamut of governmental affairs. In July 1635 he presented a report on the condition of the navy in the Mediterranean.[2] Combining reports sent from the scene with financial information given by the superintendent, it provided necessary facts for formulating policy. Often Bouthillier personally went over accounts. When Richelieu was negotiating to purchase the *charge* of general of the galleys for a nephew, Bouthillier went over the officer's accounts to see if payments made to the general had been properly disbursed, and presented the financial position of the office *vis-à-vis* the Crown. Finally, he advised Richelieu that an *arrêt de réassignation* would be necessary to terminate the affair. He then suggested that it could be prepared and sent off by the council, which would meet for consideration of finances on Saturday.[3] Such services were indispensable to Richelieu; they required an administrator with knowledge of details and patience to cope with them. In this case, when the price of the *charge* was 500,000 *livres*, the affair concerned not only the Crown but also the cardinal's own fortune.

---

[1] Normandy was then a *pays d'état*, hence the Crown was obliged to negotiate with the estates rather than simply to fix *en conseil* the taxes to be paid, as was done for the *pays d'élection*.

[2] 1 July 1635, AAE, France, 814, fol. 222. Addressed to Servien, Secretary of State for War.

[3] Bouthillier to Richelieu, 18 Jan. 1635, AAE, 813, fol. 35.

When the secretaries of state or others needed advice on financial problems, or just general information, they frequently wrote to or called on Bouthillier. On one occasion he worked with Sublet de Noyers on questions of royal debts in Provence and the outlay on captured vessels.[1] At another time he co-operated with Père Joseph and had a disagreement with him over the exact wording of the text explaining why France had declared war against Spain.[2]

Richelieu entrusted Bouthillier with personal affairs. For example, he requested him to see a certain Madame de Pontchasteau to discuss whether she wanted her second son to make a career of the 'Church or the sword'.[3] Bouthillier also worked on the marriage treaty between Richelieu and the Prince de Condé for the marriage of one of Richelieu's nieces to the Duc d'Enghien.[4]

When Bouthillier's son was away from Paris, the father assumed the task of receiving ambassadorial correspondence, presenting it *en conseil* to the king and the cardinal for their orders, and then preparing the replies. Even though Chavigny had taken over Bouthillier's functions as secretary of state, the father did not lose the power to prepare and countersign royal letters.[5] Bouthillier's dispatches were rarely vivid, for he had to write many sentences to express even the smallest idea.[6]

Both superintendents had the power to order treasury disbursements upon receiving a letter or ordonnance from

[1] Bouthillier to Sublet de Noyers, 16 July 1639, AAE, France, 833, fol. 221.

[2] Bouthillier to Père Joseph, 23 June 1635, AAE, France, 814, fol. 203; Père Joseph's reply of 27 June 1635, fol. 209 of the same volume, where we discover that Bouthillier is having the text printed.

[3] Richelieu added: 'Je suis d'advis qu'elle envoie quérir son dit fils et luy propose les deux conditions, afin de voir ses sentimens', 9 Apr. 1635, Avenel, ed. cit. viii, p. 279.

[4] See the minute in Bouthillier's hand, Feb. 1641? AAE, France, 838, fol. 55; Richelieu to Bouthillier, 30 Jan. 1641, Avenel, ed. cit. vi. ccclxxviii.

[5] This tradition resulted from the practice of sons assuming the functions of their fathers as secretaries after having received the *droit de survivance*.

[6] Bouthillier's style was even wordier than that of most of his contemporaries; for example, he wrote to Brasset, secretary to the ambassador to Holland: 'Les dernieres [letters] que j'ay receues de vous sont des 12e et 19e de ce mois esquelles je n'ay rien veu qui requiere responce pour ce qui est du service du Roy. Je vous diray donc seulement sur la premiere que pendant que j'auray le soing des depesches en l'absence de mon fils. . . .' 30 Mar. 1635, BN, MS. 17946, fol. 22.

the king countersigned by a secretary of state.[1] On one occasion, when quick action was necessary, Richelieu wrote direct to Bouthillier, because the latter combined the powers of secretary and superintendent. This was convenient. Richelieu told Servien to turn over the problem of sending medicines and linens for the Metz army to Bouthillier, because he held the power of the 'pen and the purse together'.[2] One administrative step was thus avoided, and time was saved.

The old habit of observing the court for the purpose of informing Richelieu of plots against him continued to entangle Bouthillier in important intrigues. He worked on coded messages of Marie de Médicis and her supporters in France after her exile in order to discover plots made against Richelieu;[3] and like the other creatures he was asked to advise Louis about Marie's request to return to France.[4] When Anne of Austria complained of Richelieu's harshness toward her and her followers, the cardinal sent Bouthillier to assure the queen of his favour and affection;[5] and when Chavigny was away, Bouthillier was occasionally left with the delicate task of presenting Richelieu's requests to Louis XIII. Like his son, he wrote many letters reporting all the moods and comments of the king, thus enabling Richelieu to know what to write or say at the proper moment.[6]

[1] Richelieu also had the power to order the superintendents to make a payment, but it would seem that he exercised it through the traditional formulas by having the secretaries prepare royal letters. For his power, see Bullion to Richelieu, 6 Sept. 1638, AAE, France 831, fol. 199.

[2] 5 Mar. 1635, Avenel, ed. cit. viii, p. 277.

[3] See the document in his hand in which names like Marie and Gaston d'Orléans are deciphered, 1634, AAE, France, 810, fol. 8.

[4] See the 'Advis donnez par escrit au Roy par Messieurs le Chancelier, Bullion, Bouthillier, surintendants des finances, Chavigny et des Noyers, secrétaires d'Estat, sçavoir si sa Majesté doit permettre le retour de la Reyne sa Mere en ce Royaume en Mars, 1639'; there are many copies of this document, one of which is in the BN, MS. 20547, fols. 89 f.

[5] Richelieu to Bouthillier, 18 May 1640, Avenel, ed. cit. vi. cccxlii. Bouthillier also became very involved in the struggle between Richelieu and Anne over the appointment of wet nurses for the future Louis XIV. See Richelieu to Bouthillier, 10 Aug. 1638, letter liii of the same volume.

[6] This was carefully done; for example, Bouthillier helped Richelieu on his replies to the king by going into details after saying: 'Je desirois que Vostre Eminence peust recevoir ce mot avant qu'il avoit respondu aux deux lettres que le Roy vous escrivit hier. . . .' 2 Sept. 1635, AAE, France, 815, fol. 157.

While doing these secondary but necessary tasks, Bouthillier continued to work on finance in Bullion's shadow.
Bouthillier frequently consulted Bullion before making a
decision,[1] and occasionally Bullion remarked that he had
asked his partner's advice or support on matters at hand.[2]

After Bullion's death, Bouthillier carried on alone as superintendent, in spite of Louis's misgivings about his capacity
to keep the purse strings tight.[3] In some ways more can be
learned about the duties of the office from the relatively
few letters Bouthillier wrote to Richelieu than from the
hundreds which Bullion dispatched. Bouthillier was more
straightforward than Bullion. Bouthillier co-operated and
shared responsibility with Richelieu by informing him of all
financial operations, instead of retaining a certain independence and in turn greater responsibility, as had Bullion.

Bouthillier wrote precisely, and with little emotion. He
gave his partial approval to Richelieu's suggestion that a
general subsidy be ordered to meet war costs :[4]

To inform [His Eminence] of the present state of finances and
of the sums which have been spent up to now since the beginning
of the year, about which I will only say a word here as I am writing
in detail about it to Monsieur de Noyers, who will be able to
inform you about it at a convenient time. The summary is that of
the 54 millions included in the general project of expenditure for
this year, approved and signed by the king, there are already
20,800,648 *livres* not including *subsistences*, the disbursements for
which—in regard to the *provinces d'élections*—including officers'
pay, total 13,837,477 *livres*; and for the *pays d'état* they total
3,076,896 *livres*. These expenditures—for the general project funds
as well as for the *subsistences*—are justified article by article in three

[1] Bouthillier wrote to La Valette: 'Incontinant que Monsieur Bullion sera
icy nous aviserons quel fonds il sera possible de donner pour les fortifications de Metz.' 21 May 1635, BN, MS. 6445, fol. 35.

[2] In determining the value of the queen's jewels to be purchased (?),
Bullion informed Richelieu that he had talked to Bouthillier, who had agreed
with him on not only the expenditure (40,000 *écus*), but also on his conception
of the political consequences. 12 Jan. 1635? AAE, France, 813, fol. 19.

[3] See above, p. 165.

[4] Richelieu to Bouthillier, 6 Mar. 1642: 'Si vous approuvés l'expédient
dont je vous ay escrit de Lyon, à Monsieur le chancelier et à vous, pour
l'establissement de la subvention générale, vous n'en aurez pas de besoin,
à mon avis, espérant que nous l'establirons du consentement des peuples.'
Avenel, ed. cit. VI. ccccliii.

statements which I am sending to Monsieur de Noyers. . . . I am only telling His Eminence of them in order to show him where we are, so that he may judge prudently, after Monsieur de Noyers has provided more details, where we must cut expenses. . . . His Eminence's idea to establish the general subsidy for the *pays d'état* is excellent, to have the *ferme* collected by the cities at the rate and time fixed; provided that, as His Eminence says, the mayors, *échevins*, and other principal [officers] of the cities fully co-operate in their own and private names with the king as individuals; and, similarly, provided that the first *fermes* having expired, we can make up new ones in the *Conseil du roy*.[1]

The cardinal answered Bouthillier's letter by expressing his pleasure that the superintendent approved his plan for a general subsidy.[2]

Richelieu did not overlook Bouthillier's qualification; though he had thought of a general subsidy for all France, the superintendent approved it only for the *pays d'état*. The cardinal continued by expressing his fear that the financial needs of the realm could not be met without a general subsidy on the *pays d'élection* as well. This difference had to be resolved, and Richelieu continued:

If you please, think this affair over carefully, and after having maturely examined it, Monsieur the Chancellor and you will send me your opinions signed by both of you, so that, upon having it shown to the king, he will be more inclined to agree with it if it is against his first views and [the views] of his servants who are there.[3]

The cardinal permitted Bouthillier to present his views to the king, and even told him what would be the most effective way to do so.

Even so, Richelieu dominated financial details much more under Bouthillier than he had under Bullion. This did not mean, however, that the constant pressure exerted by Bullion to keep expenditure down was relaxed. Bouthillier carried on in the old tradition, though more calmly. He wrote to Richelieu:

I am obliged to tell Your Eminence that on this occasion it is really necessary to look for more funds, but what afflicts me is

---

[1] 10 Mar. 1642, AAE, France, 842, fol. 72. Richelieu was in southern France on a military campaign.

[2] Richelieu to Bouthillier, 19 Mar. 1642, Avenel, ed. cit. VI. ccccliv.

[3] Ibid. ccccliv. Richelieu described the affair in more detail, especially Bordeaux's request that a general subsidy be established.

that the extraordinary revenues are for all purposes dried up. It is to be feared that the ordinary revenues will also suddenly be lacking in many places in the realm [because of the length of the war]. . . . It is necessary to think about this seriously, Monseigneur, and it is absolutely necessary to curtail expenditure to meet [available] funds. . . . Only seven months and twenty-three days have passed [this year]. I almost dare not say to Your Eminence that expenditure has climbed to more than sixty-four million *livres*. I am now speaking of expenditure made in cash from the treasury, or in quick and sure assignations. . . .[1]

When Bouthillier felt that proposals were detrimental to the cause, he saw to it that Richelieu was informed. Even after Richelieu had apparently ordered the superintendent to arrange exemptions for the postmasters, Bouthillier did not hesitate to raise objections. He wrote to his son, who was to inform Richelieu:

. . . that what he orders me . . . in favour of the postmasters is of very great consequence for the *taille* and the *subsistences*, the *taille* being 42 millions and the *subsistences* 18 millions, making 60 millions each year, which cannot come about unless those who have the means contribute now [and] only if the exemptions are revoked. If they are accorded to the postmasters, the roosters, that is to say, all the rich in the parishes, will become postmasters . . . and by this way exempt. The parish will be overwhelmed and will fall to no value. . . . His Eminence does not know that before 1635 postmasters had never been exempt from the *taille*. . . . Read this to Monsieur de Noyers and in God's name, both of you make His Eminence consider. . . .[2]

Bouthillier finished by describing the precarious finances.

Normally, Bouthillier happily executed Richelieu's orders. Sometimes they were of real importance, and at other times only minor details. Once, after congratulating Bouthillier for sending out commissioners to levy the general subsidy, and after asking him to be careful to choose a kindly and adroit one for Brittany (of which he was governor), Richelieu replied to a whole series of problems about which Bouthillier had no doubt informed him.[3] This explicit

[1] 24 Aug. 1642, AAE, France, 845, fol. 271.
[2] 24 July 1641, AAE, France, 839, fol. 92. See Jean Tournyol du Clos, *Richelieu et le clergé de France* (Paris, 1912), pp. 452 ff.
[3] Richelieu to Bouthillier, 19 June 1641, Avenel, ed. cit. VI. ccccxii.

discussion included negotiations on gunpowder, disapproval of a favourite's intention to import 400,000 *livres* worth of canvasses without paying duty,[1] pension problems, and finally navy finances.[2] Richelieu gave Bouthillier orders freely and affectionately, and without the care and formal courtesy he had usually used with Bullion. The cardinal also co-operated to relieve Bouthillier's difficulties where possible, as in the case where Richelieu found an expedient permitting Bouthiller to delay a payment of 500,000 *francs* for galleys to a later and more convenient date.[3]

When the General Assembly of the Clergy took place in Mantes in the spring of 1641, Bouthillier kept Richelieu informed on the temperament of the clergy and on the negotiations over the subsidies.[4] Although the cardinal was clearly the leader in the negotiations for the Crown, Bouthillier was not far behind, as he urged Richelieu to hold firm to the figure of two million for the *fabriques*, parish revenues from the Church.[5] Richelieu answered: 'I wrote to you yesterday *via* the gentlemen of the clergy with whom I disputed, as you will do yourself. Your *fabriques* are saved. Your gold mark will remain in use just as things were before you were in charge of them.'[6] The end of the affair came in August, when—after the clergy had voted the subsidy—Bouthillier was left with the task of paying the bribes granted to gain needed votes. Richelieu warned him to be careful: 'Regarding the 18,000 *livres* which you have promised to distribute underhandedly to some individuals in the assembly under the pretext of council pensions, I have nothing to say except that you must do it as you are pledged to it. Take care that there is no roguishness in this matter....'[7]

---

[1] The text reads *toiles*, which could be linen cloth, or sail canvas.

[2] Richelieu to Bouthillier, 19 June 1641, Avenel, ed. cit. vi. ccccxii.

[3] Richelieu finished his letter: 'Je suis très-aise que vous battiés monnoye comme vous faictes. Vous vous assurerés, s'il vous plaist, de mon affection pour l'avenir comme pour le passé.' 8 June 1641, ibid. vi. ccccvii.

[4] See Richelieu to Bouthillier, 6 June 1641, ibid. vi. ccccv.

[5] Bouthillier to Richelieu, 16 July 1641, ibid. vi. ccccxxii. Richelieu himself had suggested the figure of two millions a year as extraordinary help from the clergy as early as 15 Mar., p. 758 of the same volume.

[6] 16 July 1641, ibid. vi. ccccxxii.

[7] Richelieu to Bouthillier, 18 Aug. 1641, ibid. vi. ccccxxix. Is the list of ecclesiastics in Bouthillier to Richelieu, 1 Oct. 1641—each of whom received 1,000 *livres*—the group in question? AAE, France, 839, fol. 272.

When the military campaign of 1641 was momentarily endangered by the plot and flight of the Duc de Bouillon and the Comte de Soissons, Bouthillier kept right on working to raise more and more troops for the royal armies.[1] Once the affair was over, and a new pact of obedience was prepared between the king and Bouillon, the superintendent was asked to review the assignations given for the defence of Sedan (over which Bouillon had great powers) beginning from 1637.[2] The all-important power of making assignations remained with Bouthillier, as it had under Bullion. There is no evidence to indicate that Richelieu ever personally took the initiative in this domain.

When Louis and Richelieu both left the Île de France to go campaigning in southern France early in 1642, the Prince de Condé was invited by the king to attend the administrative councils that still continued to meet in Paris. Bouthillier kept Richelieu minutely informed on the more important sessions, and as a result left to posterity some of the best descriptions of the council at work in the whole reign of Louis XIII. Bouthillier wrote:

I am charged by the council to render account to His Eminence about what happened last Wednesday on the subject of the latest lease [to collect] the *aides* granted to the Sieur de Forcoal, clerk in the *Conseil des parties*, and the company joined with him; upon which a bid was made again at 100,000 *livres* for each year over and above what is stated in the last lease, for which even those who made the bid offered to deposit 300,000 *livres* in the treasury, or even up to 500,000 *livres*, so they said. This offer was placed in the hands of Monseigneur the Prince [Condé], (who comes to our *conseils de finances et direction* every day). We apologize, Monsieur the Chancellor and I, for having the bid brought into a full council session, and for hearing [in council] the Sieur de Forcoal (who is called Saint-André and speaks for those who were making the bid with him). . . . Saint-André, who up to that moment had named few acceptable backers, proposed that the 300,000 *livres* or 500,000 *livres* which he had offered to deposit in the treasury fall as a complete loss to him and his company, if he did not give acceptable backers. He had previously proposed what were very good ones,

---

[1] Richelieu to Bouthillier, 16 July 1641, Avenel, ed. cit., VI. ccccxxii.

[2] On the Béthune copy is the title: 'Premier accommodement de Monsieur le duc de Bouillon avec le Roy.' 5 Aug. 1641, ibid. VI. ccccxxviii.

including Rambouillet and Tallement [Talmond], but having sent to inquire two days before, they told us that they had never thought about it, and that they had a big enough task with the *cinq grosses fermes*. The Council, therefore, on what was amply presented from both sides, having deliberated whether the bid should be accepted, rejected it unanimously—except for Monseigneur the Prince, Messieurs de Machault and de Mauroy, whom Saint-André and his company had assured at his house before the entrance of the council, that I would be content with the backers which they had presented me, which was not the case. It [the council] rejected the bid by twenty-eight voices to three; it would be too boring to tell His Eminence all the reasons upon which the Council based [its decision].[1]

To this problem Richelieu replied: 'Being far away as I am . . . and considering the little experience that I have in financial matters, it would be impossible for me to judge if we should accept or reject the new bid made for the general [tax farm] of the *aides*.' After noting that in his absence Louis had established a council for just such problems, Richelieu continued: 'His Majesty will always approve what they [the councillors] have resolved by the plurality of voices.'[2] This incident, and the description of it, permits a glimpse into the manner in which contracts to raise taxes were let; and, above all, it indicates the real role played by the councillors in the government.[3]

Indeed, negotiating for raising taxes was one of the principal occupations of Bouthillier. He received humble supplications from the *Chambre des comptes* of Brittany regarding cuts in the income of the officers by as much as one-fourth.[4] He also received orders from Louis to speak about cutting the *rentes* of Paris on the *gabelles*, *aides* and the *cinq grosses fermes*, but not on the others, as they belonged to the clergy.[5] On another occasion Bouthillier wrote specific

[1] Bouthillier to Richelieu, 1 Feb. 1642, AAE, France, 842, fol. 33.
[2] 28 Feb. 1642, Avenel, ed. cit. vii, p. 302.
[3] See Richelieu's reply to another letter of Bouthillier's describing a split in the council, where Condé and Machaut again disagreed with the group. 13 Feb. 1642, Avenel, ed. cit. vi. ccccli.
[4] See the letter, with a note in the margin by Bouthillier, 1641, AAE, France, 1506, fol. 16.
[5] Bouthillier to Richelieu, 24 Aug. 1642: 'Le Roy leur parla tres bien . . . de sorte que Sa Majesté m'aiant commandé de leur parler ensuite, je n'eus presqu'autre chose à leur dire. . . .' AAE, France, 845, fol. 271.

instructions to the president and treasurers at Caen on how to enforce tax legislation from the king's council.[1]

Even the condition of the roads was partly Bouthillier's responsibility. He wrote to Richelieu: 'His Eminence has given me the honour of informing me . . . that the road between la Charité and Nevers was found to be detestable. He will recognize, if it pleases him, that I have not yet been able to repair the cobblestones in that region, not having enough time, and what is worse, not enough money.'[2]

Like Bullion before him, Bouthillier worked constantly with the chancellor, the secretary of state for war, and particularly with the intendants of finance. But all of them were not kept informed of the details of financial policy. After describing a meeting with Sublet and the intendants, Bouthillier wrote to Richelieu:[3]

We did not talk at all about the last *mémoire* on the general state of finances that I sent to Your Eminence. This is not for the knowledge of those gentlemen, and should be known by very few people. Only Monsieur de Tubeuf, who does almost alone with me the tasks that he did with Monsieur de Bullion knows about it, and I do not even talk about it to my son because that would be of no help. . . .[4]

Thus, in spite of co-operation between the ministers on certain problems, the superintendent stood almost alone *vis-à-vis* Richelieu and Louis XIII on matters concerning the financial condition of the realm.

When du Houssay, one of the intendants of finance, died, Bouthillier asked Richelieu not to appoint another. In explaining his request, he really described the broad powers which the superintendent had over these officers, who

[1] Dec. 1641, BN, nouvelles acquisitions, MS. 240, fol. 80.

[2] 24 Feb. 1642, AAE, France, 842, fol. 55. This was not the first time that Richelieu had complained about the state of the roads, particularly in Paris. See Richelieu to Bullion, 18 Nov. 1638, Avenel, ed. cit. vi. cxliii.

[3] Bouthillier wrote to Richelieu: 'Nous ne traistasmes hier ches Monsieur de Noyers, Messieurs les Intendans presens, que des moiens de parvenir aux establissemens de la subvention generale du sol pour livre chacun en leur departement aux lieux où il n'est pas, de quoy Monsieur de Noyers prit memoire bien ample pour le resoudre avec Vostre Eminence.' 21 Nov. 1641, AAE, France, 839, fol. 360.

[4] Ibid., fol. 360.

provided the administrative link between the councils and the provincial administration. He wrote:

I believe that for the *service du roi*, and for better order in the finances, no one else should be appointed, and not for comptroller general either. The three intendants that we have are capable, at a good age, of serving well, and in truth they are doing so. If Your Eminence informs me of His Majesty's and his intention on the matter, I will tell them [the intendants] of their [Louis's and Richelieu's] esteem for them, and I will divide the department of the deceased Monsieur du Houssay among them, without giving them more income than they have.[1]

But just in case Richelieu had made up his mind to fill the position, Bouthillier finished: 'I know some very capable men for that position if His Eminence decides to fill it.'[2] Patronage and influence over appointments were a constant concern with Bouthillier, just as they were with the other creatures. On this occasion Richelieu answered that he had not thought of replacing du Houssay, and commented: 'I have known for a long time that with that kind, three do as much as four.'[3]

Bouthillier probably showed less sympathy with the *traitants* than Bullion. When the Sieur Sabathier ran into difficulty in meeting his engagements to the Crown, Bouthillier did little to save him from bankruptcy. In March 1641 Richelieu wrote to Bouthillier: 'Regarding the Sieur Sabathier, he spoke this morning to Monsieur de Noyers. He proposes to satisfy you, and my opinion is that providing the king receives his money, your best interest is to hinder his ruin.'[4] But by August Sabathier and a certain Barbier were bankrupt. To discover just what had occurred, and to establish the position of the Crown in the bankruptcy, a commission was established, about which Bouthillier wrote to Richelieu:

Your Eminence could not imagine how the bankruptcies of Barbier and Sabathier, and the apparently reasonable remedies

---

[1] Bouthillier to Richelieu, 1 Oct. 1641, ibid., fol. 272; Avenel, ed. cit. vi, p. 880.
[2] Ibid., fol. 272.
[3] Richelieu to Bouthillier, 3 Oct. 1641, Avenel, ed. cit. vi. ccccxli.
[4] 20 Mar. 1641, ibid. vi. ccclxxxii.

that we wished to give them have brought and are still bringing prejudice every day to affairs. This is inconceivable; our *traitants* scarcely find credit any more, and they are afraid that soon one will no longer say 'scarcely,' because money-changers and re-changers, who are really notorious usurers, are afraid that—by the commissions that we have established to discover the results and the debts of those who are becoming insolvent—their usuries and excessive interest will be discovered. And [they fear] that we are preparing an inquest on usury against them, which would really be just, according to good morals and the observance of good faith. But we are constrained to tolerate them as they do at Rome . . . to avoid worse. . . .[1]

The affair was a long one. Finally, in September, Bouthillier wrote to Richelieu: 'I am sure that Your Eminence will gladly give me the honour of believing that I have no grudge against the Sieur Sabathier. In holding firm against him, we have [collected] a good third of his receipts on the deposits [*receptes des consignations*], and we have pulled public money out of his hands. . . .'[2]

Though Bouthillier lacked the stature of Bullion, the financial administration of the Crown, with all its difficulties, remained the same. Richelieu was carefully informed, and as a result played a more active part in making policy. The mutual respect and affection of the two men who had risen to power together transformed the direction of finances, permitting Richelieu to exercise real control. Whether on questions of great or minor importance, opinions were respected, as was the ultimate power of the cardinal with the king. Richelieu expressed himself freely and negotiated affectionately with Bouthillier, as in the case of the office of a dead bishop. Richelieu wrote to Bouthillier:

I am really quite vexed about the death of the [Bishop of Angoulême?]. . . . I had seriously thought of granting his priory to Monsieur d'Esclaux. However, if it is in your interest, and you absolutely wish that I do otherwise with it, I will do it. Those that I love as [I do] you have more power over me than I have on myself.[3]

[1] 17 Aug. 1641, AAE, France, 839, fol. 173.
[2] 13 Sept. 1641, ibid., fol. 246.
[3] 29 Dec. 1634, Avenel, ed. cit. IV. cccxxxix.

There was an element of truth in what appeared to be only exaggerated sentiment.

Through Richelieu, Claude le Bouthillier, his brother, his son, and his wife rose from a very lowly position to become momentarily one of the great families of France. It was no accident that the first grandson born to Bouthillier was named Armand, Richelieu's first name.[1] The cardinal returned favour for fidelity, something which Bouthillier and his entire family gave him on all matters, whether of great or small importance.

After the cardinal's death, Bouthillier was named minister of state, a title held only by Richelieu in the last decade of the reign. He was part of the Council of the Regency, but after several years of alternate favour and disfavour with Anne of Austria and Mazarin, Bouthillier was obliged to retire to his home at Caves, where he died in 1652.[2]

[1] Just as the second son of Chavigny was named Gaston, perhaps to please Gaston d'Orléans, for whom Chavigny was chancellor. Louis Moreri, *Grand Dictionnaire historique* (Paris, 1699), 'Bouthillier'.

[2] Bouthillier had continued to build and refurbish his château at Ponts and Caves, even during the difficult war years. See the interesting letters relative to the importation of lead from England for the roofs of Ponts and Caves, without payment of customs. BN, MS. 15915, fol. 105 and *passim*.

Conclusion

IN the reign of Louis XIII institutions and offices were a mixture of customs and practices given meaning by the personalities representing them at the time. Many customs were not as old as those seeking to raise their prestige claimed them to be, but together with royal legislation such as the *règlements* they determined the behaviour and functions of the king's ministers. Both formed the basis for disputes when ambitious officers sought to increase their powers at the expense of their colleagues. This framework of customs and *règlements* also determined the relationships of the central administration, centred in the *Conseil*, with the sovereign courts and the military, foreign, and provincial administrations. There was considerable flexibility in these relationships, which varied according to the king's will; or, when the king did not take the initiative, officers often changed them in his name, with the same results. Because of the energy and ambition of his ministers, the reign of Louis XIII saw marked changes in the very nature of the royal government. The most striking example of this was the ascent of Cardinal Richelieu to a place second only to the king's, even though before his entry into the court he had possessed neither great wealth, titles, nor offices. This transformation took place without a radical modification in the structure of royal institutions, but the exterior concealed important precedents that later on were to play an important role.

Richelieu accomplished this transformation by inspiring confidence in a well-meaning but unimaginative king. To safeguard his power and to help him with the administrative details, the cardinal saw to it that his friends and favourites were appointed to the highest offices in the realm. It therefore became unnecessary to modify institutions to improve their effectiveness as instruments for governing, because Richelieu and his creatures controlled the central administration, and these favourites, eager to aid their benefactor, assured the smooth working of the *conseil*.

Though the flexibility of institutions permitted Richelieu to exercise great powers without structural changes, this did not bar other officers from modifying their positions in the government in a more permanent way. The cardinal's policies and relations with the king's other councillors were responsible for changes which were to become more important than those he himself made in the capacity of principal minister. Certain newcomers, such as the secretaries of state and the intendants, took advantage of very favourable circumstances to raise their offices in prestige and power. Benefitting from the cardinal's favouritism and eagerness to get things done, they helped trace new administrative lines in the relationships of the central administration with military, foreign, and provincial affairs. The breakdown of the old geographical jurisdictions of the secretaries had started earlier, but it was hastened by the ministerial government of Richelieu and the crisis of open war to such a point that never again were the departments of war and foreign affairs challenged.

With Richelieu's friends at the controls, the divided councils which had characterized the 1620's disappeared. The king had traditionally relied upon the existence of more than one party among his ministers to maintain a freedom of action. Louis XIII did not lose control of the situation, however, once Richelieu arose to dominate the councils. In such circumstances the king turned to other methods by holding Richelieu responsible for the actions of his favourites; and while combining assurances of affection with a long history of ministerial disgraces, Louis insisted on being informed of all decisions made in his name, and in having the last word.

For aid in the task, Richelieu turned to Chavigny and Sublet de Noyers who, in his absence, faithfully served his interests and theirs also. Louis XIII was very aware of the friendships among his ministers, but his confidence in Richelieu, and the assistance which the latter gave to his creatures, obliged Louis to accept and work with secretaries who were probably not always pleasing to him. At the same time, Bullion and Bouthillier directed the labours of the councils in co-operation with the chancellor who, because of his relatively little experience, probably played a lesser role than the superintendents of finance.

These men were all administrators with relatively humble beginnings. The princes of the blood, great nobles, and hereditary officers were either brushed aside or relegated to positions of secondary importance. As Louis XIV was later to do so admirably, Richelieu chose capable, experienced, and loyal individuals to help him impose his will on opposition parties as he pursued his conception of *gloire*. This coincided with an institutional and material transformation in France brought on by the threat of Spanish hegemony and the eventual declaration of open war in 1635.

It had long been a policy of the monarchy to centralize royal powers in the person of the king and his council, to the detriment of governors, provincial parlements, and other royal officers. This effort increased not only the prestige but also the duties of the secretaries of state and the chief councillors. They turned to royal commissioners and intendants, first for the army and later for general affairs, to administer the realm in the king's name. These newly traced administrative relationships dominated what had formerly been quite independent segments of the royal government; the work of Richelieu and his creatures provided a foundation for the far more sophisticated bureaucratic structure of the *ancien régime* of the late seventeenth century.

Within the central administration itself, the struggle between the royal council and the sovereign courts temporarily favoured the council, and provided a precedent for a new form of government, where these courts would have a less important role. Richelieu's favourites, particularly Bullion, pushed the prerogatives of the Crown and the councils to subdue opposition to the sale of offices, and at the same time they undertook the almost impossible task of finding means to pay for the war.

From this point of view the most striking aspect of Richelieu's ministerial government was his reliance on the creatures in both personal and purely administrative affairs. This was overlooked by historians, when they described Richelieu as a virtual wizard who ruled France alone in the name of Louis XIII. Richelieu's great power rested not so much on a mastery of details, or even upon his administrative genius, but rather on the force of his personality, which enabled him to dominate and use not only the king but also the other ministers to develop a unified and effective political instrument which worked for him.

APPENDIX A

The Règlements of the Secretaries of State for the Reign of Louis XIII

THE *règlements* for the secretaries of state under Louis XIII have survived, mostly as copies in the various great manuscript collections in Paris. Among these the Cabinet des Manuscrits of the Bibliothèque Nationale is the most important, not only for the *règlements* but also for documents concerning the secretaries of state under Louis XIII in general.

Of the *règlement* of 1617 one original has survived in the form of a royal letter signed by the king and countersigned by one secretary of state. It was incorporated along with many other documents, including a copy of the same *règlement*, into one volume for the library of the third Achille de Harlay, an officer of the parlement of Paris.[1]

At least one other original was made at the time, because it served as the source for most of the later copies. The principal difference between the Harlay original and most of the later copies is that the latter indicate that the four secretaries of state were signatories of the *règlement*. However, copies bearing only the signature of one secretary have also survived, including the oldest copy found, coming from the library of Chancellor Séguier, and now MS. 17864, folio 312, at the Bibliothèque Nationale.

Copies signed by four secretaries of state are more numerous, including those from the late-seventeenth-century libraries of Charles Maurice Le Tellier, Archbishop of Rheims (now MS. 20762, folio 12); Le Tellier–Louvois (now MS. 4231, folio 2); Louvois (now MS. 18543, folio 46); Collection Clairambault, 664, folio 115; and MS. 7008, folio 2.

To establish the following text, the Harlay original has been used, for it presents no problems of diplomatics or authenticity. For the other *règlements*, the copies will be indicated in footnotes to the texts.

Règlement que le Roy veut estre doresnavant observé
par les Secretaires d'Estat pour l'expedition des placets
qui seront presentez à sa Majesté laquelle leur deffend

---

[1] It is now BN, MS. 15519, fol. 158.

tres expressement de faire aucunes depesches au contraire.

Premierement: Les Brevets des Archeveschez, Eveschez, Abbayes et Prieurez qui sont donnez par le Roy ne seront que pour benefices qui seront lors vacquans sans que l'on y puisse mettre, ou prest à vacquer, y sera faict mention expresse du nom de celuy par la mort duquel l'on pretendra que le benefice soit vacquant sans que l'on puisse mettre ces mots en quelque façon qu'il puisse vacquer, et ne seront lesdicts brevets delivrez qu'apres que ce Secretaire d'Estat qui les aura expediez aura esté certifié de la mort et aura receu nouveau commandement du Roy sur ladicte certification.

2. Que les resignations des benefices accordées par le Roy n'empescheront la vacquation desdicts benefices par le decedz des resignans qu'apres que le resignataire aura obtenu ses Bulles et qu'il y en aura clause expresse dans les Brevets desdictes resignations, lesquels ne seront expediez que sur procurations volontaires en bonne forme et non surannées des Titulaires.

3. Les Brevets de don des Archeveschez et Eveschez ne seront expediez qu'au non des personnes capables et de la qualité requise par les saincts Decrets et Ordonnances san que l'on y puisse emploier qui que ce soit en faveur d'autre quel qu'il puisse estre et lesdictes personnes capables seront tenues de se faire pourveoir dans le tems porté par les Ordonnances et à faute de se faire Iceux Archeveschez et Eveschez seront vacquans et Impetrables. Et pour les Abbayes les Brevets pourront faire mention de ceux en faveur desquels sa Majesté les accordera, mais y seront nommées les personnes capables qui en devront estre titulaires lesquelles seront aussy tenues de se faire pourveoir dans le temps porté par l'Ordonnance autrement les uns et les autres demeureront descheuz de leur droit sans qu'il soit besoing d'autre declaration que la nomination que sa Majesté fera d'autres personnes qui auront les qualitez requises.

4. Ne seront plus delivrez aucuns Brevets de don de benefices que par la mort des Titulaires et non de ceux en faveur desquels ils auroient esté donnez qui ny pourront plus pretendre aucun droit apres la provision de ceux qu'ils auront une fois nommez à sa Majesté.

5. Que pour les Evechez et Archeveschez vacquantes il ne sera expedié à qui que ce soit aucun don general des benefices en deppendans qui vacqueront en regale avis sa Majesté se reservera de pourveoir à chacun d'Iceux lors qu'ils viendront à vacquer pour en gratifier ses officiers et serviteurs.

6. Qu'il ne s'expediera aucun don de regale contre ceux qui auront possedé les benefices plus de trois ans.

7. Ne seront donnez aucuns benefices par Incapacité sinon apres qu'elle aura esté jugée et sera fait mention du Jugement dans le Brevet qui en sera expedié.

8. Qu'il ne s'expediera aucunes reserves de benefices, Charges et offices.

9. Ne seront accordées aucunes coadjutories pour les benefices qui

sont en commande, pour quelque cause que ce soit, ny pour les autres sinon en cas de droit d'une Inquisition prealablement faicte et avec le consentement des Chapitres et Couvens.

10. Qu'il ne s'expediera aucun des Benefices affectez aux Chantres et enfans de la Chapelle de sa Majesté qu'en rapportant le roole d'Iceux signé et certifié du Maistre de ladicte Chapelle pour y estre remply de sa main du Secretaire d'Estat qui l'expediera le non de celuy qui en sera pourveu affin qu'il n'en puisse obtenir plusieurs et à faute de raporter leur roolle au commancement de chacun mois à celuy des Secretaires d'Estat qui y entrera pour veoir celuy qui sera entour de roolle dont ils doivent tous demeurer d'accord le Roy accorder les benefices vacquans à telles autres personnes qu'il jugera en estre capables.

11. Qu'il ne s'expediera aucunes pentions sur les Abayes et Prieurez des religieuses si ce n'est en faveur de quelque ancienne qui voulut resigner à laquelle on pourra reserver pour le plus jusques à trois cens livres de pention sa vie durant.

12. Que les Oeconomats ne seront renouvelez plus d'une fois ny continuez pour plus d'un an en tout et ne s'en expediera aucuns pour les benefices des religieuses ny pour tous autres benefices vacquans par resignation.

13. Qu'il ne s'expediera aucun don de Maladerye ou Leproserie par sa Majesté ou par son grand Aulmosnier s'il n'appert qu'à elle appartienne de les conferer, et à la charge que les biens en seront gouvernez comme Il est porté par les Ordonnances, et que ceux qui seront pourveus desdictes Maladeries, ne prendront sur le revenu et par les mains des administrateurs d'Icelles que la somme qui aura esté arbitrée et taxée suivant les dictes Ordonnances, ce qui sera inseré dans les provisions qui en seront expediées.

14. Et pour le regard des finances encores que l'intention de sa Majesté soit de faire les Dons et gratifications selon la qualité, les merites et les services des personnes, si n'entend elle estendre sa liberalité aux choses qu'il est prohibé par les Ordonnances et reglemens faicts sur ce sujet, comme sur les deniers des restes des Tailles taillon et autres qui se levent sur le peuple, sur ceux des restes des Magazins et Vivres, sur les bons d'Estats les restes des Comptes les deniers provenans du prix des fermes ou des tiercemens ou doublemens faictes sur Icelles dont le prix entier doit venir à l'Espargne sans fraude ni desguisement, sur le domaine soit pour en Jouir par annee ou autrement, sur les bois bruslez et Chabliz, les Amendes outrepassés et entreprises faictes sur Iceux, et sur les deniers de la creation ou composition des offices compris aux parties casuelles.

15. Ne sera faict aucun don de ceux qui sont suprimez ou ausquels n'a encores esté pourveu ny les deniers qui en pourroient provenir non plus que du suplement à faire faire par les officiers ja [déjà] establis; demembremens de leurs charges ou attribution de nouveaux droicts.

16. Auncuns dons ne seront faicts sur les deniers extraordinaires sans exprimer la nature et qualité d'Iceux et si fait estoit ne veut sa Majesté qu'on y ait aucun esgard.

17. Ny sur les deniers ordinaires qu'avec clause expresse qu'ils ne pourront estre payez qu'à la fin de l'année et toutes les charges ordinaires de l'estat prealablement acquitées sinon pour ceux qui n'excederont la somme de douze ou quinze cens livres et pour cause tres urgente.

18. Que les Dons qui auront esté faicts sur les deniers extraordinaires ne se pourront commuer sur les deniers ordinaires.

19. Tous dons excedans mil escus seront adressez à la Chambre des Comptes, sans qu'en un mesme acquit l'on puisse employer plus d'une personne pour les dons desdictes sommes de Mil escus.

20. Aucuns dons ne seront faicts des deniers procedans des recherches si Elles ne sont ordonnées au Conseil auquel les Placets seront renvoyez pour donner advis à sa Majesté.

21. Ne sera pareillement aucune resignation expediée pour acquitement de debtes s'il n'est ordonné de nouveau par Arrest du Conseil et si outre ledit Arrest il ny a Ordonnance et commandement expres du Roy.

22. Moins encores devra il estre faict pour les reassignations qui seront pretendues à cause de dons recompenses ou arrerages de gaiges ou pentions.

23. Ne seront signées aucunes lettres de validation ou restablissement de partyes rayées purement aux chambres des Comptes qu'elles n'ayent esté raportées au Conseil.

24. Ne seront expediez aucuns acquites soubz noms supposez pour quelque occasion que ce soit.

25. Ne s'accordera aucune pention sur receptes generales ny Particulieres fermes, ny ailleurs qu'à l'Espargne.

26. Ne se donnera aucun Brevet de pention par mort, resignation ou forfaicture.

27. Les Roys predecesseurs de sa Majesté ont ordinairement faict estat des deniers provenans des Lots et Rentes et autres droicts Seigneuriaux, ayant reservé la moitié des dons et le tiers des remises pour employer à leurs Bastimens, Mais sa Majesté voulant gratifier ses sujects, et specialement sa Noblesse, les veut donner liberalement sans s'en reserver aucune chose et affin qu'elle puisse preferer aux autres ceux qui seront plus dignes de ses gratifications elle entend qu'il ne s'expedie aucun Brevet de don desdicts Lots et Rentes et droicts Seigneuriaux que la rente ne soit prealablement faicte, et neantmoings les remises estans favorables, Elle en pourra faire donner des Brevets à ceux qui seront prests d'aquerir ou de vendre selon les pays où les droicts sont deus par l'acquereur ou le vendeur, et l'on y mettra cette clause pourveu que dans trois mois la vente et adjudication en soit faicte.

28. Qu'il ne sera expedié aucun don de confiscation et Amende par lettres Patentes ny par Brevet qu'il n'aparoisse du Jugement et les Placets presentez auparavant demeureront nuls sans que l'on y aye aucun esgard.

29. Tous autres Placets concernans les finances, Eaües et foretz, le domaine du Roy et la Police seront renvoyez au Conseil de sa Majesté, sans que les Dons en puissent estre depeschez que sur l'advis d'Iceluy.

30. Pour les Aubeynes et desherances en pourront estre delivrez les Brevets et Commissions pour saisir mais non les lettres de don qu'apres qu'il aura apparu de la sentence du Tresor ou des Juges des lieux.

31. Que le dernier Jour du mois le Roolle sera cloz sans qu'Iceluy passé le Secretaire d'Estat qui sort de mois puisse recevoir aucun Placet.

32. Ledit Secretaire qui sortira de mois baillera à celuy qui y entrera un extraict de son Roolle contenant les Placets qui auront esté refusez affin que l'autre ne les reçoive si l'on venoit encores à les presenter.

33. Que les arrests du Conseil qui se donneront lorsque le Roy y sera s'expediront par chacun desdicts Secretaires d'Estat qui sera en mois comme aussy la semaine et toutes autres depesches semblables.

Faict à Fontainebleau le Roy estant en son Conseil. Le xxie Jour de Juin mil six cens dix sept.

Signed Louis and Potier.

Reglement faict par le Roy entre Messieurs les secretaires d'Estat touchant la fonction de celuy qui a le departement de la guerre et les depesches que les autres ont à faire et provinces dont ils ont la charge.[1]

Le Roy veut et ordonne que celuy qui aura le departement de la guerre reçoive le commandement de sa majesté pour faire la commission, l'estat, et toutes autres expeditions necessaires pour la premiere et principalle armée qui debvra estre commandée par sa majesté ou par son lieutenant general en icelle.

Mais s'il est besoing outre ladicte premiere armée de faire quelque autre armement, ou de dresser une ou plusieurs armées dans les provinces, celuy au departement duquel elles seront ordonnées, fera les Commissions, pouvoirs, Estats, et autre Expeditions necessaires ensuitte et consequence desdictes commissions et Estatz.

Fera pareillement les pouvoirs ou commissions des offices et estats qu'il conviendra creer de nouveau pour servir esdictes armées fors et excepté pour la levée des gens de guerre tant de cheval que de pied qui appartiendra au secretaire de la guerre;

Et s'il advient que lesdictes armées ayent esté ordonnées pour servir en plusieurs provinces qui soient de divers departemens, lesdicts secretaires qui en ont le departement, conviendront entre eux de celuy qui debvra faires lesdictes Expeditions, ou bien elles appartiendront à celuy au departement duquel il y aura plus de provinces.

Les Rendez-vous et departemens pour faire les creües ou nouvelles

---

[1] For the *règlement* of 1619, the oldest (mid-seventeenth century) and best copy found originates from the library of the Loménie de Brienne family, and is now BN, nouvelles acquisitions, MS. 32, fol. 449. This is published here. Several other manuscripts already described on p. 185 n. 1 above also contain copies: BN, MS. 17864, fol. 314; BN, MS. 4231, fol. 12^v; BN, MS. 20762, fol. 25; BN, Collection Clairambault, MS. 664, fol. 123; the library of Louvois, N, MS. 18243, fol. 102; and BN, MS. 21432, fol. 129.

levées estans donnez comme il est accoustumé par les Mareschaux de France, les depesches qui s'addresseront pour ce sujet aux gouverneurs des provinces et des villes et aux habitans d'icelles seront signées par le secretaire qui aura le departement desdicts lieux et celles qui s'addresseront aux chefs et commissaires pour la conduicte desdictes troupes seront signées par celuy qui aura le departement de la guerre jusqu'à ce qu'elles soient joinctes au corps de l'armée à laquelle auront esté destinez et lors les Expeditions debvront estre faictes et signées par celuy qui aura charge de ladicte armée;

Sa Majesté voulant faire l'estat des garnisons lesdicts secretaires seront appellez Ensemble devant elle afin que chacun d'eux luy donne son advis des choses qui seront necessaires pour les provinces de son departement et des changemens qui auront esté faicts durant le Cours de l'année, afin que la-dessus sa majesté puisse arrester les Estats particuliers et le nombre des gens de guerre qui sera requis en chacune desdictes garnisons;

Et le secretaire de la guerre dressera aussy en mesme temps estat general suivant ce que sa majesté aura ordonné, sur lequel Estat general seulement sera compté en la chambre selon qu'il est accoustumé, comme aussy les Estats particuliers seront Envoyez par les secretaires qui en ont le departement, aux gouverneurs et cappitaines des places, et feront lesdicts secretaires chacun en leur departement toutes ordonnances, Excuses, reliefs, des monstres et autres expeditions en suitte et execution desdicts Estats particuliers pour ce qui sera sous la charge desdicts gouverneurs.

S'il est jugé necessaire et commandé par sa majesté de faire quelque changement esdictes garnisons durant le cours de l'année soit pour les mettre d'un lieu en autre, ou de les augmenter ou retrancher, toutes les expeditions en seront pareillement faictes par les secretaires du departement qui en advertiront le secretaire de la guerre;

Toutes depesches et expeditions pour la levée des gens de pied et de cheval qui auront à servir la campagne et sous la charge de colonels de l'infanterie et Cavalerie legere seront faicts par le secretaire de la guerre; Et quant aux autres depesches, commissions de gens de guerre levez et mis sur pied pour servir dans les places et garnisons, les autres secretaires chacun en leur departement, les feront et escriront aussy aux gouverneurs, capittaines, maires, et Eschevins des Villes pour y faire recevoir et loger toutes lesdictes trouppes;

L'Estat general de l'artillerie sera faict par le secretaire de la guerre comme aussy ceux qu'il conviendra faire pour l'armée royalle, mais si au courant d'Icelle il survenoit quelque depesche à faire, soit pour changement, fonte, remontage, augmentation de pieces, confection de poudres et boulets pour la seureté et conservation des places, les secretaires du departement les feront.

Les Provisions des Estats et offices de Connestable, grand maistre de l'artillerie et de colonel de l'infanterie, seront faicts par le secretaire de la guerre et celles des autres officiers de la couronne ou de la maison par les autres secretaires qui ont accoustumé de les faire comme dependantes de leur departement et pour celles des mareschaux de France elles seront faictes par celuy qui sera en mois lors que le Roy en commandera la depesche;

Le secretaire qui a la maison en son departement fera toutes les depesches concernans les archers de la garde du corps, les cens et deux cent gentillhommes tant pour l'ordinaire qu'extraordinaire;

Je veux que ce reglement soit observé,

signé Louis

Faict à Saint Germain en Laye
le 29e avril 1619 par commandement du Roy
signé
Derets et P. Jeannin

Reglement entre Messieurs les Secretaires d'Estat du 11 mars 1626.[1]

Le Roy jugeant qu'il est à propos et tres expedient pour le bien de ses affaires que les provinces Estrangers soient toutes entre les mains d'un seul de ses Secretaires d'Estat, pour faire les depesches et expeditions qui luy seront commandées, Sa Majesté a resolu de changer les departements suivant lesquels ils ont travaillé jusques à present, afin de donner aux trois autres un honnorable employ pour exercer tous quatre en bonne intelligence et amitié leurs charges, selon la dignité d'icelles, et a voulu et ordonné que doresnavant le Sieur de Lomenie ou le Sieur de Ville-aux-Clercs son filz receu à sa survivance aura la maison de sa Majesté, Paris, Isle de France, Orleans, Berry, Soissons et le Parlement de Navarre, que le Sieur d'Herbault aura tous les estrangers, et outre aura dans le Royaume, Le Languedoc, La Guyenne, Brouage, Aulnix, La Rochelle, et les affaires generalles des huguenots; Que le Sieur D'auquerre aura L'auvergne, Bourbonnois, Nivernois, Bourgogne, Champagne, Bresse, Picardie, Normandie, Bretagne, Les Trois Eveschez de Metz, Toul et Verdun, La Lorraine et La Marine du Ponant; Et que le Sieur de Beauclerc aura la guerre suivant le Reglement de l'an Mil six centz dix neuf pour le dedans du Royaume Mais toute entiere pour les Estrangers, Le Taillon, et l'artillerie, sans qu'aucun autre desdicts Secretaires d'Estat y aye part; et outre cela il aura le Poictou, la Marche, Limousin, Angoumois, Xaintonge, Lyonnois, Dauphiné, Provence et la Marine du Levant; et pour le regard des fortiffications chacun en fera les Estats en ce qui sera de son departement,

Faict à Paris le Unzieme mars mil six cents vingt six et plus bas et escrit de la main du Roy : Je veux que le present reglement soit suivy.

[1] The *règlement* of 1626 also appears as a late-seventeenth-century copy in the following manuscripts already discussed above: BN, MS. 20762, fol. 26ᵛ; BN, MS. 21432, fol. 131; BN, MS. 18243, fol. 111; BN, MS. 4231, fol. 16ᵛ; and BN, Collection Clairambault, MS. 664, fol. 129. After a careful comparison of the various copies, it was decided to publish the one from the Collection Clairambault. No significant differences in the texts were discovered which would merit a detailed description of them.

Reglement entre les Secretaires d'Estat des Etrangers et de la Guerre . . . Septembre 1633.[1]

Le Roy voulant prevenir les inconveniens que les differens qui pouroient naistre entre ses Secretaires d'Estat qui ont le departement des Etrangers, et celuy de la guerre apporteroient au bien de son service; et sçachant combien en la pluspart des grandes affaires, la celerité y donne d'avantages et qu'il importe de retrancher tout ce qui peut y apporter du trouble, voulant qu'ils exercent l'un et l'autre leurs charges avec la dignité et honneur qu'il convient et qu'un chacun d'eux reglé en sa fonction n'aye d'autres pensées que ce qui peut advantager le bien de ses affaires sans innover, ny alterer les anciens reglemens faits ez années 1619 et 1626 lesquels demeureront en leur force et vigueur, Sa Majesté en les interpretant et pour oster à l'avenir tout sujet ou pretexte de division les a reglés ainsy qu'il ensuit.

Que celuy des Secretaires d'Etat qui aura en son departement la guerre expediera tous les pouvoirs, commissions et instructions qui seront données par sa Majesté à ceux auxquels elle commettra la conduitte de ses armées hors le Royaume, les Etats desdites armées, et generalement tous les ordres et Reglemens qu'il conviendra faire soit pour leur subsistance, payemens, licentiemens et tout ce qui concernera les fait desdites armées sans que celuy desdits Secretaires d'Etat qui aura en son departement les pays etrangers puisse pretendre que l'autre n'ait que la Royalle et principalle et au contraire, ne prendra aucune connoissance de ce qui concernera lesdites armées les Generaux d'icelles ou autres officiers, lesquels recevront les ordres et commandemens de Sa Majesté par l'entremise dudit Secretaire d'Etat ayant le departement de la guerre soit pour marcher, combattre ou attaquer et s'adresseront à luy pour rendre compte à Sa Majesté de ce qu'ils auront avancé ensemble l'informer des succes qu'il aura plu à Dieu de donner aux

[1] Only one copy of the *règlement* of 1633 has been found along with a rough draft of the same document in the BN, Collection Cangé, MS. 70, fols. 253 and 260. This collection of copies and engravings made by Cangé in the early eighteenth century is a valuable source for administrative history in the *ancien régime*. The authenticity and care in copying have proved to be excellent when other original documents have been compared with the copies by Cangé; hence there is every reason to accept as correct his statement, 'depost du Louvre', as the source of the copy. The document as well as the rough draft of it (fol. 253), however, present other problems. They are not presented in the form of a royal letter, nor is a specific date given to the document. This could be for one or two reasons: either the *règlement* was never presented to and signed by the king, but was rather a statement of an agreement made among the secretaries, or in copying Cangé simply left off the details which would have given the *règlement* its traditional form. The absence of other copies or of comment on the *règlement* in contemporary history might lead one to believe that it was never enacted. But at the end of the copy of the rough draft, Cangé added: 'le vray reglement est cy apres', indicating that he accepted the second document as such and that he simply neglected to copy the exact title, date, place, and signatures which appear on royal legislation.

armes de sa Majesté, et luy faire entendre les avis qui luy seront donnés de l'etat des Ennemis tant par les espions qu'autres, et pour sçavoir ses volontés et commandemens sur les occurences qui se pourront presenter.

Luy seront envoyés les capitulations accordées par lesdits generaux soit aux habitans des places qu'ils auront prises, qu'aux gens de guerre qui en seront sortis et par son ordre seront conclües les treves ou suspensions dont lesdits generaux luy ayant donné avis, il en avertira celuy qui a le departement des Etrangers en luy donnant copie tant desdites capitulations que des traités de treves ou suspensions.

Les places conquises, esquelles lesdits generaux l'airront des troupes de l'armée et quelqu'un soit marechal, Maistre de Camp ou Capitaine pour y commander tant et si longuement qu'elles demeureront en cet etat seront sous la direction dudit Secretaire d'Etat ayant la guerre en departement. Mais dès l'heure qu'il y aura vu Gouverneur etably avec une garnison reglée non tirée du corps dont l'armée sera composée ou d'autres sous la charge et authorité des colonels tant de cavalerie que d'infanterie française, suisse, ou autres etrangers estant à la solde de sa Majesté le pouvoir dudit Gouverneur sera expedié par ledit Secretaire d'Etat qui aura les etrangers ensuitte l'Etat de la garnison pour la Direction de laquelle sera observé entre-eux le meme ordre que pour les garnisons du Royaume.

Les places qui seront consignées en depost à Sa Majesté ou confiées à son garde, sera l'ordre cydessus prescrit pareillement observé.

Tout ordre de garnison et distribution de troupes de l'armée, en Pays conquis, ou envoy de troupes vers les Alliés commandées par un general, Marechal de Camp ou autres officiers sera expedié par ledit Secretaire ayant le departement de la guerre auquel ils aurront à s'adresser tant pour donner compte de ce qu'ils auront fait, que pour recevoir par luy les ordres de Sa Majesté sur le fait de la guerre, les routes pour marcher d'un lieu à l'autre seront expediées par luy et l'autre s'adressera les Commandemens aux Gouverneurs des Places pour les y recevoir les ordres necessaires pour faire dresser les Estapes ainsy qu'il se pratique en ce Royaume.

Privatement et seul audit Secretaire d'Etat ayant le departement des affaires etrangeres appartiendra d'expedier les Commissions et Instructions pour conclure paix, ou association avec quelque Potentat que ce soit, encor que ledit Traité fut avancé par le general de l'armée, sans qu'aucun autre s'en puisse mesler.

Comme aussy s'il jugeoit qu'il fut avantageux aux armes de Sa Majesté ou necessaire d'entrer en l'Etat de quelque Prince soit voisin de ce Royaume; ou pays esquels ils se trouveroit avec l'armée ce qu'il ne doit sans avoir sçu les intentions de sa Majesté telle action pouvant donner lieu à une Rupture avec le voisin, ou autres Princes non declarés ennemis, sera tenu d'en ecrire au meme Secretaire d'Etat lequel lui mandera les volontés de sa Majesté si elle desapprouve son dessein; mais si les raisons donnoient occasion de le luy permettre ou commander, en sera informé par ledit Secretaire et recevra en meme tems les ordres par l'autre, auquel il donnera compte du succes et progres des choses, dores on la continuera à luy ecrire ainsy qu'il fait de ce qui concerne sa charge de General.

L'adresse des couriers qui seront envoyés par lesdits Generaux d'armée ou autres chefs, qui n'auront autre pouvoir que de commander les armées sera faitte au Secretaire d'Etat ayant le departement de la guerre et si lesdits Lieutenans generaux sont en meme tems chargés de quelque negociation l'adresse en ce cas sera faite selon la qualité du sujet pour lequel lesdits courriers seront despeschés, en sorte que si le point le plus pressant de sa depesche concerne le fait de la guerre, pour en avoir promptement la resolution de sa Majesté le courier sera adressé au Secretaire d'Etat qui a le departement de la guerre; ou s'agissant d'un point de negociation l'adresse en sera faitte à celuy qui a les Etrangers, et au cas que le contenu au present ordre ne fut observé par lesdits Lieutenans Generaux et autres lesdits Secretaires d'Etat seront tenus de se renvoyer les despesches l'un à l'autre.

Si lesdits Generaux ou autres chefs commandans les troupes etoient obligés de traiter pour la nourriture passager d'icelles contributions, fournitures de vivres etappes, munitions de guerre et autres choses de semblable nature pour la subsistance de l'armée encore qu'ils le fassent avec potentats, Republiques ou autres etrangers ils en donneront avis à sa Majesté et apprendront ses volontés par ledit Secretaire ayant le departement de la guerre à la charge neanmoins que si les mesmes choses etoient traitées par les ambassadeurs ou agens de sa Majesté ou autre que lesdits Lieutenans generaux chefs de gens de guerre ou autres par eux deputés elles passeront par les mains de celuy qui a les affaires etrangeres.

Administrative changes in the duties of the Secretaries of State by royal letter.[1]

Monsieur,

J'ay eu commandement du Roy de vous donner advis que Sa Majesté a resolu que desormais tous ceux qui demanderont des cures, prébendes, prevostez, chapelles, priorez, et autres benefices d'autres qualitez estant à sa collation ne pourront s'adresser qu'à Messieurs les Secretaires d'Estat que [qui?] seront de mois, lesquels recevront leurs placetz et en feront raport à Sa Majesté pour, en suitte du commandement qu'elle leur feroit en faveur de celuy à qui elle accordera le benefice, donner au supliant au bas de son placet un [*illegible*] au Reverend Pere confesseur pour l'examiner en personne et luy delivrer un certifficat de s'emparer(?). Ensuitte de quoy les expeditions du benefice seront delivrées aux supplians sans difficulté . . . etc.

[1] The document has survived as a minute to a royal letter from the department of war (to be countersigned by Sublet) addressed to the other three secretaries of state: Chavigny, La Ville-aux-Clercs, and La Vrillière. 5 Jan. 1638, AG, A¹, 43, fol. 32. Owing to the rapidity with which it was written, the minute presents considerable palaeographical difficulty. It ends with what is apparently the secretary's abbreviation for the usual closing of a royal letter.

APPENDIX B

Two Documents concerning the Office of Superintendent of Finance in the 1630's

WHEN Bullion and Bouthillier took office on 4 August 1632[1] the latter prepared a *mémoire* describing the first decisions and plans which they made for administering the royal finances. This *mémoire* provides an insight into the important political and economic role of a finance minister under Louis XIII, and is a convenient measure for the study of the development of a modern bureaucracy in the *ancien régime*. As is indicated by the title written on a little tab projecting from the page, which probably served to classify it in the Superintendent's own archives,[2] the document, entirely in Bouthillier's hand, was never meant for the public.

The second document is the *règlement* upon which Bullion and Richelieu negotiated, where the latter attempted to circumscribe the power of the superintendent by obliging him to act *en conseil*; it is entirely in Bullion's hand.[3]

[1] See the seventeenth-century copy of their *lettres patentes* in BN, nouvelles acquisitions, MS. 7226, fol. 426, where, after the formalized phrases, one finds: '. . . estre à propos pour le bien de nostre service et jouir de ladicte charge aux mesmes honneurs, auctorités, prerogatives, preeminences, fonctions, estatz et appointements telz et semblables qu'en a jouy nostre dict cousin [Effiat] et les autres cy devant estably en ladicte charge sans que de ladicte administration vous soyez tenus ny obligés de rendre compte à nostre chambre des comptes de Paris ny ailleurs qu'à nostre propre personne dont nous vous avons de noz grace specialle plaine puissance et auctorité relevez et dispensés rellevons et dispensons par ces dicts presentes de ce faire nous avons donné et donnons plain pouvoir, auctorité, commission et mandement special, Mandons et ordonnons aux tresoriers de nostre espargne presents et advenir et autres noz officiers de finances et comptables generalement quelz conques qu'il apprendra(?) en ce faisant vous obeir et entendre diligemment ces choses touchans et concernans ladicte charge ausquels comptables nous deffendons d'acquicter aucunes parties soient de dons ou autrement quelque acquitz qui leur soient expediéz s'ilz ne sont ni visez ou acompagnés de vos ordonnances particulieres. . . .' See also the *brevet de séance* giving them precedence over all other councillors save the traditional great officers, BN, nouvelles acquisitions, MS. 7226, fol. 428. Note that the office of superintendent did not yet automatically bring such honours, as they had to be bestowed apart from the *lettres patentes*. This served to honour the man and not the office, an important distinction in the *ancien régime*.

[2] While the document is easy to read, the ravages of time have effaced and blurred some words beyond recognition.

[3] Compare with the very interesting copy of the 'Ordre à proposer lorsqu'il

Memoire faict par moy le 15^{esme} du mois d'aoust 1632
touchant ce que nous avons faict Monsieur de Bulion
et moy au commencement que nous sommes entrés en
la charge de Surintendant des Finances

Le Roy nous aiants appelés Monsieur de Bullyon et moy à la charge
[*illegible*] surintandan ses Finances, Nous avons commencé à travailler
ensemble le 6e jour du present mois d'aoust 1632.

Pour faire cognoistre au vray le fonds que Monseigneur le Marechal
d'Effiat a laissé lors de son deces arrivé à la Petite Pierre en Alemagne
le 27 Juillet 1632, et pour verifier l'Estat que le Sieur Tubeuf a apporté
pour le monstre au Roy. La plus grande partie du fonds que l'on dict
avoir esté laissé debvant estre prise sur les deniers extraordinaires, Nous
avons desiré que Messieurs les Intendants et Controleurs generaux des
Finances receurrent(?) tous les traictés faicts depuis l'année 1626 que feu
Monsieur le Mareschal d'Effiat fut establi surintendant des finances, et
qu'ils facent compter tous les traictants depuis ledit temps pour voir
s'ils ont satisfait à leur traictés, en suite de quoy lesdicts Sieurs intendants feront un Estat de ce qui en restera.

A cet effect pour n'obmettre aucun traicté Ils se feront representer
par les Thresoriers des parties casuelles un Estat abregé de leurs
receptes affin de les faire compter s'ils ont receu au deniers des [*illegible*] traictés, ou bien faire controler les traictants si ils leur ont donné
leur Quittances.

Il est à propos que lesdicts Sieurs intendants facent aussy compter
par estat tous les Receveurs generaux, et fermiers de leur departements
des années dernieres, et particulierement de 1630, et 1631, de la premiere demie année [*illegible*] le 15 du present mois d'aoust 1632.

Les despences de l'Espargne des mois du janvier, fevrier, mars et
avril de la presente année 1632, et celles du May et Juin de l'armée
d'Alemagne, et Juin de la Cour aiants esté arrestées par feu Monsieur
le Marechal d'Effiat, nous avons Monsieur de Bullion et moy com-
mancer à examiner les depenses du mois de May, Juin et Juillet pour
Paris seulement, ce que nous avons faict exactement, et avant que de
rien arrester nous avons chargé Monsieur le Thresorier de l'Espargne
Gueznegaud de mettre à la fin de l'Estat de chacun mois sa recepte
entiere, et la nature des deniers sur laquelle il a fait lesdictes despences
suivant les ordres du feu Monsieur le Mareschal d'Effiat, affin de
cognoistre ce qu'il en a receu, ce qui luy reste entre les mains de chacune
nature, et ce qui restera deub au Roy.

Nous avons en outre desiré que ledit Sieur Thresorier de l'Espargne
fist un Estat certifié de tous les deniers qu'il a receu de l'Espargne
pendant la presente année, apres lequel Monsieur de Bullyon et moy

plaira à Dieu donner la Paix au Royaume' by Bullion, where he outlined his
proposals for a better financial administration. BN, Collection Cinq Cents
Colbert, MS. 194, fol. 273. In many ways he was administratively looking
backward rather than proposing new measures.

pourrons faire un Estat et le ferons en [*illegible*] de tous ce qui reste à recouvrer tant des Receptes, generalités, et fermes, que des traictés, creations d'offices, et autres deniers extraordinaires.

Ces verifications estants faictes au vrai, l'on verra ce qui est certain du contenu audit Memoire de Monsieur le Mareschal d'Effiat, l'on verra de plus le fonds restant pour les charges et despenses de cette année, lesquelles j'estime estre encore pour la plupart à acquitter.

Sur ce fonds il faudra assigner les despenses ordinaires et inevitables, [*illegible*] sera donné estat audict Sieur de Guenegaud pour ce qui reste à paier de cette année, lequel estat nous ferons sur celuy que nous luy avons ordonné de faire, par ce moien nous nous dechargerons de cet ordinaire une fois pour toutes, et eviterons le travail qu'il pourroit donner si nous n'y travaillions dès le commencement.

Les deniers revenants bons de l'ordinaire, avec les moiens extraordinaires qui sont des [*illegible*] qui pourront estre trouvés seront emploiés à la guerre, marine, pensions, et autres dispenses. Il fault pour cet effect achever les traictés commancés. Il convient songer dès à present à l'année prochaine, et pour cet effect faire envoier promptement les commissions aux Generalités si [*illegible*] reste aucuns, arrester les Estats de la valeur des finances, affin que ce peuple ait de la facilité de [*illegible*] quatre termes, ce que ce retardement le soutient de paier en deux ans(?).

Pour venir à l'ordre qui a esté egalement observé ainsy que Monsieur de Bullyon a proposé qui est de faire un estat general des finances au [*illegible*] de chacune année. Il est à propos d'ordonner au Thresorier de l'Espargne qui entrera en exercice l'année prochaine de faire un projet de recepte, et despense de ladicte année, et le preserver tout le plus tost qu'il pourra affin que nous ayons le temps de l'examiner et de faire ledict Estat General.

Il faut faire promptement tenir les Estats de Normandie, ou par Monsieur de Longueville s'il est demeuré ou par Monsieur de [*illegible*] Lieutenant du Roy, ou bien il fault mander aux thresoriers de France tout ainsy que si les Estats avoient esté tenus.[1]

Reglement que le Roy veult estre à l'advenir inviolablement observé en ses finances

Aucun de messieurs du conseil ne recepvront plus outres deniers par an que ceulx qui sont portés dans les Estats du Roy et ne prendront aucune recompense par extraordinaire et par content.

Il ne s'expediera plus aucun contant que par les Secretaires d'estat qui seront nommés par Sa Majesté.

Il ne se fera plus aucun content appellé aux finances content par rolle auxquels on mettra diverses gratifications pour les particuliers.

Quant aus contents qui s'expedient au Conseil pour les remises des traitants Messieurs le Chancelier et surintendants en retiendront un

[1] AAE, France, 806, fol. 178.

extrait ou menu lequel ils feront voir à Sa Majesté quand il luy plaira le comander ou à tel autre qu'elle trouvera bon ordoner.

Les bauls à ferme seront faicte au conseil selon qu'entiennement on avoit acoustumé sans qu'aucun puisse destourner ceulx qui se presenteront pour encherir à peine d'en courir l'indignation du Roy et ne sera acordé aucun rabais aux fermiers et traitants sans que Messieurs le Chancelier et Surintendants en ayent premierement pris ordre de Sa Majesté mesme.

Les articles des traités seront raportés et examinés au conseil et mesme Messieurs le Chancelier et Surintendants et intendants en auront chacun une copie pour s'en instruire en sorte qu'ils sachent auparavant que la resolution s'en prenne s'ils sont utiles et les traités estants passés les secretaires du conseil seront tenus de les communiquer durant trois jours à touts ceulx qui le desireront pour faire la condition du Roy meilleure.

Les petites directions le service du Roy les requerant se tiendront regulierement touts les mardis et vendredis depuis les huit heures jusques à onze heures du matin affin que toutes les affaires qui se doibvent resoudre au conseil de la direction come traités, baulx et autres semblables y soyent auparavant examinées.

Messieurs de Chavigny et de Noyers signeront seuls les contents qui seront commandés par Sa Majesté assavoir le Sieur de Chavigny les contents qui s'expedieront pour les pentions et affaires d'estat et le Sieur de Noyers les contents pour toutes les affaires de la guerre soit du dedan ou dehors.

Sa Majesté veult et entend que le Règlement pour la direction de ses finances du mois de janvier 1629 tres advantageux pour son service et publié en sa presence au parlement soit ponctuellement executé par ceulx de son conseil.

J'obeiray au present Reglement et executeray de tout mon pouvoir.

Fait à Paris xix juillet mil vi^c xxxviii.

Bullion[1]

[1] AAE, France, 830, fol. 261.

BIBLIOGRAPHY

I. *Manuscript Sources*

Archives des Affaires Etrangères (AAE), Quai d'Orsay: *Mémoires et documents, France.*

801	1610–40		832	1638–9
802	1632		833	1639
807	1633		834	1639
808	1633		835	1640 (January–July)
809	1633		836	1640 (July–December)
810	1634		837	1640
811	1634		838	1641 (January–June)
812	1543–1634		839	1641
813	1635		840	1641
814	1635		841	1641
815	1635		842	1642–3
816	1635		843	1642
817	1635		844	1642
818	1635		845	1642
819	1635–6		846	1643 (January–August)
820	1636 (January–May)			
821	1636 (June–October)		244	1617–42
822	1636 (October–December)		288	1642
823	1613–36		1476	1638–53
824	1636		1481	1600–49
825	1636		1491	1636–53
826	1637 (January–April)		1546	1200–1639
827	1637		1548	1640–57
828	1637 (September–December)		1579	1629–1747
			1677	1637–41
829	1637		1703	1635 (January–October)
830	1638 (January–July)		1705	1636–7
831	1638 (August–December)		1708	1642–4

Correspondance Politique

Angleterre		46	1636–7
		47	1638–9
		48	1640–1
Grisons		9	1636–47
Hollande		18	1636 (January–December)
		19	1636–7
Pays-Bas		12	1637
Rome		59	1637 (January–May)

Sardaigne	25	1637
	26	1638
	27	1639
	28	1639 (January–June)
	29	1639 (July–December)
	31	1641 (September–December)
Suisse	28	1635–41

Archives du Ministère de la Guerre (AG), Château de Vincennes: *Series A¹*, Dispatches of the department of the secretary of state for war.

24	1635 (minutes)		49	1638
25	1635		50	1639 (Louvre)
26	1635		51	1639
27	1636 (minutes)		52	1639 (navy)
28	1636		53	1639
29	1636		54	1639 (forests)
30	1636		55	1639
31	1636		56	1639
32	1636		57	1640 (minutes)
33	1636–7		58	1640 (ecclesiastical)
34	1637 (minutes)		59	1640 (Louvre)
35	1637 (minutes)		60	1640 (minutes)
36	1637 (ecclesiastical)		61	1640
37	1637		62	1640
38	1637 (minutes)		63	1641 (finance)
39	1637 (judicial)		64	1641
40	1637 (navy)		65	1641
41	1631–7		66	1641
42	1637 (minutes)		67	1641
43	1638		68	1642
44	1638 (commerce)		69	1642 (finance)
45	1638 (minutes)		70	1642 (minutes)
46	1638 (judicial)		71	1642
47	1638 (ecclesiastical)		72	1610–43
48	1638 (minutes)			

The manuscripts are classified chronologically in each volume; the short indications above mention outstanding aspects of the volumes which contain royal correspondence of all types, but predominantly military.

Archives Nationales (AN), Hôtel Soubise:

Series

E 2665, council *arrêts*, 1629 (not minutes).

K 113–17, collection of charters for the reign of Louis XIII. 539, *maison du roi*.

881–892, collection of documents on finances (mostly for the eighteenth century).

U 945A–947, *mémoires* on the royal councils.
951, *mémoire* on the *cour des aides*.
989, *mémoire* on the *conseillers du Parlement*.
992, finances.

3AP 164–89, private archives of the de Nicolai family, for the *Chambre des comptes*.

Bibliothèque Nationale (BN), Cabinet des Manuscrits, rue de Richelieu, *fonds français*; for convenience the following have been divided into correspondence and administrative documents, but there are many exceptions as well as omissions, for only the more important manuscripts are cited.

Correspondence

Claude Bouthillier: 3216, 3257, 3673–5, 4071, 4137, 5190, 10246, 17369, 17371, 17375, 17386, n.a. 238–40, n.a. 3232, n.a. 5246, n.a. 6293, n.a. 9576.
Claude de Bullion: 4106, 4112, 5158 (Le Tellier), 5190 (Rohan), 3762 (Chastillon), 6556, 6627, 15582–4, 15621, n.a. (Séguier), 6210.
Chavigny: 3445, 3721, 3760 (Chastillon), 3762, 3765, 3767, 3770, 4067 (Coeuvres), 4072, 4106, 4211, 4220, 5158, 5159, 5190, 6642, 6644, 6645–9 (la Valette), 6650, 6880, 9354, 10733, 15523, 15915, 15935, 15962, 17370, 17375 (Séguier), 17946–7 (Brasset), 20480, 20546, 20989, 22334, n.a. 5154, n.a. 6210 (Séguier).
La Ville-aux-Clercs: the numerous catalogue references to his correspondence are all for before 1635 or after 1642.
La Vrillière: the catalogue references to his correspondence are all before 1635 or after 1642.
Louis XIII: 3703, 3721, 3724, 3736, 3833, 3843, 3844, 4071 (Coeuvres), 4091, 4133 (Sabran), 4590, 5202, 6556, 6619, 6627, 6642, 6643, 6644–9 (la Valette), 6880 (Le Tellier), 9354, 10211, 11904, 17374, 20651, 20866, 28346, 23355, 25746, n.a. 240, n.a. 9637.
Séguier: 6914, 10215, 15601, 15621, 16890, 17367–75, 18047, 18100, 18432, n.a. 1473, n.a. 3232, n.a. 6210.
Sublet de Noyers: 3721, 3759–67 (Séguier), 3843–4, 4140–1, 6642, 6644, 6646–50 (La Valette), 6880, 9354, 16537, 17369, 17374, 17378, 17946, 18518, n.a. 3232, n.a. 5130, n.a. 6210.

Administrative documents

3441 copies, commissions, &c., for superintendents.
7008 jurisdictions and *règlements* for secretaries.
10211 *lettres patentes*, &c., for Sublet de Noyers.
15519 jurisdictions and *règlements* for secretaries.
16219 list of council deans.
16240 secretarial formularies from Séguier library.

16626 finances, brevets, &c., for superintendents.
17864 *règlements* for secretaries from Séguier library.
18236 *mémoire* on origins of secretaries.
18239 documents on the secretaries of the king.
18240 finances.
18243 secretaries (fol. 178) 'Estat et Cahier des expéditions qui ont esté faites par moy', de la Barde.
18504 finances, Sublet de Noyers (copy).
18543 councils, secretaries, superintendents.
20762 *règlements*, secretaries.
21432 *règlements*, secretaries.
21564 *mémoire* on the secretaries (late seventeenth or early eighteenth century).
23937 *mémoire* on the secretaries.
n.a. 32   *règlements*, secretaries (Brienne library).
n.a. 164–5 finances, treasury rolls.
n.a. 7225   *maison du roi*.
n.a. 7226   councils, secretaries.
n.a. 9735   secretaries.

Collection Clairambault

384 correspondence, Bouthillier, Chavigny, Sublet de Noyers, finances, military history, and secretaries.
385 Mazarin and Chavigny.
572 correspondence, Chavigny, Richelieu.
647 secretaries.
649 councils.
664 secretaries.

Collection Dupuy

218 secretaries.
224 secretaries.

Collection Châtre de Cangé (reserve reading-room).

22 secretaries.
23 secretaries and military administration.
24 military administration.
68 secretaries.
69 secretaries.
70 secretaries.
71 superintendents.

Bibliothèque de l'Arsenal, Boulevard Henri IV, *manuscrits*: 3738, 4058, 5298.
Bibliothèque de l'Institut, Quai de Conti, *Collection Godefroy*: 310.

The other collections of manuscripts in Paris, the Bibliothèque Sainte-Geneviève, Bibliothèque de la Sorbonne, Bibliothèque Mazarine, Bibliothèque du Sénat, Bibliothèque de la Chambre des Députés, and

the Archives du Ministère de la Marine, do not have documents pertinent to the subject.

Public Record Office, Chancery Lane, London, *State Papers*, series 78,
volumes 96, 97, 98, 99, 100, 101, 102, 103, 104, 105, 106, 107.

British Museum, Great Russell Street, London, *manuscripts*: Additions,
9291, Harleian 4472, Egerton 1687–9.

II. *Printed Sources*

AUBERY, *Mémoires pour servir à l'histoire du Cardinal Duc de Richelieu*,
Cologne, 1667, vols. i, ii, iii, iv, v.

BEAUNE, C., *Traité de la chambre des comptes . . .*, Paris, 1647.

BOISLISLE, A. de, ed., *Chambre des comptes de Paris, pièces justificatives
pour servir à l'histoire des premiers présidents (1506–1751), histoire de la
maison de Nicolai*, Nogent le Rotrou, 1873.

BRIENNE, H. A. (the elder), *Mémoires du Comte de Brienne*, ed. by Michaud
and Poujoulat, séries 3, Paris, 1833.

BRIQUET, M., *De l'origine et du progrès des charges de secrétaire d'Etat*, La
Haye, 1747.

DUCHESNE, A., *Histoire des chanceliers et gardes des sceaux de France . . .*,
Paris, 1680.

DUCROT, L., *Traité des aides, tailles, gabelles . . .*, Paris, 1636.

DUPLEIX, S., *Histoire de Louis le Juste XIII du nom, roy de France et de
Navarre*, Paris, 1654.

FAUVELET-DU-TOC, A., *Histoire des secrétaires d'Etat*, Paris, 1668.

GIRARD, E., and JOLY, *Trois livres des offices de France*, Paris, 1638,
I and II.

GODEFROY, D., *Histoire des connestables, chanceliers, et mareschaux . . .*,
Paris, 1658.

GRISELLE, E., ed., *Formulaire de lettres de François I à Louis XIV, dressé
en 1642*, Paris, 1919.

GUILLARD, *Histoire du conseil du roi*, Paris, 1718.

GUYOT, P., *Traité des droits, fonctions, franchises, exemptions, prérogatives et
privilèges annexés en France à chaque dignité, à chaque office, et à chaque état*,
Paris, 1787, vols. i, ii, iii, iv.

HARDY, S., *et al.*, *Le Guidon général des finances*, Paris, 1644.

LA VALETTE (Louis de Nogaret, cardinal de La Valette), *Mémoires*,
Paris, 1771.

LOUIS XIII, *Louis XIII d'après sa correspondance avec le Cardinal de Richelieu*, ed. by Comte de Beauchamp, Paris, 1902.

MORERI, L., *Grand Dictionaire historique*, Paris, 1699, vols. i, ii, iii, iv.

MOUSNIER, R., ed., 'Les Règlements du conseil du roi', *Annuaire-
Bulletin de la Société de l'histoire de France*, Paris, 1948.

RÉMOND, N., *Sommaire Traité de revenue*, Paris, 1622.

RICHELIEU, *Lettres, instructions diplomatiques et papiers d'Etat*, ed. by
M. Avenel, Paris, 1853–77, vols. iii, iv, v, vi, vii, viii.

—— *Testament politique*, ed. by L. André, Paris, 1947.

SÉGUIER, P., *Diare du Chancelier Séguier*, ed. by Floquet, Rouen, 1842.

SILHON, J., *Ministre d'Etat avec le véritable usage de la politique moderne*, Paris, 1631–43, vols. i, ii.

SOURDIS (Henri d'Escoubleau de Sourdis, Archbishop of Bordeaux), *Correspondance*, ed. by E. Sue, Paris, 1839, vols. i, ii.

TALON, O., *Mémoires d'Omer Talon*, ed. by Michaud and Poujoulat, Paris, 1838, vol. i.

VERON DE FORBONNAIS, *Recherches et considérations sur les finances de France*, Basel, 1758.

VERTHAMONT, *Relation du voyage du Chancelier Séguier dans la Normandie*, ed. by Floquet, Rouen, 1842.

Secondary Works

Only the important secondary works used in the preparation of this monograph are included.

ANDRÉ, L., *Michel Le Tellier et l'organisation de l'armée monarchique*, Paris, 1906.

AUDOUIN, X., *Histoire de l'administration de la guerre*, Paris, 1811, vols. i, ii.

D'AVENEL, Vicomte, *Richelieu et la monarchie absolue*, Paris, 1884, vols. i, ii, iii, iv.

CAILLET, J., *L'Administration en France sous le ministère du Cardinal de Richelieu*, Paris, 1863.

CHÉRUEL, A., *Histoire de l'administration monarchique*, Paris, 1855.

—— *Histoire de France pendant la minorité de Louis XIV*, Paris, 1879–80, vol. i.

DELISLE, L., *Le Cabinet des manuscrits de la Bibliothèque nationale*, Paris, 1868.

DELOCHE, M., *La Maison du Cardinal de Richelieu*, Paris, 1912.

DOUCET, R., *Les Institutions de la France au XVIe siècle*, Paris, 1948, vols. i, ii.

ELLUL, J., *Histoire des institutions*, Paris, 1956.

GALARD, Marquis de, *Monographie du château de Wideville*, Paris, 1879.

GRIFFET, le Père, *Histoire du règne de Louis XIII, Roi de France et de Navarre*, Paris, 1758, vols. i, ii, iii.

GRISELLE, E., *Les Tribulations d'un ambassadeur en Suisse*, Paris, 1920.

HARSIN, P., *Doctrines monétaires*, Paris, 1928.

HAUSER, H., *La Pensée, et l'action économique du Cardinal de Richelieu*, Paris, 1944.

JOUVENCEL, M. de, *Le Contrôleur général des finances sous l'ancien régime*, Paris, 1901.

KERVILER, R., *Le Chancelier Séguier*, Paris, 1874.

LA FORCE, Duc de, *Histoire du Cardinal de Richelieu*, Paris, 1933 (in collaboration with Gabriel Hanotaux), vols. i, ii, iii, iv, v, vi.

LA PORTE, A. de, *Histoire généologique des familles nobles du nom de la Porte*, Poitiers, 1882.

LE CLERT, L., *Notice généologique sur les Bouthillier de Chavigny, seigneurs de Ponts-sur-Seine, de Rancé et de Beaujeu*, Troyes, 1907.

LE VASSOR, *Histoire du règne de Louis XIII*, Amsterdam, 1757, vols. i, ii, iii.

LUÇAY, Comte de, *Les Secrétaires d'Etat depuis leur institution jusqu'à la mort de Louis XV*, Paris, 1881.

MARIÉJOL, J., *Histoire de France*, ed. by E. Lavisse, Paris, 1911, vol. vi-part 2.

MOUSNIER, R., *La Vénalité des offices sous Henri IV et Louis XIII*, Rouen, 1945.

PAGÈS, G., *Les Institutions monarchiques sous Louis XIII et Louis XIV*, Paris, 1937.

PICCIONI, C., *Les Premiers Commis des affaires étrangères au XVIIe et XVIIIe siècles*, Paris, 1928.

PRÉCLIN, E., and TAPIÉ, V., *Le XVIIe siècle*, Paris, 1955.

ROBIN, P., *La Compagnie des secrétaires du roi*, Paris, 1933.

SÉE, H., RÉBEILLON, A., and PRÉCLIN, E., *Le XVIe siècle*, Paris, 1950.

VIOLLET, *Le Roi et ses ministres*, Paris, 1912.

ZELLER, G., *Les Institutions de la France, au XVIe siècle*, Paris, 1948.

Articles

MOUSNIER, R., 'Le Conseil du roi de la mort de Henri IV au gouvernement personnel de Louis XIV', *Études d'Histoire Moderne et Contemporaine*, 1947.

—— 'Recherches sur la création des intendants des provinces (1634–1648)', *Forschungen zu Staat und Verfassung, Festgabe für Fritz Hartung*, Berlin, 1958.

PAGÈS, G., 'Le Conseil du roi sous Louis XIII', *Revue d'Histoire Moderne*, Paris, 1937, vol. xii.

SCHMIDT, C., 'Le Rôle et les attributions d'un intendant des finances aux armées, Sublet de Noyers, de 1632–1636', *Revue d'Histoire Moderne et Contemporaine*, Paris, 1901, vol. ii.

INDEX

Aides, 176.
Ambassadors, 6, 77, 94, 161.
André, Louis (historian), 46, 118.
Angoulême, le duc de, 67.
Anne of Austria, 160, 170.
Antibes, 84.
Argencourt, le sieur de, 59.
Army, administration, 104–19, 156.
— Louis's supervision, 19.
— munitioners, 20.
— Richelieu's supervision, 24.
Arpajon, Vicomte de, 81.
Arras, 117.
Arrêt de réassignation, 168.
Arrêts du conseil, 5, 10 n. 2, 162, 168.
— preparation, 9, 127 n. 2, 124.
Arrière-ban, 62, 109.
Assembly of the Clergy, 12, 174.
Assembly of Saumur (1611), 37.
Assignations, 127.
l'Aubespine family, 51.
Audiger, le président, 66.
Augier, 77, 85 n. 1.
Avenel, Vicomte de (historian), 45.

Baillis, 56, 110.
Barbier, Louis, see La Rivière.
Bellièvre, le sieur de, Nicolas (ambassador to Italy), 161.
Bochart family, 42.
Bochart, Magdaleine, 40.
Bochetel family, 51.
Bonnelles, Claude de, 164.
Bordeaux, archbishop of (Sourdis), 80, 101 n. 2.
Bouillon, duc de, 175.
Bouthillier, Claude le, superintendent of finance, 166–79, 196–8.
— biography, 32–35, 166.
— negotiating to raise taxes, 176.
— observes the court for Richelieu, 170.
— responsible for road repairs, 177.
— secretary of state and superintendent of finance, 169.
— and Bullion, 162, 171–3, 179.
— and Père Joseph, 169.
— and Richelieu, 166, 170, 179–80.

Bouthillier, Denis le, seigneur of Feuilletourte, 32.
Bouthillier, Denis le, seigneur de Rancé, 32, 35.
Bouthillier, Léon de, see Chavigny.
Bouthillier, Sébastien, 33 n. 3.
Bouthillier, Victor, 33 n. 3.
Bragelonne, Marie de, 34, 77.
Brézé, Urbain, duc de, maréchal, 133.
Bribing (Assembly of the Clergy), 174.
Brienne, comte de, Antoine de Loménie, 68.
Brienne, comte de, Henri-Auguste de Loménie, see La Ville-aux-Clercs.
Budget preparation, 125, 171.
Bullion, Claude de, superintendent of finance, 108, 143–60, 196–8.
— biography, 37, 144, 164.
— Chavigny speculates on his disgrace, 153 n. 5.
— controls military expenses, 149.
— influences Assembly of the Clergy, 12.
— influence on foreign affairs, 161.
— intervenes in a quarrel between trésoriers, 127 n. 2.
— personal fortune, 164.
— reviews proposals in the conseil, 124.
— role in budget making, 125.
— role in the ministry, 20, 161.
— representative, Assembly of Saumur, 37.
— supposed irregularity of his death, 164.
— and Claude le Bouthillier, 168, 171.
— and Chavigny, 89, 95, 153 n. 5, 163.
— and Louis XIII, 134, 145–8.
— and Richelieu, 37–39, 145–8, 150–9.
— and Sublet de Noyers, 169.
— and traitants, 145.
Bullion, Pierre de, 164.
Bussy de Vère, le sieur de, 73.

3018

DATE DUE

JAN 5 1988		
JAN 22 1988		
DEC 19 1989		